OECD/G20 Base Erosion and Profit Shifting Project

Prevention of Tax Treaty Abuse – Fourth Peer Review Report on Treaty Shopping

INCLUSIVE FRAMEWORK ON BEPS: ACTION 6

OECD
BETTER POLICIES FOR BETTER LIVES

Please cite this publication as:
OECD (2022), *Prevention of Tax Treaty Abuse – Fourth Peer Review Report on Treaty Shopping : Inclusive Framework on BEPS: Action 6*, OECD/G20 Base Erosion and Profit Shifting Project, OECD Publishing, Paris, https://doi.org/10.1787/3dc05e6a-en.

ISBN 978-92-64-82658-8 (print)
ISBN 978-92-64-59267-4 (pdf)
ISBN 978-92-64-59322-0 (HTML)
ISBN 978-92-64-86273-9 (epub)

OECD/G20 Base Erosion and Profit Shifting Project
ISSN 2313-2604 (print)
ISSN 2313-2612 (online)

Photo credits: Cover © ninog-Fotolia.com.

Corrigenda to publications may be found on line at: www.oecd.org/about/publishing/corrigenda.htm.

Foreword

Digitalisation and globalisation have had a profound impact on economies and the lives of people around the world, and this impact has only accelerated in the 21st century. These changes have brought with them challenges to the rules for taxing international business income, which have prevailed for more than a hundred years and created opportunities for base erosion and profit shifting (BEPS), requiring bold moves by policy makers to restore confidence in the system and ensure that profits are taxed where economic activities take place and value is created..

In 2013, the OECD ramped up efforts to address these challenges in response to growing public and political concerns about tax avoidance by large multinationals. The OECD and G20 countries joined forces and developed an Action Plan to address BEPS in September 2013. The Action Plan identified 15 actions aimed at introducing coherence in the domestic rules that affect cross-border activities, reinforcing substance requirements in the existing international standards, and improving transparency as well as certainty.

After two years of work, measures in response to the 15 actions, including those published in an interim form in 2014, were consolidated into a comprehensive package and delivered to G20 Leaders in November 2015. The BEPS package represents the first substantial renovation of the international tax rules in almost a century. As the BEPS measures are implemented, it is expected that profits will be reported where the economic activities that generate them are carried out and where value is created. BEPS planning strategies that rely on outdated rules or on poorly co-ordinated domestic measures will be rendered ineffective.

OECD and G20 countries also agreed to continue to work together to ensure a consistent and co ordinated implementation of the BEPS recommendations and to make the project more inclusive. As a result, they created the OECD/G20 Inclusive Framework on BEPS (Inclusive Framework), bringing all interested and committed countries and jurisdictions on an equal footing in the Committee on Fiscal Affairs and its subsidiary bodies. With over 140 members, the Inclusive Framework monitors and peer reviews the implementation of the minimum standards and is completing the work on standard setting to address BEPS issues. In addition to its members, other international organisations and regional tax bodies are involved in the work of the Inclusive Framework, which also consults business and the civil society on its different work streams.

Although implementation of the BEPS package is dramatically changing the international tax landscape and improving the fairness of tax systems, one of the key outstanding BEPS issues – to address the tax challenges arising from the digitalisation of the economy – remained unresolved. In a major step forward on 8 October 2021, over 135 Inclusive Framework members, representing more than 95% of global GDP, joined a two-pillar solution to reform the international taxation rules and ensure that multinational enterprises pay a fair share of tax wherever they operate and generate profits in today's digitalised and globalised world economy. The implementation of these new rules is envisaged by 2023.

This report was approved by the Inclusive Framework on 9 February 2022 and prepared for publication by the OECD Secretariat.

Acknowledgements

This document was prepared by the Tax Treaty Unit of the OECD Centre for Tax Policy and Administration. The data included in this document was submitted by the delegates of Working Party 1 (WP1), in its Inclusive Framework on BEPS (IF) format, of each jurisdiction that is a member of the IF. The fourth edition of this report was prepared by Jessica Di Maria and Sara Shearmur, advisors in the Tax Treaty Unit of the OECD Centre for Tax Policy and Administration. The authors would like to thank the delegates of WP1 for their input.

The authors would also like to thank Lee Harley, Head of the Tax Treaty Unit, and Théo Leclercq, Yves Van Brussel and Kazuya Shimizu for analysing the relevant data and for their contribution in preparing the report; to Caroline Devlin-Genin for her help with matters relating to the *Multilateral Convention to Implement Tax Treaty Related Measures to Prevent BEPS*; to Andrew Dawson and Edward Barret for their comments on the draft report; and to Raphaël Clément for his help with the French version of the report. The authors are especially grateful to Ria Sandilands for her assistance with coordination and communication, as well as to Karena Garnier and Carrie Tyler for their help in preparing this publication.

Table of contents

TABLES

Executive Summary

1. The minimum standard on treaty shopping included in the Report on Action 6 is one of the four BEPS minimum standards. Action 6 of the BEPS Project identified treaty abuse, and in particular treaty shopping, as one of the principal sources of BEPS concerns. Owing to the seriousness of treaty shopping, jurisdictions have agreed to adopt, as a minimum standard, measures to address it, and to subject their efforts to an annual peer review (OECD, 2017[1]). (OECD, 2021[2]). The Inclusive Framework on BEPS published reports for each of the three peer review processes carried out in 2018, 2019 and 2020 (OECD, 2019[3]) (OECD, 2020[4]) (OECD, 2021[5]).

2. This 2021 peer review report reflects the fourth peer review process on the implementation of the Action 6 minimum standard. It contains the aggregate results of the peer review, background information on treaty shopping in Chapter 7, and the 139 "jurisdictional sections" which provide detailed information on the implementation of the minimum standard for each member of the Inclusive Framework in Chapter 8. This fourth peer review process was governed by a revised peer review methodology, discussed in Section 2 below.

3. In 2021, the *Multilateral Convention to Implement Tax Treaty Related Measures to Prevent Base Erosion and Profit* Shifting (MLI) has continued to significantly expand the implementation of the minimum standard for the jurisdictions that have ratified it.

4. Indeed, the number of compliant agreements concluded between members of the Inclusive Framework and covered by the MLI almost doubled, from approximately 350 to more than 650 (out of around 710 compliant agreements), between the 2020 and 2021 peer reviews. More than 960 additional agreements will shortly become compliant under the MLI, once all Signatories to the MLI will have ratified it. In total, nearly 70% of the agreements concluded among the members Inclusive Framework is being brought into compliance under the MLI. Jurisdictions that have not signed or ratified the MLI have generally made significantly slower progress compared with those that have.

5. In total, as at 30 June 2021, around 2,330 agreements concluded between members of the Inclusive Framework are either compliant, subject to a complying instrument, subject to steps taken by at least one treaty partner to implement the minimum standard, or the object of a general statement by one treaty partner that it intends to use the detailed Limitation-on-benefits rule (LOB) to implement the minimum standard in all its bilateral agreements.

6. This year's peer review further reveals jurisdictions' plans to implement the minimum standard in non-compliant agreements concluded with other members of the Inclusive Framework, that are not already subject to a complying instrument or general statement on the detailed LOB, and in respect of which no steps have been taken to implement the minimum standard (and where no reasons were provided why, for that member, the tax agreement does not give rise to material treaty-shopping concerns). The vast majority of these plans involve the application of the MLI to the concerned agreements. Once all plans to implement the minimum standard are in effect, the minimum standard will be implemented, or on course to being implemented, in nearly all of the agreements concluded between members of the Inclusive Framework.

7. Finally, recommendations were made in this year's peer review to jurisdictions that must formulate a plan for the implementation of the minimum standard, and to those that have signed the MLI but have not yet completed the steps for the entry into effect of its provisions.

Context and background to the peer review

8. This fourth report on the implementation of the Action 6 minimum standard reflects the first peer review process carried out under the revised peer review methodology.

9. The peer review processes for 2018, 2019 and 2020 were carried out following an agreed approach that was set out in a document published on 29 May 2017, and that formed the basis on which the peer review process was undertaken (the 2017 Peer Review Documents) (OECD, 2017[1]). The 2017 Peer Review Documents included the Terms of Reference which set out the criteria for assessing the implementation of the Action 6 minimum standard, and the methodology setting out the procedural mechanism by which the review would be conducted.

10. In 2021, members of the Inclusive Framework on BEPS approved a revised methodology in the 2021 Peer Review Document (OECD, 2021[2])[1], which governs the conduct of this year's and future years' peer reviews of the Action 6 minimum standard.

11. As in previous years, jurisdictions were required to complete a peer review questionnaire by 31 May 2021, reporting on the status of the implementation of the minimum standard in all of their comprehensive income tax agreements in force on that date (including agreements with jurisdictions that are not Inclusive Framework members). For each tax agreement listed, members indicated whether or not it complied with the minimum standard and, if not, whether it was on course to becoming compliant with the minimum standard.

12. However, under the revised methodology, jurisdictions' progress in implementing the minimum standard has been measured in greater detail.

13. The changes to the peer review methodology were agreed as part of the review process that was set out in of the 2017 Peer Review Documents. Paragraph 14 of the 2017 Peer Review Documents provided that the methodology for the review of the implementation of the minimum standard on treaty shopping would be reviewed in 2020 in light of the experience in conducting that review.

14. The objective of the revised methodology (explained in further detail in Chapter 7) is to establish a framework through which assistance would be given to a member jurisdiction that had non-compliant agreements with members of the Inclusive Framework that could, on its own assessment, create treaty-shopping opportunities and for which the jurisdiction had not yet taken steps to bring them into compliance with the minimum standard.

15. This year's peer review process resulted in a new and expanded data set on the status of jurisdictions' implementation of the Action 6 minimum standard. Jurisdictions have reported on their progress in the implementation of the minimum standard in much greater detail. In particular, jurisdictions have been invited to report additional information for every agreement with a jurisdiction member of the Inclusive Framework that neither complied with the minimum standard nor was subject to a complying instrument (e.g. the MLI or a signed amending instrument resulting from bilateral negotiations). Jurisdictions that have signed the MLI but not ratified it have also been invited to provide additional information on their ratification process.

16. As part of the new framework, jurisdictions have formulated plans, where relevant, for the implementation of the minimum standard in certain of their agreements. This concerns agreements concluded with other members of the Inclusive Framework that are not compliant or subject to a complying instrument, for which no steps have yet been taken to implement the minimum standard, and where no

statement has been made that a treaty partner intends to use a detailed limitation-on-benefits provision as part of the implementation of the minimum standard in all its bilateral tax agreements.

17. The assistance provided to jurisdictions under the revised methodology also includes the issuance of recommendations, contained in this report. These recommendations are, where relevant: to formulate a plan for the implementation of the minimum standard if one was not already in existence; and to complete the steps to have the MLI take effect where a jurisdiction is using the MLI to implement the minimum standard.

18. The implementation plans and recommendations are further discussed, respectively, in Sections 4 and 5 below, as well as the jurisdictional sections of the concerned jurisdictions, in Chapter 8.

References

OECD (2021), *BEPS Action 6 on Preventing the Granting of Treaty Benefits in Inappropriate Circumstances – Revised Peer Review Documents*, OECD/G20 Base Erosion and Profit Shifting Project, OECD, Paris, www.oecd.org/tax/beps/beps-action-6-preventing-the-granting-of-treaty-benefits-in-inappropriate-circumstances-revised-peer-review-documents.pdf. [2]

OECD (2021), *Prevention of Tax Treaty Abuse – Third Peer Review Report on Treaty Shopping: Inclusive Framework on BEPS: Action 6*, OECD/G20 Base Erosion and Profit Shifting Project, OECD Publishing, Paris, https://doi.org/10.1787/d6cecbb8-en. [5]

OECD (2020), Prevention of Treaty Abuse – Second Peer Review Report on Treaty Shopping: Inclusive Framework on BEPS: Action 6, OECD/G20 Base Erosion and Profit Shifting Project, OECD Publishing, Paris, https://doi.org/10.1787/d656738d-en.

OECD (2019), *Prevention of Treaty Abuse - Peer Review Report on Treaty Shopping: Inclusive Framework on BEPS: Action 6*, OECD/G20 Base Erosion and Profit Shifting Project, OECD Publishing, Paris, https://doi.org/10.1787/9789264312388-en. [3]

OECD (2017), *BEPS Action 6 on Preventing the Granting of Treaty Benefits in Inappropriate Circumstances – Peer Review Documents*, OECD/G20 Base Erosion and Profit Shifting Project, OECD, Paris. www.oecd.org/tax/beps/beps-action-6-preventing-the-granting-of-treaty-benefits-in-inappropriatecircumstance-peer-review-documents.pdf. [1]

Note

[1] Approved by the Inclusive Framework in the 2021 Peer Review Document on 17 February 2021.

1 Implementation of the minimum standard: Aggregate data and key figures

19. This section sets out the aggregate data on the implementation of the minimum standard on treaty shopping included in the Report on Action 6 (OECD, 2015[1]).

20. The minimum standard requires jurisdictions to do two things in their tax agreements: include an express statement on non-taxation (generally in the preamble); and adopt one of three methods of addressing treaty shopping. It does not specify how these two things should be achieved (e.g. through the MLI or bilaterally) (OECD, 2015[1]).[1]

21. Aggregate data on the jurisdictions' progress towards implementing the minimum standard is provided below. Detailed information on each jurisdiction's progress is provided in the jurisdictional sections in Chapter 8. The information that can be found in the "Conclusion" section in some of the jurisdictional sections in Chapter 8 further highlights the following:

- Members of the Inclusive Framework that have signed but not ratified the MLI are recommended to complete the steps to have the MLI take effect as soon as possible (Section 5 below);
- Similarly, some of the parties to the MLI that have made a reservation under the MLI to delay its entry into effect until the completion of internal procedures are recommended to complete the steps to have the MLI take effect as soon as possible (Section 5 below).[2]
- An implementation plan must be developed for agreements concluded with other members of the Inclusive Framework that are not compliant, not subject to a complying instrument or to a general statement on the detailed LOB, for which no steps have been taken to implement the minimum standard and no reasons have been given on why, for a jurisdiction, the agreement does not give rise to material treaty shopping concerns. Where no implementation plan has been developed in respect of such agreements, jurisdictions are recommended to develop a plan for the implementation of the minimum standard (Sections 4 and 5 below).
- The OECD Secretariat stands ready to discuss with any jurisdiction that has developed, or that needs to develop, a plan for the implementation of the minimum standard to see how support could best be provided to bring the concerned agreements into compliance with the minimum standard.
- Jurisdictions that are parties to the CARICOM Agreement are recommended to bring that agreement up to date by commencing talks among all the treaty partners (see Section 6 below).

Aggregate data and key figures

22. In total, the 139 jurisdictions of the Inclusive Framework reported 2,390 agreements (including 5 multilateral agreements) in force on 31 May 2021 among themselves, and about 890 additional

agreements between members of the Inclusive Framework and non-members.[3] Eight member jurisdictions had no comprehensive tax agreements in force.[4]

23. The data collected on the implementation of the Action 6 minimum standard showed that, on 31 May 2021, 116 jurisdictions of the Inclusive Framework had some agreements that already complied with the minimum standard, that were subject to a complying instrument, in respect of which steps had been taken to implement the minimum standard, or that were subject to a general statement on the detailed LOB.[5]

24. The agreements between members of the Inclusive Framework and non-members are not subject to the peer review and the aggregate results in this chapter focus on the 2,390 agreements (including 5 multilateral agreements) entered into among members of the Inclusive Framework. The jurisdictional sections in Chapter 8 nevertheless indicate the reported status of the implementation of the minimum standard in agreements outside the peer review.[6]

Compliant agreements

25. On 31 May 2021, over 710 bilateral agreements between members of the Inclusive Framework complied with the minimum standard. An additional 60 agreements not subject to this review (i.e. agreements between members of the Inclusive Framework and non-members) also complied with the minimum standard. This represents a more than two-fold increase compared to 2020.

26. In all compliant agreements, the preamble statement and the principal purpose test (PPT) were implemented to meet the minimum standard. In 40 of those agreements, the PPT was supplemented with a LOB provision.

Agreements subject to compliant instrument

27. Many jurisdictions in the Inclusive Framework have agreements currently subject to a signed complying instrument that is not yet in force, but that would implement the minimum standard.

28. On 31 May 2021, over 960 bilateral agreements (of 2,385 bilateral) between members of the Inclusive Framework were set to become covered tax agreements under the MLI (i.e. both Contracting Jurisdictions had listed the agreement under the MLI and, as a result, the MLI will modify the agreement once in effect) and thereby to become compliant with the minimum standard. These agreements will comply with the minimum standard once the relevant provisions of the MLI take effect, following ratification by both Contracting Jurisdictions.[7]

29. A further 23 agreements between members of the Inclusive Framework are subject to a bilateral amending instrument that is not yet in force. The number of agreements subject to a bilateral amending instrument, when compared with those that are subject to the MLI, shows the comparative effectiveness of the MLI in implementing the minimum standard.

30. For the agreements listed under the MLI, all 93 members of the Inclusive Framework that are parties and signatories to the MLI are implementing the preamble statement and the PPT. Fifteen jurisdictions have also opted to apply the simplified LOB through the MLI to supplement the PPT when possible. Six additional jurisdictions agreed to accept a simplified LOB in agreements with partners that opted for it under the MLI.

Steps taken to implement the minimum standard (incl. general statement on the detailed LOB)

31. Many jurisdictions in the Inclusive Framework have non-compliant agreements that are not subject to a complying instrument, but in respect of which the jurisdictions have taken steps to enable the

agreement to become subject to a complying instrument. For example, according to the revised peer review methodology, a jurisdiction will be considered to have taken a step to implement the minimum standard in an agreement under the MLI if it has signed the MLI and listed that agreement to be covered, but its treaty partner has not done the same (Where both treaty partners have signed the MLI and listed an agreement to be covered, the MLI would instead be considered a complying instrument for that agreement.) Other steps also include entering into bilateral renegotiations with a treaty partner, agreeing to enter into such renegotiations, or contacting a treaty partner with a draft protocol, with these steps intended to implement the minimum standard.

32. While some jurisdictions have chosen only one method in their steps to implement the minimum standard (e.g. by listing all their agreements under the MLI), other jurisdictions have tailored their approach across their treaty network (e.g. by pursuing bilateral renegotiations of some agreements, and using the MLI for other agreements). The MLI remains the more widely applied step taken for the implementation of the minimum standard in non-compliant agreements, covering more than 470 agreements. Jurisdictions have also taken steps other than under the MLI to implement the minimum standard in about 240 agreements (including about 90 agreements for which a treaty partner has taken concurrent steps under the MLI). As discussed further below (Section 6) treaty partners may have taken different steps to implement the minimum standard in a given agreement, and may at this stage still be in the process of deciding which method to pursue (e.g. MLI or bilateral negotiations).

33. An additional two jurisdictions, the United States and Trinidad and Tobago, have made a general statement that they intend to use the detailed LOB as part of their commitment to implement the minimum standard in all their bilateral agreements (these two countries have between them concluded a total of 79 agreements with other members of the Inclusive Framework). The detailed LOB provision is not included in the MLI and requires substantive bilateral discussions and customisation to each tax agreement, which could take several years. If a jurisdiction makes such a statement, its treaty partners will not generally provide any additional information about their tax agreement with that jurisdiction.

34. In total, this year, around 2,330 agreements concluded between members of the Inclusive Framework are compliant, subject to a complying instrument or to steps taken by at least one treaty partner to implement the minimum standard, or are the object of a general statement by a treaty partner on the detailed limitation-on-benefits provision.

Provisions used to implement the minimum standard

35. As with previous years, this year's peer review shows that among the three alternative methods to implement the second component of the minimum standard[8], the PPT alone remains much the most widely used. The majority of jurisdictions have chosen to implement the minimum standard using this alternative. Indeed, it is the only provision capable on its own of satisfying the second component of the minimum standard, and can be implemented using the MLI.

36. About 65 agreements are or will be brought into compliance with the minimum standard using the PPT supplemented by a detailed or simplified LOB. The MLI can be used to implement the PPT together with a simplified LOB and 14 jurisdictions have chosen this option. An additional six have agreed to implement the simplified MLI LOB in cases where their treaty partner has chosen to adopt that measure[9].

37. As mentioned above, two jurisdictions, the United States and Trinidad and Tobago, have made a general statement that they intend to use the detailed LOB as part of their commitment to implement the minimum standard in all their bilateral agreements. In total, these statements concern 83 agreements (including 79 agreements concluded with other members of the Inclusive Framework).

Methods of implementation

38. The MLI has proven to be an effective way – indeed, the preferred way – of implementing the minimum standard. However, a jurisdiction that prefers to implement the minimum standard through a detailed limitation on benefits provision cannot use the MLI to do so. Ninety-six jurisdictions have joined the MLI (including 93 members of the Inclusive Framework), 68 have ratified it, and the MLI would, once fully in effect, implement the minimum standard in more than 1,700 bilateral agreements, thus modifying the majority of agreements concluded between members of the Inclusive Framework.

39. The efforts made by most members of the Inclusive Framework in tackling treaty shopping started to show in 2020 for those that ratified the MLI. Jurisdictions that have not signed or ratified the MLI have generally made significantly slower progress compared with those that have.

40. Nevertheless, for a number of agreements, while one jurisdiction may have signed the MLI and listed the agreement as one to be covered, its treaty partner may prefer to enter into bilateral renegotiations. As specified in the Terms of Reference, the way in which the minimum standard will be implemented in each bilateral agreement must be agreed between the contracting jurisdictions; participation in the MLI is not a minimum standard and jurisdictions may have different preferences.

References

OECD (2015), *Preventing the Granting of Treaty Benefits in Inappropriate Circumstances, Action 6 - 2015 Final Report*, OECD/G20 Base Erosion and Profit Shifting Project, OECD Publishing, Paris, https://dx.doi.org/10.1787/9789264241695-en. [1]

Notes

[1] The Action 6 Final Report further states that (i) a jurisdiction is required to implement the minimum standard in a treaty only if asked to do so by another member of the Inclusive Framework; (ii) the decision on which of the three methods to adopt has to be agreed (a solution cannot be imposed); and (iii) reflecting treaties' bilateral nature, there is no time limit within which a jurisdiction has to attain the minimum standard.

[2] The reservation under Article 35(7) MLI delays the entry into effect of the provisions of the MLI with respect to a Covered Tax Agreement until the reserving Party notifies (under Article 35(7)(b) MLI) that it has completed its internal procedures for such entry into effect. Several Parties to the MLI have made this reservation but have not yet made any notification under Article 35(7)(b) MLI. As a result, their agreements cannot yet be brought into compliance with the minimum standard under the MLI.

[3] In 2020, the Inclusive Framework reported 2,295 agreements entered into between members of the Inclusive Framework. The additional 88 agreements reviewed in 2021 include new agreements entered into between members of the Inclusive Framework between 1 July 2020, and 31 May 2021, and the relevant existing agreements of the two new members of the Inclusive Framework, which agreements were not subject to the 2020 Peer Review.

[4] Anguilla, the Bahamas, the Cayman Islands, the Cook Islands, Djibouti, Haiti, Honduras and Turks and Caicos Islands have no agreements in force.

[5] On 31 May 2021, 95 jurisdictions were signatories or parties to the MLI, but three of them (Cyprus, Fiji and Kuwait) are not members of the Inclusive Framework. Thus, as of 31 May 2021, 92 members of the Inclusive Framework were signatories or parties to the MLI; Namibia signed the MLI on 30 September 2021, bringing this number to 93. A number of additional members of the Inclusive Framework, although not signatories or parties to the MLI, have concluded amending protocols to implement the minimum standard.

[6] A "complying instrument" could be the MLI or a suitable new amending protocol yet to enter into force. It could also be a completely new agreement that has not yet entered into force.

[7] And, where relevant, the notification pursuant to Article 35(7)(b) MLI (see further explanations in footnote 7).

[8] These are: the PPT, the PPT supplemented by a detailed or simplified LOB, or a detailed LOB together with an anti-conduit mechanism.

[9] As allowed under Article 7(7) MLI.

2 Key role of the MLI

Ratification of the MLI

41. The MLI started to show its effect and to strengthen the bilateral tax treaty network of jurisdictions that ratified it in the course of 2020. The number of agreements that became compliant with the MLI increased from 60 to over 350 between 2019 and 2020. In 2021, this number has surpassed 650. The peer review continues to reveal an important difference in the progress made on implementing the minimum standard by jurisdictions that have ratified the MLI compared with other jurisdictions.

42. Over the past year, 21 jurisdictions have ratified the MLI: Albania, Andorra, Barbados, Bosnia-Herzegovina, Burkina Faso, Chile, Costa Rica, Croatia, Egypt, Estonia, Germany, Greece, Hungary, Jordan, Kazakhstan, Malaysia, Oman, Pakistan, Panama, the Seychelles and Spain.

43. On average, nearly 50% of the treaty networks of jurisdictions for which the MLI started to take effect as of 1 January 2021,[1] are compliant with the minimum standard in 2021, as shown in the Table 2.1.

44. For the jurisdictions that ratified the MLI after October 2020,[2] the relevant provisions of the MLI had generally not yet started to take effect for their agreements on 31 May 2021. This is because provisions of the MLI can generally only start to take effect for an agreement after a period of time that follows the latest of the dates on which the MLI enters into force for each of the partners to an agreement. This period could roughly amount to a year from the latest ratification.[3]

45. While the jurisdictions that ratified the MLI made good progress in the implementation of the minimum standard, those that did not sign or ratify the MLI generally made little progress in implementing the minimum standard. Only around 8% of the agreements concluded by those jurisdictions are compliant.

46. The 2021 peer review thus continues to show the importance of swift ratification of the MLI. All signatories to the MLI that have not yet ratified it are therefore encouraged to do so.

47. The OECD Secretariat has liaised with the signatories of the MLI that, at the time of the drafting of this report, had not yet ratified it and notes that Bulgaria, Cameroon, Jamaica and North Macedonia are aiming to deposit their instrument of ratification of the MLI during the fourth quarter of 2021.[4]

Table 2.1. Treaty networks and ratification of the MLI

Jurisdiction	Date of MLI Ratification	Agreements in force	Compliant agreements on 31 May 2021	% of network compliant	% of network with IF members compliant
Albania	22 September 2020	42	18	43%	44%
Australia	26 September 2018	45	22	49%	54%
Austria	22 September 2017	90	26	29%	33%
Belgium	27 June 2019	95	39	41%	49%
Bosnia and Herzegovina	16 September 2020	38	16	42%	47%
Canada	29 August 2019	94	36	38%	45%
Costa Rica	22 September 2020	3	0	0%	0%
Curaçao	29 March 2019	4	1	25%	25%
Czech Republic1	13 May 2020	92	35	38%	43%
Denmark	30 September 2019	76	30	39%	49%
Egypt	30 September 2020	59	24	41%	49%
Finland	25 February 2019	73	40	54%	61%
France	26 September 2018	119	41	34%	44%
Georgia	29 March 2019	56	23	41%	45%
Guernsey	12 February 2019	14	10	71%	69%
Iceland	26 September 2019	45	29	64%	63%
India	25 June 2019	95	42	44%	53%
Indonesia	28 April 2020	70	21	30%	38%
Ireland	29 January 2019	73	40	55%	57%
Isle of Man	25 October 2017	10	6	60%	60%
Israel	13 September 2018	58	28	48%	55%
Japan	26 September 2018	75	44	59%	66%
Jersey	15 December 2017	15	8	53%	54%
Jordan	29 September 2020	37	15	41%	58%
Kazakhstan	24 June 2020	55	23	42%	49%
Korea	13 May 2020	94	41	44%	50%
Latvia	29 October 2019	62	34	55%	61%
Liechtenstein	19 December 2019	21	16	76%	76%
Lithuania	11 September 2018	56	33	59%	65%
Luxembourg	9 April 2019	83	46	55%	57%
Malta	18 December 2018	77	43	56%	59%
Mauritius	18 October 2019	44	12	27%	33%
Monaco	10 January 2019	10	6	60%	67%
Netherlands	29 March 2019	94	45	48%	54%
New Zealand	27 June 2018	40	21	53%	57%
Norway	17 July 2019	89	24	27%	30%
Oman	7 July 2020	35	9	26%	33%
Poland	23 January 2018	82	38	46%	54%
Portugal	28 February 2020	78	35	45%	50%
Qatar	23 December 2019	78	29	37%	45%
Russia2	18 June 2019	85	36	42%	52%
San Marino	11 March 2020	23	10	43%	43%
Saudi Arabia	23 January 2020	54	22	40%	52%
Serbia	5 June 2018	61	35	57%	63%
Singapore	21 December 2018	88	45	51%	60%
Slovak Republic	20 September 2018	69	32	46%	53%
Slovenia	22 March 2018	59	34	58%	63%
Sweden3	22 June 2018	85	7	8%	9%
Switzerland4	29 August 2019	107	14	13%	15%

Ukraine	8 August 2019	75	31	41%	48%
United Arab Emirates	29 May 2019	105	38	36%	46%
United Kingdom	29 June 2018	131	53	40%	50%
Uruguay	6 February 2020	22	14	64%	67%

1. The Czech Republic has 92 agreements in force. These 92 agreements relate to 93 jurisdictions, because the Czech Republic continues to apply the agreement with former Serbia and Montenegro to both Serbia and Montenegro. The Czech Republic has listed this agreement to be covered under the MLI only in respect of Serbia. The agreement complies with the minimum standard only in relation to Serbia.
2. The Russia Federation made a reservation under Article 35(7) of the MLI to delay the entry into effect of the MLI after completing its domestic procedures.
3. Sweden made a reservation under Article 35(7) of the MLI to delay the entry into effect of the MLI after completing its domestic procedures.
4. Switzerland made a reservation under Article 35(7) of the MLI to delay the entry into effect of the MLI after completing its domestic procedures.

Gaps in coverage of MLI

48. Throughout the 2021 peer review, gaps in the coverage of the MLI were identified. These gaps exist because the MLI is a flexible instrument that allows each signatory to decide which of its agreements it wishes to cover under the MLI. Thus, at the time of signature, signatories are required to deposit lists of agreements they want to modify. The MLI only modifies bilateral agreements listed by both treaty partners.

One-way agreements

49. Where an agreement has been listed under the MLI by only one of its treaty partners when both treaty partners have signed the MLI, the minimum standard would not be implemented in the agreement. The revised methodology has made it explicit that where both partners have signed the MLI, but only one has listed the agreement, listing the agreement would be interpreted as a request to implement the minimum standard. The parties would have an obligation to implement the minimum standard in the agreement and agree bilaterally how it would be done.

50. The 2021 peer review reveals that about 160 bilateral agreements, concluded between pairs of signatories to the MLI that are members of the Inclusive Framework, would not be modified by the MLI because, at this stage, only one jurisdiction had listed the agreement under the MLI ("one-way agreements").[5]

51. In some cases, the treaty partner that has not listed a "one-way agreement" to be covered under the MLI has formulated a plan to implement the minimum standard in that agreement by expanding its list of covered tax agreements under the MLI to include that agreement. In other cases, those "one-way agreements" have not been listed under the MLI because the parties are pursuing bilateral renegotiations to implement the minimum standard. These parties may also be intending to cover elements that go beyond the implementation of the minimum standard and other treaty-related BEPS measures.

Waiting agreements

52. The 2021 peer review reveals that there are about 390 bilateral agreements concluded between pairs of jurisdictions that are members of the Inclusive Framework where only one of them has signed the MLI ("waiting agreements"). For that reason, none of these agreements would, at this stage, be modified by the MLI. Nearly all these agreements would become covered under the MLI if the treaty partner that has not yet signed the MLI would do so and would list the agreement.

In the course of this peer review, the OECD Secretariat liaised with some of the jurisdictions that were working towards signature of the MLI as part of their plan to implement the minimum standard (see Section 4 below). Those included Botswana, Mongolia, Montenegro, Thailand and Viet Nam, which between them have more than 140 waiting agreements that would become covered agreements under the MLI following their signatures. Thus, the signature of the MLI by jurisdictions with large treaty networks would materially improve the coverage of the MLI.

Notes

[1] The MLI generally started to take effect as of 1 January 2021, with respect to agreements of jurisdictions that ratified it before the end of September 2020.

[2] Andorra, Barbados, Burkina Faso, Chile, Croatia, Estonia, Germany, Greece, Hungary, Malaysia, Pakistan, Panama, the Seychelles and Spain deposited their instruments of ratification of the MLI after October 2020.

[3] Article 35 of the MLI provides for the rules on its entry into effect and divides modifications into two categories based on the type of taxation to which they apply. In general, under Article 35(1)(a), with respect to taxes withheld at source on amounts paid or credited to non-residents, the MLI enters into effect on or after the first day of the next calendar year that begins on or after the latest of the dates on which the Convention enters into force for each of the Contracting Jurisdictions to a Covered Tax Agreement. As for all the other taxes levied by a jurisdiction, Article 35(1)(b) provides that the MLI generally enters into effect with respect to taxable periods beginning on or after the expiration of a period of six calendar months from the latest of the dates on which the Convention enters into force for each of the Contracting Jurisdictions to a Covered Tax Agreement.

[4] China expects that the MLI ratification process will be accomplished before the end of 2021, and that the instrument of ratification of the MLI will be deposited in 2022. The deposit of China's instrument of ratification will also cover Hong Kong (China).

[5] The MLI can only modify bilateral agreements that have been listed by both treaty partners under the MLI.

3 Plans for the implementation of the minimum standard and support provided to jurisdictions

Framework for the development of plans to implement the minimum standard

53. A number of jurisdictions reported agreements, concluded with other members of the Inclusive Framework, that are not compliant, not subject to a complying instrument or to a general statement on the detailed LOB, and in respect of which no steps have been taken to implement the minimum standard. These agreements are included in the table titled 'Other agreements' in the jurisdictional sections.

54. Where a jurisdiction did not provide reasons why, for that jurisdiction, such agreements do not give rise to material treaty-shopping concerns, it was invited to develop a plan to implement the minimum standard in those agreements concluded with another member of the Inclusive Framework.[1]

55. The information included in an implementation plan concerns the way in which the minimum standard will be implemented – for example, that the jurisdictions will:

- include the agreements in their list of covered tax agreements under the MLI;
- enter into bilateral negotiations for the implementation of the minimum standard; or
- sign and ratify the MLI and list the agreements as a covered tax agreements.

56. Jurisdictions will be invited to provide an annual update on their implementation plan if changes occur. The jurisdiction that is facing any difficulty in implementing the plan will also be able to report such difficulty to the Secretariat.

57. In cases where a jurisdiction did not make a plan (or provide an update on the plan) to implement the minimum standard where a plan was called for, a recommendation to provide one has been made. These recommendations are discussed in Section 6 below.

Status of plans to implement the minimum standard

58. As mentioned above, implementation plans can take a variety of forms. While some jurisdictions have developed the same implementation plan for all concerned agreements, others have developed tailored plans for each agreement. Five jurisdictions have also stated that their plan, which was discussed with the OECD Secretariat, at this stage, remains under internal deliberation and therefore detail has not been included in this report.

59. In total, 28 jurisdictions have developed a plan for the implementation of the minimum standard, covering around 350 non-compliant agreements. The table below broadly sets out the different categories of implementation plans developed by the concerned jurisdictions:

Table 3.1. Plans to implement the minimum standard

Jurisdiction	MLI		Other	Under internal deliberation
	Plan to join the MLI	Plan to expand list of covered tax agreements		
Albania		X		
Antigua and Barbuda	X			
Austria		X	X	
Belize		X		
Benin				X
Botswana	X			
Bulgaria			X	
Cabo Verde			X	
Czech Republic		X	X	
Democratic Republic of the Congo	X			
Eswatini				X
Gabon		X		
Georgia		X	X	
Germany			X	
Indonesia		X		
Italy		X		
Kenya		X		
Maldives				X
Mongolia	X			
Montenegro	X			
Norway			X	
Paraguay				X
Saint Kitts and Nevis				X
South Africa				X
Sri Lanka			X	
Thailand	X			
Viet Nam	X			
Zambia				X

Note: Detail on each jurisdiction's plan to implement the minimum standard is included in that jurisdiction's jurisdictional section.

60. Most of the plans that have been developed to implement the minimum standard involve the application of the provisions of the MLI. Indeed, 15 out of the 21 jurisdictions that have confirmed their plan intend to implement the minimum standard in the relevant agreements by way of an extension of their existing lists of covered tax agreements, or in the context of a plan to join the MLI. In the light of the experience gathered by many members of the Inclusive Framework in signing, ratifying and implementing the MLI, the MLI evidently continues to be a key recourse for the implementation of the minimum standard. Many jurisdictions note that a majority or their agreements are, or would become, matched agreements under the MLI and seek out the efficiency, in terms of time and resources, offered by the MLI.

61. Jurisdictions choosing to implement the minimum standard by other means, such as bilateral discussions, do so for several reasons. Sometimes, this plan forms part of a wider effort to renegotiate different aspects of an agreement, beyond the implementation of the minimum standard. It may also be that their treaty partner has indicated that it does not intend to use the MLI to implement the minimum standard in that agreement. Jurisdictions with small treaty networks are also more likely to consider bilateral negotiations to implement the minimum standard.

62. An update will be provided in the 2022 Action 6 peer review report on the status of each of each implementation plan.

Note

[1] The Secretariat contacted the jurisdictions that have agreements for which a plan for the implementation of the minimum standard had to be developed to offer its support in developing and giving effect to such a plan. Where a jurisdiction wants to implement the minimum standard through the PPT and some or all of its treaty partners are already signatories to the MLI, the Secretariat has encouraged the jurisdiction to sign and ratify the MLI. Where a jurisdiction has already joined the MLI, the Secretariat similarly encouraged the jurisdiction to expand its list of agreements to be covered under the MLI in order to include the concerned agreements. For tax treaties that would not become covered tax agreements under the MLI, the Secretariat encouraged the treaty partners to develop a plan, and where possible a joint plan, for the implementation of the minimum standard.

4 Recommendations

63. As part of the support provided to jurisdictions in the implementation of the minimum standard under the revised peer review methodology, recommendations are issued to members in two categories of cases. First, a member that is implementing the minimum standard by signing the MLI will be recommended to complete the steps to have it take effect with respect to its tax agreements. Second, where a jurisdiction has tax agreements for which a plan for the implementation of the minimum standard needs to be developed, if the jurisdiction does not make such a plan (or provide an update on the plan), a recommendation will be made to provide a plan with respect to the concerned tax agreements.

64. This year, 26 jurisdictions have been recommended to take steps to have the MLI take effect.[1] Additional recommendations have been made to 9 jurisdictions to develop a plan, or provide an update on the plan, for the implementation of the minimum standard. Further detail on the recommendations made can be found in the jurisdictional sections in Chapter 8.

65. The Secretariat has contacted the concerned jurisdictions to offer its support, as applicable, in completing the steps to have the MLI take effect and to develop a plan for the implementation of the minimum standard. As discussed in Section 4 above, the information to be included in an implementation plan is the way in which the minimum standard will be implemented – for example, that the jurisdictions will:

- include the tax agreements in their list of covered tax agreements under the MLI;
- enter into bilateral negotiations for the implementation of the minimum standard; or
- sign and ratify the MLI and list the tax agreements as a covered tax agreements.

66. Recommendations were issued to those jurisdictions that did not confirm an implementation plan in respect of the agreements for which a plan needs to be developed.

67. An update will be provided in the 2022 Action 6 peer review report on the steps taken by each jurisdiction that has received a recommendation.

Note

[1] This type of recommendation mostly concerns jurisdictions that have signed the MLI, but have not yet completed the steps to deposit the instrument of ratification of the MLI (until which time, in accordance with Articles 34 and 35 of the MLI, the provisions of the MLI cannot start to take effect). In some cases, a similar recommendation is made to jurisdictions that are Parties to the MLI but that have made a reservation under Article 35(7) MLI to delay the entry into effect of the provisions of the MLI until the completion of their internal procedures, but have not yet notified the completion of such internal procedures for any of their covered tax agreements.

5 Difficulties in implementing the minimum standard

68. The peer review provides jurisdictions that encounter difficulties in reaching agreement with another jurisdiction to implement the Action 6 minimum standard with an opportunity to raise concerns with the OECD Secretariat. This process, which is set out in paragraph 35 of the Revised Peer Review Documents, was initially put in place in the 2017 Peer Review Documents (paragraph 19) to identify cases where a jurisdiction is facing a treaty partner that is a member of the Inclusive Framework that is unwilling to respect its commitment to implement the minimum standard. The process was examined as part of the review of the peer review methodology, and it was determined that the process was adequate as it stood and no changes were needed.

Concern regarding the CARICOM Agreement

69. In the course of the 2019 peer review, a jurisdiction raised a concern about the Agreement among the Member States of the Caribbean Community (CARICOM), a multilateral agreement concluded by eleven jurisdictions, ten of which are members of the Inclusive Framework. In the 2020 peer review, jurisdictions that are parties to the CARICOM Agreement were encouraged to bring that agreement up to date by commencing talks among all the treaty partners. This concern remained this year as the parties to the CARICOM Agreement have not yet modernised it.

70. The CARICOM Agreement was concluded in 1994 to encourage regional trade and investment within the CARICOM, and contains several unusual features,[1] not found in the OECD Model Tax Convention or UN Model Double Taxation Convention, which could lead to certain income flows escaping tax altogether. These departures from standard tax treaty provisions may have encouraged greater economic integration within the CARICOM at the time, but they may also have made the Agreement more vulnerable to treaty shopping and other forms of abuse.

71. Updating the CARICOM Agreement requires agreement by all eleven jurisdictions that are parties to that agreement. Previous attempts to renegotiate the CARICOM Agreement have proven to be difficult. Recent events (e.g. natural disasters such as hurricanes and volcanic eruptions in the region, and the Covid-19 pandemic) also made it difficult to launch discussions on the modernisation of the Agreement.

72. The Secretariat has contacted the jurisdictions that are parties to the CARICOM Agreement and members of the Inclusive Framework[2] as part of the 2021 Action 6 peer review process. It was acknowledged that the CARICOM Agreement does not at this stage comply with the minimum standard and that discussions to bring this agreement up to date would be contemplated.[3] Governments have been made aware and it is expected that in time a review of the CARICOM Agreement will be conducted.

Other concerns

73. The revised peer review methodology has shed light on a number of instances where jurisdictions disagreed on the method of implementation of the minimum standard (outside the process described above on raising concerns on difficulties in reaching agreement with another jurisdiction). This typically involves cases where one jurisdiction signed the MLI and listed an agreement to be covered, while the other did not sign the MLI and expressed a preference to pursue bilateral negotiations (or where the other jurisdiction did sign the MLI but did not list an agreement to be covered, i.e. one-way agreements). As set out in paragraphs 10 to 12 of the Revised Peer Review Documents, it is understood that the way in which the minimum standard will be implemented in each bilateral agreement will need to be agreed to between the contracting jurisdictions. While the MLI provides an effective way for jurisdictions that choose to apply the PPT to implement the minimum standard swiftly, participation in the MLI is not mandatory and jurisdictions may prefer to meet the minimum standard in different ways.

74. That said, it has been observed that several members of the Inclusive Framework wishing to implement the minimum standard through bilateral renegotiations have, on the same occasion, requested that their treaty partner also introduce other elements – unrelated to the minimum standard – in their agreements. While jurisdictions will understandably want to conserve resources and renegotiate different aspects of an agreement in the course of a single renegotiation process, agreeing to implement the minimum standard should not be made conditional upon any additional amendment being made to an agreement.

Notes

[1] The CARICOM Agreement provides for an almost exclusive source-based taxation of all income, gains and profits. Some income – for instance, dividends – are also entirely exempted from tax under the CARICOM Agreement.

[2] The following eleven jurisdictions are parties to the CARICOM Agreement : Antigua and Barbuda, Barbados, Belize, Dominica, Grenada, Guyana*, Jamaica, St Kitts and Nevis, Saint Lucia, Saint Vincent and the Grenadines, and Trinidad and Tobago.

[3] Revisions to the CARICOM Agreement require an agreement from its eleven treaty partners.

6 Conclusion and next steps

75. The 2021 peer review shows that in general, most jurisdictions that are members of the Inclusive Framework are respecting their commitment to implement the minimum standard. The 2021 peer review also highlights that the MLI, which has been the main tool used to implement the minimum standard, has continued to have a significant and increased effect and is strengthening the bilateral tax treaty network of jurisdictions that ratified it.

76. As with last year's peer review, however, this year's peer review shows that the Action 6 minimum standard is being implemented unevenly and, in particular, an important difference in the progress made on its implementation between jurisdictions that have ratified the MLI and other jurisdictions is evident.

77. Indeed, the peer review shows that jurisdictions that have not signed or ratified the MLI have still generally made no or little progress in implementing the minimum standard. The 2021 peer review thus highlights that ratification of the MLI is an effective tool for the implementation of the minimum standard.

78. That said, under the revised peer review methodology, additional insight has been gained regarding steps taken other than under the MLI to implement the minimum standard. Currently, such steps have been taken in respect of around 240 agreements (including around 90 agreements for which the treaty partner has taken concurrent steps under the MLI). An additional 79 agreements concluded between members of the Inclusive Framework are the object of a general statement on one party's intention to use the detailed LOB as part of its commitment to implement the minimum standard. By comparison, steps to implement the minimum standard under the MLI have been taken in respect of over 470 agreements (including the 90 agreements, mentioned above, in respect of which the treaty partner has taken concurrent steps other than under the MLI).

79. In total, this year, around 2,330 agreements concluded between members of the Inclusive Framework are compliant, subject to a complying instrument, subject to steps taken by at least one treaty partner to implement the minimum standard, or are the object of a general statement by one treaty partner that it intends to use the detailed LOB to implement the minimum standard in all its bilateral agreements. This is an impressive number that represents more than 70% of the global tax treaty network.

80. Moreover, this year's peer review reveals jurisdictions' plans to implement the minimum standard where one was called for (see Section 4 above). The vast majority of these plans involve the application of the MLI to the concerned agreements. Once all plans to implement the minimum standard are in effect, the minimum standard will be implemented, or on course to being implemented, in nearly all of the agreements concluded between members of the Inclusive Framework.

Next steps for certain members of the Inclusive Framework

81. This year's peer review contains, in Chapter 8, recommendations to jurisdictions that have not yet completed the steps to have the MLI take effect, and to jurisdictions that have not made a plan (or provided an update on the plan) to implement the minimum standard where needed, to ensure those jurisdictions can be provided with appropriate support in the implementation of the minimum standard. The immediate next steps for jurisdictions are to take note of these recommendations and follow them in their progress towards the implementation of the minimum standard.

82. When no recommendations are made, no other implementation issues are identified with respect to a jurisdiction and no other jurisdiction has raised any concerns regarding their agreements with that jurisdiction, no immediate next steps are indicated for that jurisdiction.[1]

Next steps for the Inclusive Framework

83. The implementation of the minimum standard – in particular the actions taken to follow the recommendations made, and the progress made to give effect to the implementation plans that have been developed – will continue to be monitored. As set out in the Revised Peer Review Document, the next peer review exercise will be launched in the first half of 2022.

Note

[1] The jurisdictional section of each such jurisdiction includes the mention that "No jurisdiction has raised any concerns about their agreements with the jurisdiction."

7 Background on the Action 6 minimum standard and peer review

Context of the peer review

84. Over the last decades, bilateral tax agreements, concluded by nearly every jurisdiction in the world, have served to prevent harmful double taxation and remove obstacles to cross-border trade in goods and services, and movements of capital, technology and persons. This extensive network of tax agreements has, however, also given rise to so-called "treaty-shopping" arrangements.

85. As set out in the Action 6 Final Report, treaty shopping typically involves the attempt by a person to indirectly access the benefits of a tax agreement between two jurisdictions without being a resident of one of those jurisdictions.[1]

86. Treaty shopping is undesirable for several reasons, including:

- Treaty benefits negotiated between the parties to an agreement are economically extended to residents of a third jurisdiction in a way the parties did not intend. The principle of reciprocity is therefore breached and the balance of concessions that the parties make is altered;
- Income may escape taxation altogether or be subject to inadequate taxation in a way the parties did not intend; and
- The jurisdiction of residence of the ultimate income beneficiary has less incentive to enter into a tax agreement with the jurisdiction of source, because residents of the jurisdiction of residence can indirectly receive treaty benefits from the jurisdiction of source without the need for the jurisdiction of residence to provide reciprocal benefits.

Some previous attempts to tackle treaty shopping

87. Concerns about treaty shopping are not new. For example, in 1977, the concept of "beneficial owner" was introduced into the dividends, interest, and royalties articles of the OECD Model Tax Convention to clarify the meaning of the words "paid to", and deal with simple treaty-shopping situations where income is paid to an intermediary resident of a treaty country who is not treated as the owner of that income for tax purposes (such as an agent or nominee).[2]

88. In 1977, the Commentary on Article 1 of the OECD Model Tax Convention was also updated to include a section on the improper use of tax agreements.[3] In 1986, the Committee on Fiscal Affairs (CFA) published two reports: *Double Taxation and the Use of Base Companies* and *Double Taxation and the Use of Conduit Companies*. In 2002, the Committee published the report, *Restricting the Entitlement to Treaty Benefits*. The Commentary on Article 1 of the OECD Model Tax Convention was expanded on several occasions, notably in 2003, with the inclusion of sample provisions that countries could use to counter treaty shopping.

89. A review of jurisdictions' practices shows that they have tried to address treaty shopping in the past and have used different approaches to do so. Some have relied on specific anti-abuse rules based

on the legal nature, ownership, and general activities of residents of a jurisdiction party to a tax agreement.[4] Others have favoured a general anti-abuse rule based on the purpose of transactions or arrangements.

BEPS and treaty shopping

90. The BEPS Action Plan[5], developed by the CFA and endorsed by the G20 Leaders in September 2013[6], identified 15 actions to address base erosion and profit shifting (BEPS). It identified treaty abuse, and in particular treaty shopping, as one of the most important sources of BEPS concerns.

91. Action 6 (Prevent Treaty Abuse) of the BEPS Action Plan called for the development of treaty provisions to prevent the granting of treaty benefits in inappropriate circumstances. In parallel, Action 15 of the BEPS Action Plan called for an analysis of the possible development of a multilateral instrument "to enable jurisdictions that wish to do so to implement measures developed in the course of the work on BEPS and amend bilateral tax treaties".

92. After two years of work, the CFA, in which OECD and G20 countries work on an equal footing, produced the final BEPS Package,[7] which was endorsed by the OECD Council and the G20 Leaders in November 2015.

93. Jurisdictions agreed that four of the BEPS measures would be minimum standards that participating jurisdictions would commit to implement. The Action 6 Report sets out one of these minimum standards. The Action 6 minimum standard requires jurisdictions to commit to include in their tax treaties provisions dealing with treaty shopping to ensure a minimum level of protection against treaty abuse.

The Action 6 minimum standard

94. The minimum standard on treaty shopping requires jurisdictions to include two components in their tax agreements: an express statement on non-taxation (generally in the preamble) and one of three methods of addressing treaty shopping.

95. The minimum standard does not provide how these two components should be implemented (i.e. through the MLI or amending instruments). It recognises, however, that these provisions need to be agreed bilaterally and that a jurisdiction will be required to implement the minimum standard when requested to do so by another member of the Inclusive Framework.

The express statement

96. As set out in paragraphs 22 and 23 of the Final Report on Action 6, jurisdictions have agreed to include in their tax agreements an express statement that their common intention is to eliminate double taxation without creating opportunities for non-taxation or reduced taxation through tax evasion or avoidance, including through treaty-shopping arrangements. The following provision now appears in the 2017 OECD Model Tax Convention:

> *Intending to conclude a Convention for the elimination of double taxation with respect to taxes on income and on capital without creating opportunities for non-taxation or reduced taxation through tax evasion or avoidance (including through treaty-shopping arrangements aimed at obtaining reliefs provided in this Convention for the indirect benefit of residents of third States)*

Three methods of addressing treaty shopping

97. Jurisdictions have also committed to implement that "common intention" through the inclusion of treaty provisions in one of the following three forms:

- a principal purpose test (PPT) equivalent to paragraph 9 of Article 29 of the 2017 OECD Model Tax Convention together with either a simplified or a detailed version of the limitation on benefits (LOB) rule that appears in paragraphs 1 to 7 of the 2017 OECD Model Tax Convention; or
- the PPT alone; or
- a detailed version of the LOB rule together with a mechanism (such as a treaty rule that might take the form of a PPT rule restricted to conduit arrangements, or domestic anti-abuse rules or judicial doctrines that would achieve a similar result) that would deal with conduit arrangements not already dealt with in tax treaties.

The obligation to implement the minimum standard

98. The Action 6 Report recognised that "some flexibility in the implementation of the Action 6 minimum standard would be required, as these provisions need to be adapted to each country's specificities and to the circumstances of the negotiation of bilateral conventions." In particular:

- a jurisdiction is required to implement the minimum standard in a treaty only if asked to do so by another member of the Inclusive Framework;
- the way in which the minimum standard will be implemented in each bilateral treaty will need to be agreed to between the contracting jurisdictions.
- the commitment applies to existing and future treaties but since the conclusion of a new treaty and the modification of an existing treaty depend on the overall balance of the provisions of a treaty, this commitment should not be interpreted as a commitment to conclude new treaties or amend existing treaties within a specified period of time.
- if a jurisdiction is not itself concerned by the effect of treaty shopping on its own taxation rights as a jurisdiction of source, it will not be obliged to apply provisions such as the LOB or the PPT as long as it agrees to include in a treaty provisions that its treaty partner will be able to use for that purpose.

99. It is also understood from the Action 6 that, while the MLI provides an effective way for jurisdictions that choose to apply the PPT to implement the minimum standard swiftly, participation in the MLI is not mandatory and jurisdictions may have different preferences as to how the minimum standard should be met. However, jurisdictions that have signed the MLI are expected to take steps to ensure that it starts to take effect with respect to their Covered Tax Agreements. Where two parties to a tax treaty have signed the MLI but only one has listed the tax treaty, listing the tax treaty amounts to a request to implement the minimum standard.

100. In May 2017, the Inclusive Framework agreed the Terms of Reference for the peer review and its methodology (the 2017 Peer Review Documents) (OECD, 2017[1]) and decided that the methodology would be reviewed in 2020. In 2021, members of the Inclusive Framework on BEPS approved the 2021 Peer Review Document (OECD, 2021[2]) which is an updated version of the 2017 Peer Review Documents. The changes to the Peer Review Documents related to the methodology; changes to other sections of the Peer Review Documents were mostly conforming in nature. The Action 6 minimum standard and the way it is reflected in the Terms of Reference remained unchanged.

101. This 2021 Peer Review Document governs the conduct of the peer reviews of the Action 6 minimum standard as of 2021. It describes: the core output of the peer review and monitoring process; the process for the resolution of interpretation and application issues that might arise in the course of implementing the minimum standard on treaty-shopping; the process to be followed by jurisdictions that encounter difficulties in getting agreement from another jurisdiction member of the Inclusive Framework on BEPS in order to implement the Action 6 minimum standard; and the confidentiality of documents produced in the review process.

The 2018 peer review

102. The first peer review was conducted in 2018 and covered the 116 jurisdictions that were members of the Inclusive Framework on 30 June 2018. The Peer Review Report, which was adopted by the Inclusive Framework in January 2019, was published on 14 February 2019.

103. The 2018 peer review revealed that, as the provisions of the MLI had not taken effect at the time of the first peer review, nearly all of the agreements reviewed for this report did not at that time comply with the minimum standard. Substantial progress had, however, been made in 2017 and 2018 towards its implementation and a large majority of Inclusive Framework members had begun to translate their commitment on treaty shopping into actions and were in the process of modifying their treaty networks.

104. In total, on 30 June 2018, the peer review showed that 82 jurisdictions had some agreements that were already compliant with the minimum standard or were subject to a complying instrument that would bring their agreements into compliance.[8] The first Peer Review highlighted the effectiveness of the MLI in implementing the treaty-related BEPS measures. It was by far the preferred tool of Inclusive Framework members for implementing the minimum standard.

105. In the course of the first peer review, all concerns raised by jurisdictions on the implementation of the minimum standard in their agreements had been resolved when the Report was approved by the Inclusive Framework and therefore no recommendation was made under the first peer review.

The 2019 peer review

106. The Second peer review was conducted in 2019 and covered the 129 jurisdictions that were members of the Inclusive Framework on 30 June 2019. The Peer Review Report, which was adopted by the Inclusive Framework in January 2020, was published on 24 March 2020.

107. The 2019 peer review revealed that, by 30 June 2019, 91 Inclusive Framework members had begun to update their bilateral treaty network and were implementing the minimum standard. The data compiled for this peer review demonstrated that the MLI had been the tool used by the vast majority of jurisdictions that had begun to implement the minimum standard.

108. By 30 June 2019, the MLI had already modified around 60 bilateral agreements. The MLI's impact was expected to increase quickly as jurisdictions ratified it.

109. In the course of the Second peer review, a jurisdiction had raised a concern with respect to the CARICOM Agreement, a multilateral agreement concluded by eleven jurisdictions, ten of which were members of the Inclusive Framework. The CARICOM Agreement had been concluded in 1994 to encourage regional trade and investment within the Community, and contains several unusual features,9 not found in the OECD Model Tax Convention or the UN Model Double Taxation Convention, which could lead to certain income flows escaping tax altogether. These departures from standard tax treaty provisions may have encouraged greater economic integration within the CARICOM Community at the time. But they may also have made the CARICOM Agreement more vulnerable to treaty shopping and other forms of abuse. Previous renegotiation attempts of the CARICOM Agreement had proven to be difficult.

The 2020 peer review

110. The Third peer review was conducted in 2021 and covered the 137 jurisdictions that were members of the Inclusive Framework on 30 June 2020. The Peer Review Report, which was adopted by the Inclusive Framework in February 2021, was published on 1 April 2021.

111. The 2020 peer review revealed that, by 30 June 2020, 98 Inclusive Framework members jurisdictions of the Inclusive Framework had some agreements that already complied with the minimum standard or that were subject to a complying instrument and would therefore become compliant shortly.

The data compiled for this peer review demonstrated that the MLI had been the tool used by the vast majority of jurisdictions that had begun to implement the minimum standard.

112. By 30 June 2020, the MLI had already modified around 350 bilateral agreements. The MLI's impact was expected to increase quickly as jurisdictions ratified it.

113. Concerning the CARICOM Agreement, the concern raised in 2019 remained as the parties to the CARICOM Agreement have not yet modernised it. All Jurisdictions that are parties to the CARICOM Agreement were encouraged to bring that agreement up to date by commencing talks among all the treaty partners.

114. Moreover, encouragements were made to members of the Inclusive Framework that were signatories to the MLI but that had not yet ratified it, as the agreements listed under the MLI would only start to become compliant after their ratification.

115. The 2020 Action 6 peer review report also identified gaps in MLI coverage, or "non-covered agreements" under the MLI (agreements concluded between pairs of signatories to the MLI where one treaty partner has not listed the agreement under the MLI; and agreements concluded between jurisdictions only one of which has signed the MLI).

Conduct of the 2021 peer review

116. The review started with a questionnaire sent to members of the Inclusive Framework in April 2021. This questionnaire contained many new features compared with previous years, reflecting the revised methodology in the 2021 Peer Review Document. Similar to the questionnaires issued for 2018, 2019, and 2020,[10] each jurisdiction was asked to list all of its comprehensive income tax agreements in force.

117. For each tax agreement listed, members indicate whether or not it complies with the minimum standard described in the terms of reference at paragraph 2 above. A tax agreement complies with the minimum standard if it does so as originally signed, if an amending instrument that implements the minimum standard in that tax agreement is in force, or if the relevant provisions of the MLI have started to take effect for that tax agreement (in accordance with Article 35 of the MLI).

118. For each tax agreement listed that is non-compliant with the minimum standard, members indicate whether it is on course to become compliant with the minimum standard (i.e. whether it is subject to a complying instrument). This is satisfied if a member has signed the MLI and both jurisdictions have listed the agreement as one to be covered. It is also satisfied if an amending bilateral tax agreement implementing the minimum standard in the agreement has been signed or if a completely new treaty that complies with the Action 6 minimum standard and that would replace that treaty has been signed.

119. Members were requested to provide additional information for tax agreements that are not compliant and not subject to a complying instrument:

- *Plan to implement a detailed LOB provision*: If a member intends to use the detailed LOB as part of its commitment to implement the minimum standard in all of its bilateral tax agreements, the additional information to be provided would be a general statement that it intends to implement the minimum standard bilaterally by negotiating a detailed LOB provision and that the negotiation of its agreements will take place as time and resources permit.
- *Steps taken to enable the tax treaty to become subject to a complying instrument*: A member that does not intend to use the detailed LOB as part of its commitment to implement the minimum standard in all of its bilateral tax agreements to implement the minimum standard would provide information on the steps it has taken to implement the minimum standard for each tax agreement not compliant with the minimum standard or not subject to a complying instrument.
- *Other tax treaties*: For tax agreements not dealt with above and concluded with other members of the Inclusive Framework, a member would provide reasons why, for that member, the tax

agreement does not give rise to material treaty-shopping concerns. Where, for a tax treaty, a jurisdiction does not provide such information, it would formulate a plan to include the minimum standard in that tax agreement.

120. Each jurisdiction was invited to complete the questionnaire taking into account the agreements that were in force, or expected to be in force, by 31 May 2021.

121. Each jurisdiction was also asked to answer additional questions on ratification of complying instruments and issues described in Sections D and E of the Peer Review Document on difficulties encountered in getting agreement from another jurisdiction to implement the minimum standard. Jurisdictions were also free to add any further comments. The list of the 139 jurisdictions that were subject to the peer review and full details by jurisdiction are contained in Chapter 8.

122. The Secretariat analysed jurisdictions' responses to verify and reconcile any divergent information and produced a first draft of this report.

References

OECD (2021), *BEPS Action 6 on Preventing the Granting of Treaty Benefits in Inappropriate Circumstances – Revised Peer Review Documents*, OECD/G20 Base Erosion and Profit Shifting Project, OECD, Paris, www.oecd.org/tax/beps/beps-action-6-preventing-the-granting-of-treaty-benefits-in-inappropriatecircumstances-revised-peer-review-documents.pdf. [2]

OECD (2017), *BEPS Action 6 on Preventing the Granting of Treaty Benefits in Inappropriate Circumstances – Peer Review Documents*, OECD/G20 Base Erosion and Profit Shifting Project, OECD, Paris. www.oecd.org/tax/beps/beps-action-6-preventing-the-granting-of-treaty-benefits-in-inappropriatecircumstance-peer-review-documents.pdf. [1]

Notes

[1] See paragraph 17 of the BEPS Action 6 Final Report (2015). As the Report also notes, cases where a resident of the Contracting State in which income originates seeks to obtain treaty benefits (e.g. through a transfer of residence to the other Contracting State or through the use of an entity established in that other State) could also be considered a form of treaty shopping.

[2]See paragraph 2 of Articles 10 and 11, and paragraph 1 of Article 12 of the OECD Model Tax Convention.

[3] See paragraphs 7-10 of the Commentary on Article 1 of the 1977 Model Tax Convention.

[4] "Limitation on benefits" provisions commonly found in agreements concluded by the United States are the best-known example.

[5] https://www.oecd.org/ctp/BEPSActionPlan.pdf.

[6] http://www.g20.utoronto.ca/2013/2013-0906-declaration.html.

[7] In October 2015, the CFA, including OECD and G20 countries working on an equal footing, produced the Final BEPS Package, in the form of reports on each of the 15 actions accompanied by an Explanatory Statement. The Final BEPS Package gives countries and economies the tools they need to ensure that profits are taxed where economic activities generating the profits are performed and where value is created, while at the same time giving businesses greater certainty by reducing disputes over the application of international tax rules and standardising compliance requirements.

[8] A further seven jurisdictions had no comprehensive tax agreements and were outside the scope of this exercise.

[9] The CARICOM Agreement provides for an almost exclusive source-based taxation of all income, gains and profits. Some income – for instance dividends – are also entirely exempted from tax under the CARICOM Agreement.

[10] See, for example, the 2018 Action 6 peer review questionnaire.

8 Jurisdictional Sections

Inclusive Framework members on 31 May 2021

1	Albania	51	Gabon	101	Panama
2	Andorra	52	Georgia	102	Papua New Guinea
3	Angola	53	Germany	103	Paraguay
4	Anguilla	54	Gibraltar	104	Peru
5	Antigua and Barbuda	55	Greece	105	Poland
6	Argentina	56	Greenland	106	Portugal
7	Armenia	57	Grenada	107	Qatar
8	Aruba	58	Guernsey	108	Romania
9	Australia	59	Haiti	109	Russian Federation
10	Austria	60	Honduras	110	Saint Kitts and Nevis
11	The Bahamas	61	Hong Kong, China	111	Saint Lucia
12	Bahrain	62	Hungary	112	Saint Vincent and the Grenadines
13	Barbados	63	Iceland	113	Samoa
14	Belarus	64	India	114	San Marino
15	Belgium	65	Indonesia	115	Saudi Arabia
16	Belize	66	Ireland	116	Senegal
17	Benin	67	Isle of Man	117	Serbia
18	Bermuda	68	Israel	118	Seychelles
19	Bosnia-Herzegovina	69	Italy	119	Sierra Leone
20	Botswana	70	Jamaica	120	Singapore
21	Brazil	71	Japan	121	Slovak Republic
22	British Virgin Islands	72	Jersey	122	Slovenia
23	Brunei Darussalam	73	Jordan	123	South Africa
24	Bulgaria	74	Kazakhstan	124	Spain
25	Burkina Faso	75	Kenya	125	Sri Lanka
26	Cabo Verde	76	Korea	126	Sweden
27	Cameroon	77	Latvia	127	Switzerland
28	Canada	78	Liberia	128	Thailand
29	Cayman Islands	79	Liechtenstein	129	Trinidad and Tobago
30	Chile	80	Lithuania	130	Tunisia
31	China (People's Republic of)	81	Luxembourg	131	Turks and Caicos Islands
32	Colombia	82	Macau, China	132	Turkey
33	Congo	83	Malaysia	133	Ukraine
34	Cook Islands	84	Maldives	134	United Arab Emirates
35	Costa Rica	85	Malta	135	United Kingdom
36	Côte d'Ivoire	86	Mauritius	136	United States
37	Croatia	87	Mexico	137	Uruguay
38	Curaçao	88	Monaco	138	Viet Nam
39	Czech Republic	89	Mongolia	139	Zambia
40	Democratic Republic of the Congo	90	Montenegro		
41	Denmark	91	Montserrat		

42	Djibouti	92	Morocco		
43	Dominica	93	Namibia		
44	Dominican Republic	94	Netherlands		
45	Egypt	95	New Zealand		
46	Estonia	96	Nigeria		
47	Eswatini	97	North Macedonia		
48	Faroe Islands	98	Norway		
49	Finland	99	Oman		
50	France	100	Pakistan		

Note: The jurisdictional sections include tax agreements with jurisdictions that are not members of the Inclusive Framework. Such agreements are indicated with an asterisk (*).

Albania

A. Progress in the implementation of the minimum standard

Albania has 42 tax agreements in force, as reported in its response to the Peer Review questionnaire. Eighteen of those agreements comply with the minimum standard.

Albania signed the MLI in 2019 and deposited its instrument of ratification on 22 September 2020. The MLI entered into force for Albania on 1 January 2021. The agreements modified by the MLI come into compliance with the minimum standard once the provisions of the MLI take effect.

Albania has not listed its agreement with Saudi Arabia under the MLI, but indicated in its response to the Peer Review questionnaire that this agreement did not give rise to material treaty-shopping concerns for Albania. Saudi Arabia has listed its agreement with Albania to be covered under the MLI.

Albania is implementing the minimum standard through the inclusion of the preamble statement and the PPT.[1]

B. Conclusion

Saudi Arabia has listed its agreement with Albania under the MLI, which amounts to a request to implement the minimum standard in that agreement. Albania indicated in its response to the Peer Review questionnaire that while this agreement did not give rise to material treaty-shopping concerns for Albania, Albania intends to implement the minimum standard in this agreement by listing it to be covered in its list of covered tax agreements under the MLI, which will require completion of domestic procedures.

Summary of the jurisdiction response - Albania

	1.Treaty partners	2. Compliance with the standard	3. Signature of a complying instrument	4. Minimum standard provision used
1	Austria	No	No	PPT
2	Belgium	Yes MLI		PPT
3	Bosnia-Herzegovina	Yes MLI		PPT
4	Bulgaria	No	Yes MLI	PPT
5	China (People's Republic of)	No	Yes MLI	PPT
6	Croatia	No	Yes MLI	PPT
7	Czech Republic	No	No	PPT
8	Egypt	Yes MLI		PPT
9	Estonia	No	Yes MLI	PPT
10	France	Yes MLI		PPT
11	Germany	No	No	PPT
12	Greece	No	Yes MLI	PPT
13	Hungary	No	Yes MLI	PPT
14	Iceland	Yes MLI		PPT
15	India	Yes MLI		PPT
16	Ireland	Yes MLI		PPT

[1] For its agreements listed under the MLI, Albania is implementing the preamble statement (Article 6 of the MLI) and the PPT (Article 7 of the MLI).

17	Italy	No	No	PPT
18	Korea	No	No	PPT
19	Kosovo*	Yes other		PPT
20	Kuwait*	No	No	PPT
21	Latvia	Yes MLI		PPT
22	Macedonia	No	Yes MLI	PPT
23	Malaysia	No	Yes MLI	PPT
24	Malta	Yes MLI		PPT
25	Moldova*	No	No	PPT
26	Montenegro	No	No	PPT
27	Netherlands	Yes MLI		PPT
28	Norway	No	No	PPT
29	Poland	Yes MLI		PPT
30	Qatar	Yes MLI		PPT
31	Romania	No	Yes MLI	PPT
32	Russian Federation	No	Yes MLI	PPT
33	Serbia	Yes MLI		PPT
34	Singapore	Yes MLI		PPT
35	Slovenia	Yes MLI		PPT
36	Spain	No	Yes MLI	PPT
37	Sweden	No	Yes MLI	PPT
38	Switzerland	No	No	PPT
39	Turkey	No	Yes MLI	PPT
40	United Arab Emirates	Yes MLI		PPT
41	United Kingdom	Yes MLI		PPT

Other agreements

	1.Treaty partners	2. Inclusive Framework member
1	Saudi Arabia	Yes

Andorra

A. Progress in the implementation of the minimum standard

Andorra has eight tax agreements in force, as reported in its response to the Peer Review questionnaire. One of those agreements, the agreement with Cyprus*, complies with the minimum standard.

Andorra signed the MLI in 2017 and deposited its instrument of ratification on 29 September 2021, listing its non-compliant agreements. The MLI enters into force for Andorra on 1 January 2022. The agreements modified by the MLI come into compliance with the minimum standard once the provisions of the MLI take effect.

Andorra is implementing the minimum standard through the inclusion of the preamble statement and the PPT.[2]

B. Conclusion

No jurisdiction has raised any concerns about their agreements with Andorra.

Summary of the jurisdiction response - Andorra

	1.Treaty partners	2. Compliance with the standard	3. Signature of a complying instrument	4. Minimum standard provision used
1	Cyprus*	Yes other		PPT
2	France	No	Yes MLI	PPT
3	Liechtenstein	No	Yes MLI	PPT
4	Luxembourg	No	Yes MLI	PPT
5	Malta	No	Yes MLI	PPT
6	Portugal	No	Yes MLI	PPT
7	Spain	No	Yes MLI	PPT
8	United Arab Emirates	No	Yes MLI	PPT

[2] For its agreements listed under the MLI, Andorra is implementing the preamble statement (Article 6 of the MLI) and the PPT (Article 7 of the MLI). Andorra has made a reservation pursuant to Article 7(15)(b) of the MLI not to apply Article 7(1) of the MLI with respect to agreements that already contain a PPT (covering two agreements).

Angola

A. Progress in the implementation of the minimum standard

Angola has two tax agreements in force, as reported in its response to the Peer Review questionnaire. Both of those agreements comply with the minimum standard.

Angola is implementing the minimum standard through the inclusion of the preamble statement and the PPT.

B. Conclusion

No jurisdiction has raised any concerns about their agreements with Angola.

Summary of the jurisdiction response - Angola

	1.Treaty partners	2. Compliance with the standard	3. Signature of a complying instrument	4. Minimum standard provision used
1	Portugal	Yes other		PPT
2	United Arab Emirates	Yes other		PPT

Anguilla

A. Progress in the implementation of the minimum standard

Anguilla has no tax agreements, as reported in its response to the Peer Review questionnaire.

B. Conclusion

No jurisdiction has raised any concerns about Anguilla.

Antigua and Barbuda

A. Progress in the implementation of the minimum standard

Antigua and Barbuda has three tax agreements in force as reported in its response to the Peer Review questionnaire, including the multilateral agreement among the members of the CARICOM concluded with ten treaty partners (the CARICOM Agreement).[3] None of those agreements comply with the minimum standard.

Antigua and Barbuda has not signed the MLI.

In its response to the Peer Review Questionnaire, Switzerland indicated that its agreement with Antigua and Barbuda did not give rise to material treaty shopping concerns for Switzerland.

B. Conclusion

Antigua and Barbuda has developed a plan for the implementation of the minimum standard in its agreement with the United Kingdom. Antigua and Barbuda indicated in its response to the Peer Review questionnaire that it intends to sign the MLI and list that agreement.

The CARICOM Agreement does not at this stage comply with the minimum standard and discussions to bring this agreement up to date should be contemplated. [4]

Other agreements

This Table shows the agreements that are not compliant, not subject to a complying instrument, not covered by a general statement on the implementation of the detailed LOB and for which no steps have been taken to implement the minimum standard.

	1.Treaty partners	2. Inclusive Framework member
1	Barbados	Yes
2	Belize	Yes
3	Dominica	Yes
4	Grenada	Yes
5	Guyana*	No
6	Jamaica	Yes
7	Saint Kitts and Nevis	Yes

[3] Agreement Among the Governments of the Member States of the Caribbean Community for the Avoidance of Double Taxation and the Prevention of Fiscal Evasion with Respect to Taxes on Income, Profits or Gains and Capital Gains and for the Encouragement of Regional Trade and Investment, St. Michael Barbados, 6 July 1994; between: Antigua and Barbuda (18 February 1998), Barbados (7 July 1995), Belize (30 November 1994), Dominica (19 June 1996), Grenada (1 March 1996), Guyana* (26 November 1997), Jamaica (16 February 1995), St. Kitts/Nevis (8 May 1997), St. Lucia (22 May 1995) St. Vincent (12 February 1998) and Trinidad & Tobago (29 November 1994). In total, Antigua and Barbuda identified twelve "agreements" in its List of Tax agreements: two bilateral agreements and the CARICOM Agreement concluded with ten of its treaty partners.

[4] Revisions to the CARICOM Agreement require an agreement from its eleven treaty partners.

8	Saint Lucia	Yes
9	Saint Vincent and the Grenadines	Yes
10	Switzerland	Yes
11	Trinidad and Tobago	Yes
12	United Kingdom	Yes

Argentina

A. Progress in the implementation of the minimum standard

Argentina has 21 tax agreements in force, as reported in its response to the Peer Review questionnaire. Four of those agreements comply with the minimum standard.

Argentina signed the MLI in 2017. The agreements modified by the MLI will come into compliance with the minimum standard once the provisions of the MLI take effect.

Argentina has not listed its agreement with Germany under the MLI but indicated in its response to the Peer Review questionnaire that steps have been taken (other than under the MLI) to implement the minimum standard in this agreement.

Argentina is implementing the minimum standard through the inclusion of the preamble statement and the PPT combined with the LOB. [5]

B. Conclusion

Recommendation

It is recommended that Argentina completes the steps to have the MLI take effect with respect to its agreements listed under the MLI as those agreements will only be modified by the MLI (and come into compliance with the minimum standard) once the provisions of the MLI take effect.

Summary of the jurisdiction response - Argentina

	1.Treaty partners	2. Compliance with the standard	3. Signature of a complying instrument	4. Minimum standard provision used
1	Australia	No	Yes MLI	PPT
2	Belgium	No	Yes MLI	PPT
3	Brazil	Yes other		PPT + LOB
4	Canada	No	Yes MLI	PPT
5	Chile	Yes other		PPT + LOB
6	Denmark	No	Yes MLI	PPT + LOB
7	Finland	No	Yes MLI	PPT
8	France	No	Yes MLI	PPT
9	Germany	No	No	
10	Italy	No	Yes MLI	PPT

[5] For 15 of its agreements listed under the MLI, Argentina is implementing the preamble statement (Article 6 of the MLI) and the PPT (Article 7 of the MLI). Argentina has made a reservation pursuant to Article 6(4) of the MLI not to apply Article 6(1) of the MLI with respect to agreements that already contain the relevant preamble language (covering two agreements). Argentina has also made a reservation pursuant to Article 7(15)(b) of the MLI not to apply Article 7(1) of the MLI with respect to agreements that already contain a PPT (covering four agreements). Argentina has also adopted the simplified LOB under Article 7(6) of the MLI.

11	Mexico	Yes other		PPT + LOB
12	Netherlands	No	Yes MLI	PPT
13	Norway	No	Yes MLI	PPT + LOB
14	Qatar	Yes other		PPT
15	Russian Federation	No	Yes MLI	PPT + LOB
16	Spain	No	Yes MLI	PPT
17	Sweden	No	Yes MLI	PPT
18	Switzerland	No	Yes MLI	PPT
19	United Arab Emirates	No	Yes MLI	PPT
20	United Kingdom	No	Yes MLI	PPT

Other agreements

	1.Treaty partners	2. Inclusive Framework member
1	Bolivia*	No

Armenia

A. Progress in the implementation of the minimum standard

Armenia has 49 tax agreements in force, as reported in its response to the Peer Review questionnaire. None of those agreements comply with the minimum standard.

Armenia signed the MLI in 2017. The agreements modified by the MLI will come into compliance with the minimum standard once the provisions of the MLI take effect.

Armenia has not listed its agreement with Japan under the MLI.[6] This agreement will therefore not, at this stage, be modified under the MLI. In its response to the Peer Review Questionnaire, Japan indicated that its agreement with Armenia did not give rise to material treaty shopping concerns for Japan.

Armenia is implementing the minimum standard through the inclusion of the preamble statement and the PPT combined with the LOB.[7]

B. Conclusion

Recommendation

It is recommended that Armenia completes the steps to have the MLI take effect with respect to its agreements listed under the MLI as those agreements will only be modified by the MLI (and come into compliance with the minimum standard) once the provisions of the MLI take effect.

Summary of the jurisdiction response - Armenia

	1.Treaty partners	2. Compliance with the standard	3. Signature of a complying instrument	4. Minimum standard provision used
1	Austria	No	No	PPT
2	Belarus	No	No	PPT
3	Belgium	No	Yes MLI	PPT
4	Bulgaria	No	Yes MLI	PPT
5	Canada	No	Yes MLI	PPT
6	China (People's Republic of)	No	Yes MLI	PPT
7	Croatia	No	Yes MLI	PPT
8	Cyprus*	No	Yes MLI	PPT
9	Czech Republic	No	Yes MLI	PPT
10	Denmark	No	No	PPT

[6] While Armenia has not listed its agreements with Denmark and Israel in its provisional list of reservations and notifications under the MLI (MLI Position), Armenia has included these agreements to be covered under the MLI in its draft definitive MLI Position, for deposit upon Armenia's deposit of its instrument of ratification of the MLI.

[7] For its agreements listed under the MLI, Armenia is implementing the preamble statement (Article 6 of the MLI) and the PPT (Article 7 of the MLI). Armenia has also adopted the simplified LOB under Article 7(6) of the MLI.

11	Estonia	No	Yes MLI	PPT
12	Finland	No	Yes MLI	PPT
13	France	No	Yes MLI	PPT
14	Georgia	No	No	PPT
15	Germany	No	No	PPT
16	Greece	No	Yes MLI	PPT+LOB
17	Hungary	No	Yes MLI	PPT
18	India	No	Yes MLI	PPT+LOB
19	Indonesia	No	Yes MLI	PPT
20	Iran*	No	No	PPT
21	Ireland	No	Yes MLI	PPT
22	Italy	No	Yes MLI	PPT
23	Kazakhstan	No	Yes MLI	PPT+LOB
24	Kuwait*	No	Yes MLI	PPT
25	Latvia	No	Yes MLI	PPT
26	Lebanon*	No	No	PPT
27	Lithuania	No	Yes MLI	PPT
28	Luxembourg	No	Yes MLI	PPT
29	Moldova*	No	No	PPT
30	Netherlands	No	Yes MLI	PPT
31	Poland	No	Yes MLI	PPT
32	Qatar	No	Yes MLI	PPT
33	Romania	No	Yes MLI	PPT
34	Russian Federation	No	Yes MLI	PPT+LOB
35	Serbia	No	Yes MLI	PPT
36	Slovak Republic	No	No	PPT+LOB
37	Slovenia	No	Yes MLI	PPT
38	Spain	No	Yes MLI	PPT
39	Sweden	No	Yes MLI	PPT
40	Switzerland	No	No	PPT
41	Syrian Arab Republic*	No	No	PPT
42	Tajikistan*	No	No	PPT
43	Thailand	No	No	PPT
44	Turkmenistan*	No	No	PPT
45	Ukraine	No	Yes MLI	PPT
46	United Arab Emirates	No	Yes MLI	PPT
47	United Kingdom	No	Yes MLI	PPT
48	Israel	No	No	PPT

Other agreements

	1.Treaty partners	2. Inclusive Framework member
1	Japan	Yes

Aruba

A. Progress in the implementation of the minimum standard

Aruba has one tax agreement in force, the agreement with Netherlands, as reported in its response to the Peer Review questionnaire. The agreement does not comply with the minimum standard.

Aruba has not joined the MLI.

Aruba's agreement with Netherlands is an arrangement governed by the domestic law of the Kingdom of Netherlands.[8] Aruba indicated in its response to the Peer Review questionnaire that steps have been taken (other than under the MLI) to implement the minimum standard in its agreement with Netherlands.

B. Conclusion

No jurisdiction has raised any concerns about Aruba.

Summary of the jurisdiction response - Aruba

	1.Treaty partners	2. Compliance with the standard	3. Signature of a complying instrument	4. Minimum standard provision used
1	Netherlands	No	No	

[8] Aruba indicated in its response that the current tax arrangement for the Kingdom of Netherlands applies between Aruba and Netherlands (including the Caribbean part of Netherlands), Curaçao and Sint Maarten*. In light of the implementation of the minimum standards Aruba has drafted a tax arrangement separately with Netherlands. After the ratification of the tax arrangement with Netherlands Aruba will take steps to start the negotiations for a separate tax arrangement with Curaçao and Sint Maarten*, which will be similar to the one with Netherlands.

Australia

A. Progress in the implementation of the minimum standard

Australia has 45 tax agreements in force, as reported in its response to the Peer Review questionnaire. Twenty-two of those agreements comply with the minimum standard.

Australia signed the MLI in 2017 and deposited its instrument of ratification on 26 September 2018, listing its non-compliant agreements concluded with other members of the Inclusive Framework. The MLI entered into force for Australia on 1 January 2019. The agreements modified by the MLI come into compliance with the minimum standard once the provisions of the MLI take effect.

Australia is implementing the minimum standard through the inclusion of the preamble statement and the PPT.[9]

B. Conclusion

No jurisdiction has raised any concerns about their agreements with Australia.

Summary of the jurisdiction response - Australia

	1.Treaty partners	2. Compliance with the standard	3. Signature of a complying instrument	4. Minimum standard provision used
1	Argentina	No	Yes MLI	PPT alone
2	Austria	No	No	
3	Belgium	Yes MLI		PPT alone
4	Canada	Yes MLI		PPT alone
5	Chile	No	Yes MLI	PPT alone
6	China (People's Republic of)	No	Yes MLI	PPT alone
7	Czech Republic	Yes MLI		PPT alone
8	Denmark	Yes MLI		PPT alone
9	Fiji*	No	Yes MLI	PPT alone
10	Finland	Yes MLI		PPT alone
11	France	Yes MLI		PPT alone
12	Germany	Yes other		PPT alone
13	Hungary	No	Yes MLI	PPT alone
14	India	Yes MLI		PPT alone
15	Indonesia	Yes MLI		PPT alone
16	Ireland	Yes MLI		PPT alone
17	Israel	Yes other		PPT alone
18	Italy	No	Yes MLI	PPT alone
19	Japan	Yes MLI		PPT and LOB
20	Kiribati*	No	No	
21	Korea	Yes MLI		PPT alone

9 For its agreements listed under the MLI, Australia is implementing the preamble statement (Article 6 of the MLI) and the PPT (Article 7 of the MLI). In the case of the agreement concluded with Japan, Australia has supplemented the PPT with an LOB.

22	Malaysia	No	Yes MLI	PPT alone
23	Malta	Yes MLI		PPT alone
24	Mexico	No	Yes MLI	PPT alone
25	Netherlands	Yes MLI		PPT alone
26	New Zealand	Yes MLI		PPT alone
27	Norway	Yes MLI		PPT alone
28	Papua New Guinea	No	Yes MLI	PPT alone
29	Philippines*	No	No	
30	Poland	Yes MLI		PPT alone
31	Romania	No	Yes MLI	PPT alone
32	Russian Federation	Yes MLI		PPT alone
33	Singapore	Yes MLI		PPT alone
34	Slovak Republic	Yes MLI		PPT alone
35	South Africa	No	Yes MLI	PPT alone
36	Spain	No	Yes MLI	PPT alone
37	Sri Lanka	No	No	
38	Sweden	No	No	
39	Switzerland	No	No	
40	Thailand	No	No	
41	Turkey	No	Yes MLI	PPT alone
42	United Kingdom	Yes MLI		PPT alone
43	United States	No	No	
44	Viet Nam	No	No	

Other agreements

	1.Treaty partners	2. Inclusive Framework member
1	Chinese Taipei*	No

Austria

A. Progress in the implementation of the minimum standard

Austria has 90 tax agreements in force, as reported in its response to the Peer Review questionnaire[10]. Twenty-six of those agreements comply with the minimum standard.

Austria signed the MLI in 2017 and deposited its instrument of ratification on 22 September 2017, listing 37 of its agreements in force at that time. The MLI entered into force for Austria on 1 July 2018. The agreements modified by the MLI come into compliance with the minimum standard once the provisions of the MLI take effect.[11]

Austria has not listed its agreement with Albania, Argentina, Armenia, Australia, Bahrain, Barbados, Belarus, Belize, Bosnia-Herzegovina, Brazil, Denmark, Egypt, Georgia, Iceland, Indonesia, Kazakhstan, Korea, Malaysia, Mongolia, Montenegro, Morocco, New Zealand, North Macedonia, Norway, Qatar, San Marino, Saudi Arabia, Sweden, Thailand, Tunisia, Ukraine, the United Arab Emirates, and Viet Nam under the MLI. These agreements will therefore not, at this stage, be modified by the MLI. Albania, Armenia, Australia, Bahrain, Barbados, Belize, Bosnia-Herzegovina, Denmark, Egypt, Kazakhstan, Malaysia, Morocco, New Zealand, North Macedonia, San Marino, Saudi Arabia, Tunisia, Ukraine and the United Arab Emirates have listed their agreements with Austria under the MLI.

Austria has signed a bilateral complying instrument with respect to its agreements with Argentina[12] and Ukraine[13].

Austria further indicated that steps have been taken (other than under the MLI) to implement the minimum standard in its agreements with Australia, Bahrain, Brazil, Indonesia, Korea[14], Kuwait*, New Zealand, Norway, Qatar, the United Arab Emirates, the United States and Uzbekistan*.

Austria is implementing the minimum standard through the inclusion of the preamble statement and the PPT.[15]

B. Conclusion

Albania, Armenia, Australia, Bahrain, Barbados, Belize, Bosnia-Herzegovina, Denmark, Egypt, Kazakhstan, Malaysia, Morocco, New Zealand, North Macedonia, San Marino, Saudi Arabia, Tunisia and

[10] Austria indicated in its response that the agreement with Chinese Taipei is an Arrangement for the Avoidance of Double Taxation and the Prevention of Fiscal Evasion with Respect to Taxes on Income between the Austrian Chamber of Commerce and the Taipei Chamber of Commerce.

[11] Austria has made a reservation under Article 35(3) of the MLI (Entry into Effect).

[12] Austria ratified the complying instrument with respect to the agreement with Argentina on 17 December 2020.

[13] The complying instrument with respect to the agreement with Ukraine entered into force on 25 June 2021.

[14] A complying instrument was signed with respect to the agreement with Korea on 14 June 2021. Austria indicated in its response that the parliamentary process to ratify this instrument is expected to be completed in the 4th quarter of 2021.

[15] For its agreements listed under the MLI, Austria is implementing the preamble statement (Article 6 of the MLI) and the PPT (Article 7 of the MLI). In the case of the agreement concluded with Japan, Austria has supplemented the PPT with an LOB.

the United Arab Emirates have listed their agreements with Austria under the MLI, which amount to a requests to implement the minimum standard in those agreements.

Austria is preparing to give effect to its plan to implement the minimum standard in its agreements with Albania, Armenia, Barbados, Belarus, Belize, Bosnia-Herzegovina, Denmark, Egypt, Georgia, Iceland, Kazakhstan, North Macedonia, Malaysia, Mongolia, Montenegro, Morocco, San Marino, Saudi Arabia, Thailand, Tunisia and Viet Nam by making a notification to expand its list of agreements to be covered under the MLI to include these agreements.

Austria has developed a plan for the implementation of the minimum standard in its agreement with Sweden. Austria indicated in its response to the Peer Review questionnaire that bilateral negotiations would be pursued with respect to that agreement.

Summary of the jurisdiction response - Austria

	1.Treaty partners	2. Compliance with the standard	3. Signature of a complying instrument	4. Minimum standard provision used
1	Argentina	No	Yes other	PPT
2	Australia	No	No	N/A
3	Bahrain	No	No	N/A
4	Belgium	Yes MLI		PPT
5	Brazil	No	No	N/A
6	Bulgaria	No	Yes MLI	PPT
7	Canada	Yes MLI		PPT
8	Chile	No	Yes MLI	PPT
9	China (People's Republic of)	No	Yes MLI	PPT
10	Croatia	No	Yes MLI	PPT
11	Cyprus*	Yes MLI		PPT
12	Czech Republic	Yes MLI		PPT
13	Estonia	No	Yes MLI	PPT
14	Finland	Yes MLI		PPT
15	France	Yes MLI		PPT
16	Germany	No	Yes MLI	PPT
17	Greece	No	Yes MLI	PPT
18	Hong Kong (China)	No	Yes MLI	PPT
19	Hungary	No	Yes MLI	PPT
20	India	Yes MLI		PPT
21	Indonesia	No	No	N/A
22	Ireland	Yes MLI		PPT
23	Israel	Yes MLI		PPT
24	Italy	No	Yes MLI	PPT
25	Japan	Yes other		PPT + LOB
26	Korea	No	No	PPT
27	Kosovo*	Yes other		PPT
28	Kuwait*	No	No	N/A
29	Latvia	Yes MLI		PPT
30	Liechtenstein	Yes other		PPT
31	Lithuania	Yes MLI		PPT
32	Luxembourg	Yes MLI		PPT
33	Malta	Yes MLI		PPT
34	Mexico	No	Yes MLI	PPT
35	Netherlands	Yes MLI		PPT
36	New Zealand	No	No	N/A

37	Norway	No	No	N/A
38	Pakistan	Yes MLI		PPT
39	Poland	Yes MLI		PPT
40	Portugal	Yes MLI		PPT
41	Qatar	No	No	N/A
42	Romania	No	Yes MLI	PPT
43	Russian Federation	Yes MLI		PPT
44	Serbia	Yes MLI		PPT
45	Singapore	Yes MLI		PPT
46	Slovak Republic	Yes MLI		PPT
47	Slovenia	Yes MLI		PPT
48	South Africa	No	Yes MLI	PPT
49	Spain	No	Yes MLI	PPT
50	Switzerland	No	Yes MLI	PPT
51	Turkey	No	Yes MLI	PPT
52	Ukraine	No	Yes, other	PPT
53	United Arab Emirates	No	No	N/A
54	United Kingdom	Yes other		PPT
55	United States	No	No	N/A
56	Uzbekistan*	No	No	N/A

Other agreements

	1.Treaty partners	2. Inclusive Framework member
1	Albania	Yes
2	Algeria*	No
3	Armenia	Yes
4	Azerbaijan*	No
5	Barbados	Yes
6	Belarus	Yes
7	Belize	Yes
8	Bosnia-Herzegovina	Yes
9	Chinese Taipei*	No
10	Cuba*	No
11	Denmark	Yes
12	Egypt	Yes
13	Georgia	Yes
14	Iceland	Yes
15	Iran*	No
16	Kazakhstan	Yes
17	Kyrgyzstan*	No
18	Malaysia	Yes
19	Moldova*	No
20	Mongolia	Yes
21	Montenegro	Yes
22	Morocco	Yes
23	Nepal*	No
24	North Macedonia	Yes
25	Philippines*	No
26	San Marino	Yes
27	Saudi Arabia	Yes
28	Sweden	Yes

29	Tajikistan*	No
30	Thailand	Yes
31	Tunisia	Yes
32	Turkmenistan*	No
33	Venezuela*	No
34	Viet Nam	Yes

The Bahamas

A. Progress in the implementation of the minimum standard

The Bahamas has no tax agreements, as reported in its response to the Peer Review questionnaire.

B. Conclusion

No jurisdiction has raised any concerns about the Bahamas.

Bahrain

A. Progress in the implementation of the minimum standard

Bahrain has 44 tax agreements in force,[16] as reported in its response to the Peer Review questionnaire. None of those agreements comply with the minimum standard.

Bahrain signed the MLI in 2020 and listed its non-compliant agreements. The agreements modified by the MLI will come into compliance with the minimum standard once the provisions of the MLI take effect.

Bahrain indicated in its response to the Peer Review questionnaire that steps have been taken (other than under the MLI) to implement the minimum standard in its agreements with Austria and Bermuda.

Bahrain is implementing the minimum standard through the inclusion of the preamble statement and the PPT.[17]

B. Conclusion

Recommendation

It is recommended that Bahrain completes the steps to have the MLI take effect with respect to its agreements listed under the MLI as those agreements will only be modified by the MLI (and come into compliance with the minimum standard) once the provisions of the MLI take effect.

Summary of the jurisdiction response - Bahrain

	1.Treaty partners	2. Compliance with the standard	3. Signature of a complying instrument	4. Minimum standard provision used
1	Algeria*	No	No	PPT
2	Austria	No	No	PPT
3	Bangladesh*	No	No	PPT
4	Barbados	No	Yes MLI	PPT
5	Belarus	No	No	PPT
6	Belgium	No	Yes MLI	PPT
7	Bermuda	No	No	PPT
8	Brunei Darussalam	No	No	PPT
9	Bulgaria	No	Yes MLI	PPT
10	China (People's Republic of)	No	Yes MLI	PPT
11	Cyprus*	No	Yes MLI	PPT
12	Czech Republic	No	No	PPT

16 Bahrain has also concluded an agreement with Switzerland, which entered into force on 27 July 2021. Therefore, as of that date, Bahrain has 45 tax agreements in force. The agreement with Switzerland complies with the minimum standard.

17 For its agreements listed under the MLI, Bahrain is implementing the preamble statement (Article 6 of the MLI) and the PPT (Article 7 of the MLI).

13	Egypt	No	Yes MLI	PPT
14	Estonia	No	Yes MLI	PPT
15	France	No	Yes MLI	PPT
16	Georgia	No	No	PPT
17	Hungary	No	Yes MLI	PPT
18	Iran*	No	No	PPT
19	Ireland	No	Yes MLI	PPT
20	Isle of Man	No	Yes MLI	PPT
21	Jordan	No	Yes MLI	PPT
22	Korea	No	Yes MLI	PPT
23	Lebanon*	No	No	PPT
24	Luxembourg	No	Yes MLI	PPT
25	Malaysia	No	Yes MLI	PPT
26	Malta	No	Yes MLI	PPT
27	Mexico	No	Yes MLI	PPT
28	Morocco	No	Yes MLI	PPT
29	Netherlands	No	Yes MLI	PPT
30	Pakistan	No	Yes MLI	PPT
31	Philippines*	No	No	PPT
32	Portugal	No	Yes MLI	PPT
33	Seychelles	No	Yes MLI	PPT
34	Singapore	No	Yes MLI	PPT
35	Sri Lanka	No	No	PPT
36	Sudan*	No	No	PPT
37	Syrian Arab Republic*	No	No	PPT
38	Tajikistan*	No	No	PPT
39	Thailand	No	No	PPT
40	Turkey	No	Yes MLI	PPT
41	Turkmenistan*	No	No	PPT
42	United Kingdom	No	Yes MLI	PPT
43	Uzbekistan*	No	No	PPT
44	Yemen*	No	No	PPT

Barbados

A. Progress in the implementation of the minimum standard

Barbados has 31 tax agreements in force as reported in its response to the Peer Review questionnaire, including the multilateral agreement among the members of the CARICOM concluded with ten treaty partners (the CARICOM Agreement).[18] One of those agreements, the agreement with Mauritius, complies with the minimum standard.

Barbados signed the MLI in 2018 and deposited its instrument of ratification on 21 December 2020, listing its non-compliant bilateral agreements concluded with other members of the Inclusive Framework. The MLI entered into force for Barbados on 1 April 2021. The agreements modified by the MLI come into compliance with the minimum standard once the provisions of the MLI take effect.

Barbados is implementing the minimum standard through the inclusion of the preamble statement and the PPT.[19]

B. Conclusion

The CARICOM Agreement does not at this stage comply with the minimum standard and discussions to bring this agreement up to date should be contemplated.[20]

Summary of the jurisdiction response – Barbados

	1.Treaty partners	2. Compliance with the standard	3. Signature of a complying instrument	4. Minimum standard provision used
1	Austria	No	No	PPT
2	Bahrain	No	Yes MLI	PPT
3	Botswana	No	No	PPT
4	Canada	No	Yes MLI	PPT
5	China (People's Republic of)	No	Yes MLI	PPT
6	Cyprus*	No	Yes MLI	PPT
7	Czech Republic	No	No	PPT
8	Finland	No	Yes MLI	PPT

[18] Agreement Among the Governments of the Member States of the Caribbean Community for the Avoidance of Double Taxation and the Prevention of Fiscal Evasion with Respect to Taxes on Income, Profits or Gains and Capital Gains and for the Encouragement of Regional Trade and Investment, St. Michael Barbados, 6 July 1994; between: Antigua and Barbuda (18 February 1998), Barbados (7 July 1995), Belize (30 November 1994), Dominica (19 June 1996), Grenada (1 March 1996), Guyana* (26 November 1997), Jamaica (16 February 1995), St. Kitts/Nevis (8 May 1997), St. Lucia (22 May 1995) St. Vincent (12 February 1998) and Trinidad & Tobago (29 November 1994). In total, Barbados identified 40 "agreements" in its List of Tax agreements: 30 bilateral agreements and the CARICOM Agreement concluded with ten of its treaty partners.

[19] For its agreements listed under the MLI, Barbados is implementing the preamble statement (Article 6 of the MLI) and the PPT (Article 7 of the MLI).

[20] Revisions to the CARICOM Agreement require an agreement from its eleven treaty partners.

9	Iceland	No	Yes MLI	PPT
10	Italy	No	Yes MLI	PPT
11	Luxembourg	No	Yes MLI	PPT
12	Malta	No	Yes MLI	PPT
13	Mauritius	Yes MLI		PPT
14	Mexico	No	Yes MLI	PPT
15	Netherlands	No	Yes MLI	PPT
16	Norway	No	No	PPT
17	Panama	No	Yes MLI	PPT
18	Portugal	No	Yes MLI	PPT
19	Qatar	No	Yes MLI	PPT
20	San Marino	No	Yes MLI	PPT
21	Seychelles	No	Yes MLI	PPT
22	Singapore	No	Yes MLI	PPT
23	Spain	No	Yes MLI	PPT
24	Sweden	No	Yes MLI	PPT
25	Switzerland	No	No	PPT
26	United Arab Emirates	No	Yes MLI	PPT
27	United Kingdom	No	Yes MLI	PPT
28	United States	No	No	PPT
29	Venezuela*	No	No	PPT

Other agreements

	1.Treaty partners	2. Inclusive Framework member
1	Antigua and Barbuda	Yes
2	Belize	Yes
3	Cuba*	No
4	Dominica	Yes
5	Grenada	Yes
6	Guyana*	No
7	Jamaica	Yes
8	Saint Kitts and Nevis	Yes
9	Saint Lucia	Yes
10	Saint Vincent and the Grenadines	Yes
11	Trinidad and Tobago	Yes

Belarus

A. Progress in the implementation of the minimum standard

Belarus has 72 tax agreements in force, as reported in its response to the Peer Review questionnaire. Two of those agreements comply with the minimum standard.

Belarus has not signed the MLI.

Belarus is implementing the minimum standard through the inclusion of the preamble statement and the PPT.

In their responses to the Peer Review questionnaire, Germany, Italy and Japan indicated that their agreements with Belarus did not give rise to material treaty shopping concerns for their respective jurisdictions.

B. Conclusion

Recommendation

It is recommended that Belarus formulates a plan for the implementation of the minimum standard in its agreements for which no steps have yet been taken and that were concluded with members of the BEPS Inclusive Framework (Armenia, Austria, Bahrain, Belgium, Bulgaria, China (People's Republic of), Croatia, Czech Republic, Denmark, Egypt, Estonia, Finland, France, Georgia, Hungary, India, Indonesia, Ireland, Israel, Kazakhstan, Korea, Latvia, Lithuania, North Macedonia, Malaysia, Mongolia, Montenegro, Netherlands, Oman, Pakistan, Poland, Qatar, Romania, Russian Federation, Saudi Arabia, Serbia, Singapore, Slovak Republic, Slovenia, South Africa, Spain, Sri Lanka, Sweden, Switzerland, Thailand, Turkey, Ukraine, United Arab Emirates, and Viet Nam).

Summary of the jurisdiction response – Belarus

	1.Treaty partners	2. Compliance with the standard	3. Signature of a complying instrument	4. Minimum standard provision used
1	Hong Kong (China)	Yes other		PPT
2	United Kingdom	Yes other		PPT
3	United States	No	No	D-LOB

Other agreements

	1.Treaty partners	2. Inclusive Framework member
1	Armenia	Yes
2	Austria	Yes
3	Azerbaijan*	No
4	Bahrain	Yes
5	Bangladesh*	No

6	Belgium	Yes
7	Bulgaria	Yes
8	China (People's Republic of)	Yes
9	Croatia	Yes
10	Cyprus*	No
11	Czech Republic	Yes
12	Democratic People's Republic of Korea	No
13	Denmark	Yes
14	Ecuador*	No
15	Egypt	Yes
16	Estonia	Yes
17	Finland	Yes
18	France	Yes
19	Georgia	Yes
20	Germany	Yes
21	Hungary	Yes
22	India	Yes
23	Indonesia	Yes
24	Iran*	No
25	Ireland	Yes
26	Israel	Yes
27	Italy	Yes
28	Japan	Yes
29	Kazakhstan	Yes
30	Korea	Yes
31	Kuwait*	No
32	Kyrgyzstan*	No
33	Laos*	No
34	Latvia	Yes
35	Lebanon*	No
36	Lithuania	Yes
37	Malaysia	Yes
38	Moldova*	No
39	Mongolia	Yes
40	Montenegro	Yes
41	Netherlands	Yes
42	North Macedonia	Yes
43	Oman	Yes
44	Pakistan	Yes
45	Poland	Yes
46	Qatar	Yes
47	Romania	Yes
48	Russian Federation	Yes
49	Saudi Arabia	Yes
50	Serbia	Yes
51	Singapore	Yes
52	Slovak Republic	Yes
53	Slovenia	Yes
54	South Africa	Yes
55	Spain	Yes
56	Sri Lanka	Yes
57	Sweden	Yes
58	Switzerland	Yes

59	Syria*	No
60	Tajikistan*	No
61	Thailand	Yes
62	Turkey	Yes
63	Turkmenistan*	No
64	Ukraine	Yes
65	United Arab Emirates	Yes
66	Uzbekistan*	No
67	Venezuela*	No
68	Viet Nam	Yes

Belgium

A. Progress in the implementation of the minimum standard

Belgium has 95 tax agreements in force, as reported in its response to the Peer Review questionnaire. Thirty-nine of those agreements comply with the minimum standard.

Belgium signed the MLI in 2017 and deposited its instrument of ratification on 26 June 2019. The MLI entered into force for Belgium on 1 October 2019. The agreements modified by the MLI come into compliance with the minimum standard once the provisions of the MLI take effect.

Belgium has not listed its agreements with Germany, Norway and Switzerland under the MLI but indicated in its response to the Peer Review questionnaire that steps have been taken (other than under the MLI) to implement the minimum standard in those three agreements.

Belgium is implementing the minimum standard through the inclusion of the preamble statement and the PPT.[21]

B. Conclusion

No jurisdiction has raised any concerns about their agreements with Belgium.

Summary of the jurisdiction response - Belgium

	1.Treaty partners	2. Compliance with the standard	3. Signature of a complying instrument	4. Minimum standard provision used
1	Albania*	No	Yes MLI	PPT
2	Algeria*	No	No	PPT
3	Argentina	No	Yes MLI	PPT
4	Armenia	No	Yes MLI	PPT
5	Australia	Yes MLI		PPT
6	Austria	Yes MLI		PPT
7	Azerbaijan*	No	No	PPT
8	Bahrain	No	Yes MLI	PPT
9	Bangladesh*	No	No	PPT
10	Belarus	No	No	PPT
11	Bosnia-Herzegovina	Yes MLI		PPT
12	Brazil	No	No	PPT
13	Bulgaria	No	Yes MLI	PPT
14	Canada	Yes MLI		PPT
15	Chile	No	Yes MLI	PPT
16	China (People's Republic of)	No	Yes MLI	PPT
17	Democratic Republic of the Congo	No	No	PPT
18	Côte d'Ivoire	No	Yes MLI	PPT

21 For its agreements listed under the MLI, Belgium is implementing the preamble statement (Article 6 of the MLI) and the PPT (Article 7 of the MLI). In the case of the agreement concluded with Japan, Belgium has supplemented the PPT with an LOB.

19	Croatia	No	Yes MLI	PPT
20	Cyprus*	Yes MLI		PPT
21	Czech Republic	Yes MLI		PPT
22	Denmark	Yes MLI		PPT
23	Ecuador*	No	No	PPT
24	Egypt	Yes MLI		PPT
25	Estonia	No	Yes MLI	PPT
26	Finland	Yes MLI		PPT
27	France	Yes MLI		PPT
28	Gabon	No	Yes MLI	PPT
29	Georgia	Yes MLI		PPT
30	Germany	No	No	PPT
31	Ghana*	No	No	PPT
32	Greece	No	Yes MLI	PPT
33	Hong Kong (China)	No	Yes MLI	PPT
34	Hungary	No	Yes MLI	PPT
35	Iceland	Yes MLI		PPT
36	India	Yes MLI		PPT
37	Indonesia	Yes MLI		PPT
38	Ireland	Yes MLI		PPT
39	Israel	Yes MLI		PPT
40	Italy	No	Yes MLI	PPT
41	Japan	Yes other		PPT and LOB
42	Kazakhstan	Yes MLI		PPT
43	Korea	Yes MLI		PPT
44	Kosovo*	No	No	PPT
45	Kuwait*	No	Yes MLI	PPT
46	Kyrgyzstan*	No	No	PPT
47	Latvia	Yes MLI		PPT
48	Lithuania	Yes MLI		PPT
49	Luxembourg	Yes MLI		PPT
50	Malaysia	No	Yes MLI	PPT
51	Malta	Yes MLI		PPT
52	Mauritius	Yes MLI		PPT
53	Mexico	No	Yes MLI	PPT
54	Moldova*	No	No	PPT
55	Mongolia	No	No	PPT
56	Montenegro	No	No	PPT
57	Morocco	No	Yes MLI	PPT
58	Netherlands	No	No	PPT
59	New Zealand	Yes MLI		PPT
60	Nigeria	No	Yes MLI	PPT
61	North Macedonia	No	Yes MLI	PPT
62	Norway	No	No	PPT
63	Pakistan	Yes MLI		PPT
64	Philippines*	No	No	PPT
65	Poland	Yes MLI		PPT
66	Portugal	Yes MLI		PPT
67	Romania	No	Yes MLI	PPT
68	Russian Federation	Yes MLI		PPT
69	Rwanda*	No	No	PPT
70	San Marino	Yes MLI		PPT
71	Senegal	No	Yes MLI	PPT

72	Serbia	Yes MLI		PPT
73	Seychelles	No	Yes MLI	PPT
74	Singapore	Yes MLI		PPT
75	Slovak Republic	Yes MLI		PPT
76	Slovenia	Yes MLI		PPT
77	South Africa	No	Yes MLI	PPT
78	Spain	No	Yes MLI	PPT
79	Sri Lanka	No	No	PPT
80	Sweden	No	Yes MLI	PPT
81	Switzerland	No	No	PPT
82	Tajikistan*	No	No	PPT
83	Thailand	No	No	PPT
84	Tunisia	No	Yes MLI	PPT
85	Turkey	No	Yes MLI	PPT
86	Turkmenistan*	No	No	PPT
87	Ukraine	Yes MLI		PPT
88	United Arab Emirates	Yes MLI		PPT
89	United Kingdom	Yes MLI		PPT
90	United States	No	No	PPT
91	Uruguay	Yes MLI		PPT
92	Uzbekistan*	No	No	PPT
93	Venezuela*	No	No	PPT
94	Viet Nam	No	No	PPT

Other agreements

	1.Treaty partners	2. Inclusive Framework member
1	Chinese Taipei*	No

Belize

A. Progress in the implementation of the minimum standard

Belize has five tax agreements in force as reported in its response to the Peer Review questionnaire, including the multilateral agreement among the members of the CARICOM concluded with ten treaty partners (the CARICOM Agreement).[22] None of those agreements comply with the minimum standard.

Belize signed the MLI in 2019. The agreements modified by the MLI will come into compliance with the minimum standard once the provisions of the MLI take effect. Belize has not listed its agreement with the United Arab Emirates under the MLI. This agreement will therefore not, at this stage, be modified by the MLI. The United Arab Emirates has listed its agreement with Belize to be modified under the MLI.

Belize is implementing the minimum standard through the inclusion of the preamble statement and the PPT.[23]

B. Conclusion

The United Arab Emirates has listed its agreement with Belize to be modified under the MLI, which amounts to a request to implement the minimum standard. Belize has developed a plan for the implementation of the minimum standard in its agreement with the United Arab Emirates. Belize indicated in its response to the Peer Review questionnaire that it intends to implement the minimum standard by listing this agreement to be covered under the MLI in its definitive MLI Position, to be deposited upon the deposit of Belize's instrument of ratification of the MLI.

The CARICOM Agreement does not at this stage comply with the minimum standard and discussions to bring this agreement up to date should be contemplated.[24]

[22] Agreement Among the Governments of the Member States of the Caribbean Community for the Avoidance of Double Taxation and the Prevention of Fiscal Evasion with Respect to Taxes on Income, Profits or Gains and Capital Gains and for the Encouragement of Regional Trade and Investment, St. Michael Barbados, 6 July 1994; between: Antigua and Barbuda (18 February 1998), Barbados (7 July 1995), Belize (30 November 1994), Dominica (19 June 1996), Grenada (1 March 1996), Guyana* (26 November 1997), Jamaica (16 February 1995), St. Kitts/Nevis (8 May 1997), St. Lucia (22 May 1995) St. Vincent (12 February 1998) and Trinidad & Tobago (29 November 1994). In total, Belize identified thirteen "agreements" in its List of Tax agreements: three bilateral agreements and the CARICOM Agreement concluded with ten of its treaty partners.

[23] For its agreements listed under the MLI, Belize is implementing the preamble statement (Article 6 of the MLI) and the PPT (Article 7 of the MLI).

[24] Revisions to the CARICOM Agreement require an agreement from its eleven treaty partners.

Recommendation

It is recommended that Belize completes the steps to have the MLI take effect with respect to its agreements listed under the MLI as those agreements will only be modified by the MLI (and come into compliance with the minimum standard) once the provisions of the MLI take effect.

Summary of the jurisdiction response – Belize

	1.Treaty partners	2. Compliance with the standard	3. Signature of a complying instrument	4. Minimum standard provision used
1	Antigua and Barbuda	No	No	
2	Austria	No	No	PPT
3	Barbados	No	No	
4	Dominica	No	No	
5	Grenada	No	No	
6	Guyana*	No	No	
7	Jamaica	No	No	
8	Saint Lucia	No	No	
9	Saint Kitts and Nevis	No	No	
10	St. Vincent and the Grenadine	No	No	
11	Switzerland	No	No	PPT
12	Trinidad and Tobago	No	No	
13	United Kingdom	No	Yes MLI	PPT

Other agreements

	1.Treaty partners	2. Inclusive Framework member
1	United Arab Emirates	Yes

Benin

A. Progress in the implementation of the minimum standard

Benin has three tax agreements in force, as reported in its response to the Peer Review questionnaire, including the multilateral Regulation 08/2008/COM adopting the rules for the avoidance of double taxation within the West African Economic and Monetary Union and the rule for assistance in tax matters (the UEMOA) concluded with seven partners.[25] None of those agreements comply with the minimum standard.

Benin has not signed the MLI.

B. Conclusion

Benin is currently developing a plan, in consultation with the Secretariat, for the implementation of the minimum standard in its agreements with France and Norway.

The UEMOA does not at this stage comply with the minimum standard and discussions to bring this agreement up to date should be contemplated.[26]

Other agreements

This Table shows the agreements that are not compliant, not subject to a complying instrument, not covered by a general statement on the implementation of the detailed LOB and for which no steps have been taken to implement the minimum standard.

	1.Treaty partners	2. Inclusive Framework member
1	Burkina Faso	Yes
2	Côte d'Ivoire	Yes
3	France	Yes
4	Guinea-Bissau*	No
5	Mali*	No
6	Niger*	No
7	Norway	Yes
8	Senegal	Yes
9	Togo*	No

[25] Règlement n°08/2008/CM des pays de l'Union économique et monétaire Ouest Africaine (UEMOA) du 26 septembre 2008 portant adoption des règles visant à éviter la double imposition au sein de l'UEMOA et des règles d'assistance en matière fiscale. In total, Benin identified nine "agreements" in its list of tax agreements: two bilateral agreements and the UEMOA concluded with seven of its treaty partners.

[26] Revisions to the UEMOA require an agreement from its eight treaty partners.

Bermuda

A. Progress in the implementation of the minimum standard

Bermuda has four tax agreements in force, as reported in its response to the Peer Review questionnaire. None of those agreements comply with the minimum standard.

Bermuda concluded a bilateral complying instrument with respect to its agreement with Qatar.

Bermuda indicated in its response to the Peer Review questionnaire that steps have been taken (other than under the MLI) to implement the minimum standard in its agreement with Bahrain, the Seychelles and the United Arab Emirates.

B. Conclusion

No jurisdiction has raised any concerns about their agreements with Bermuda.

Summary of the jurisdiction response - Bermuda

	1.Treaty partners	2. Compliance with the standard	3. Signature of a complying instrument	4. Minimum standard provision used
1	Bahrain	No	No	
2	Qatar	No	Yes other	PPT
3	Seychelles	No	No	
4	United Arab Emirates	No	No	

Bosnia-Herzegovina

A. Progress in the implementation of the minimum standard

Bosnia-Herzegovina has 38 tax agreements in force, as reported in its response to the Peer Review questionnaire. Sixteen of those agreements comply with the minimum standard.

Bosnia-Herzegovina signed the MLI in 2019 and deposited its instrument of ratification on 16 September 2020, listing its non-compliant agreements concluded with other members of the Inclusive Framework. The MLI entered into force for Bosnia-Herzegovina on 1 January 2021. The agreements modified by the MLI come into compliance with the minimum standard once the provisions of the MLI take effect.

Bosnia-Herzegovina is implementing the minimum standard through the inclusion of the preamble statement and the PPT.[27]

B. Conclusion

No jurisdiction has raised any concerns about their agreements with Bosnia-Herzegovina.

Summary of the jurisdiction response – Bosnia-Herzegovina

	1.Treaty partners	2. Compliance with the standard	3. Signature of a complying instrument	4. Minimum standard provision used
1	Albania	Yes MLI		PPT
2	Algeria*	No	No	PPT
3	Austria	No	No	PPT
4	Azerbaijan*	No	No	PPT
5	Belgium	Yes MLI		PPT
6	China (People's Republic of)	No	Yes MLI	PPT
7	Croatia	No	Yes MLI	PPT
8	Cyprus*	Yes MLI		PPT
9	Czech Republic	No	No	PPT
10	Finland	Yes MLI		PPT
11	France	Yes MLI		PPT
12	Germany	No	No	PPT
13	Greece	No	Yes MLI	PPT
14	Hungary	No	Yes MLI	PPT
15	Ireland	Yes MLI		PPT
16	Italy	No	Yes MLI	PPT
17	Jordan	Yes MLI		PPT
18	Kuwait*	No	Yes MLI	PPT
19	Malaysia	No	Yes MLI	PPT
20	Moldova*	No	No	PPT
21	Montenegro	No	No	PPT
22	Netherlands	Yes MLI		PPT
23	North Macedonia	No	Yes MLI	PPT

[27] For its agreements listed under the MLI, Bosnia-Herzegovina is implementing the preamble statement (Article 6 of the MLI) and the PPT (Article 7 of the MLI).

24	Norway	No	No	PPT
25	Pakistan	Yes MLI		PPT
26	Poland	Yes MLI		PPT
27	Qatar	Yes MLI		PPT
28	Romania	No	Yes MLI	PPT
29	Serbia	Yes MLI		PPT
30	Slovak Republic	Yes MLI		PPT
31	Slovenia	Yes MLI		PPT
32	Spain	No	Yes MLI	PPT
33	Sri Lanka	No	No	PPT
34	Sweden	No	No	PPT
35	Turkey	No	Yes MLI	PPT
36	United Arab Emirates	Yes MLI		PPT
37	United Kingdom	Yes MLI		PPT

Other agreements

	1.Treaty partners	2. Inclusive Framework member
1	Iran*	No

Botswana

A. Progress in the implementation of the minimum standard

Botswana has 19 tax agreements in force, as reported in its response to the Peer Review questionnaire. One of those agreements, the agreement with the United Arab Emirates, complies with the minimum standard.

Botswana has not signed the MLI.

Botswana is implementing the minimum standard through the inclusion of the preamble statement and the PPT.

B. Conclusion

Botswana has developed a plan for the implementation of the minimum standard in its agreements with Barbados, China (People's Republic of), the Czech Republic, Eswatini, France, India Ireland, Malta, Mauritius, Namibia, Russian Federation, the Seychelles, Sweden, the United Kingdom, and Zambia. Botswana indicated in its response to the Peer Review questionnaire that it intends to sign the MLI and list those agreements.

Summary of the jurisdiction response - Botswana

	1.Treaty partners	2. Compliance with the standard	3. Signature of a complying instrument	4. Minimum standard provision used
1	United Arab Emirates	Yes other		PPT

Other agreements

	1.Treaty partners	2. Inclusive Framework member
1	Barbados	Yes
2	China (People's Republic of)	Yes
3	Czech Republic	Yes
4	Eswatini	Yes
5	France	Yes
6	India	Yes
7	Ireland	Yes
8	Malta	Yes
9	Mauritius	Yes
10	Mozambique*	No
11	Namibia	Yes
12	Russian Federation	Yes
13	Seychelles	Yes
14	South Africa	Yes
15	Sweden	Yes
16	United Kingdom	Yes
17	Zambia	Yes
18	Zimbabwe*	No

Brazil

A. Progress in the implementation of the minimum standard

Brazil has 35 tax agreements in force, as reported in its response to the Peer Review questionnaire. Three of those agreements comply with the minimum standard.

Brazil has not signed the MLI.

Brazil has signed a bilateral complying instrument with respect to its agreement with Sweden.

Brazil indicated in its response to the Peer Review questionnaire that steps have been taken (other than under the MLI) to implement the minimum standard in its agreements with Austria, Belgium, Canada, Chile, China (People's Republic of), Czech Republic, Denmark, Ecuador*, Finland, France, Hungary, India, Israel, Italy, Japan, Korea, Luxembourg, Mexico, Netherlands, Norway, Peru, Philippines*, Portugal, Russian Federation, Slovak Republic, South Africa, Spain, Trinidad and Tobago, Turkey and Ukraine.

Brazil is implementing the minimum standard through the inclusion of the preamble statement and the PPT combined with the LOB.

B. Conclusion

No jurisdiction has raised any concerns about their agreements with Brazil.

Summary of the jurisdiction response – Brazil

	1.Treaty partners	2. Compliance with the standard	3. Signature of a complying instrument	4. Minimum standard provision used
1	Argentina	Yes other		PPT + LOB
2	Austria	No	No	
3	Belgium	No	No	
4	Canada	No	No	
5	Chile	No	No	
6	China (People's Republic of)	No	No	
7	Czech Republic	No	No	
8	Denmark	No	No	
9	Ecuador*	No	No	
10	Finland	No	No	
11	France	No	No	
12	Hungary	No	No	
13	India	No	No	
14	Israel	No	No	
15	Italy	No	No	
16	Japan	No	No	
17	Korea	No	No	
18	Luxembourg	No	No	
19	Mexico	No	No	
20	Netherlands	No	No	
21	Norway	No	No	

22	Peru	No	No	
23	Philippines*	No	No	
24	Portugal	No	No	
25	Russian Federation	No	No	
26	Slovak Republic	No	No	
27	South Africa	No	No	
28	Spain	No	No	
29	Sweden	No	Yes other	PPT + LOB
30	Switzerland	Yes other		PPT
31	Trinidad and Tobago	No	No	
32	Turkey	No	No	
33	Ukraine	No	No	
34	United Arab Emirates	Yes other		PPT + LOB

Other agreements

	1.Treaty partners	2. Inclusive Framework member
1	Venezuela*	No

British Virgin Islands

A. Progress in the implementation of the minimum standard

British Virgin Islands has one tax agreement in force, the agreement with Switzerland, as reported in its response to the Peer Review questionnaire. The agreement does not comply with the minimum standard.

British Virgin Islands has not signed the MLI.

In its response to the Peer Review questionnaire, Switzerland indicated that its agreement with the British Virgin Islands did not give rise to material treaty shopping concern for Switzerland.

B. Conclusion

No jurisdiction has raised any concerns about the British Virgin Islands.

Other agreements

This Table shows the agreements that are not compliant, not subject to a complying instrument, not covered by a general statement on the implementation of the detailed LOB and for which no steps have been taken to implement the minimum standard.

	1.Treaty partners	2. Inclusive Framework member
1	Switzerland	Yes

Brunei Darussalam

A. Progress in the implementation of the minimum standard

Brunei Darussalam has 18 tax agreements in force, as reported in its response to the Peer Review questionnaire. None of those agreements comply with the minimum standard.

Brunei Darussalam has not signed the MLI.

B. Conclusion

Brunei Darussalam has developed a plan for the implementation of the minimum standard in its agreements with Bahrain, China (People's Republic of), Hong Kong (China), Indonesia, Japan, Korea, Luxembourg, Malaysia, Oman, Pakistan, Qatar, Singapore, the united Arab Emirates, the United Kingdom, and Viet Nam. Brunei Darussalam indicated in its response to the Peer Review questionnaire that it is currently amending its legal framework in order to join the MLI.

Other agreements

This Table shows the agreements that are not compliant, not subject to a complying instrument, not covered by a general statement on the implementation of the detailed LOB and for which no steps have been taken to implement the minimum standard.

	1.Treaty partners	2. Inclusive Framework member
1	Bahrain	Yes
2	Cambodia*	No
3	China (People's Republic of)	Yes
4	Hong Kong (China)	Yes
5	Indonesia	Yes
6	Japan	Yes
7	Korea	Yes
8	Kuwait*	No
9	Lao People's Democratic Republic*	No
10	Luxembourg	Yes
11	Malaysia	Yes
12	Oman	Yes
13	Pakistan	Yes
14	Qatar	Yes
15	Singapore	Yes
16	United Arab Emirates	Yes
17	United Kingdom	Yes
18	Viet Nam	Yes

Bulgaria

A. Progress in the implementation of the minimum standard

Bulgaria has 71 tax agreements in force, as reported in its response to the Peer Review questionnaire. Two of those agreements comply with the minimum standard.

Bulgaria signed the MLI in 2017. The agreements modified by the MLI will come into compliance with the minimum standard once the provisions of the MLI take effect.

Bulgaria has not listed its agreements with Finland, Malta and the Netherlands[28] under the MLI but indicated in its response to the Peer Review questionnaire that steps have been taken (other than under the MLI) to implement the minimum standard in the agreements with Finland, Germany, Luxembourg, Malta, the Netherlands, Switzerland and Uzbekistan*.

Bulgaria is implementing the minimum standard through the inclusion of the preamble statement and the PPT.[29]

B. Conclusion

Recommendation

It is recommended that Bulgaria completes the steps to have the MLI take effect with respect to its agreements listed under the MLI as those agreements will only be modified by the MLI (and come into compliance with the minimum standard) once the provisions of the MLI take effect.

Summary of the jurisdiction response - Bulgaria

	1.Treaty partners	2. Compliance with the standard	3. Signature of a complying instrument	4. Minimum standard provision used
1	Albania	No	Yes MLI	PPT
2	Algeria*	No	No	PPT
3	Armenia	No	Yes MLI	PPT
4	Austria	No	Yes MLI	PPT
5	Azerbaijan*	No	No	PPT
6	Bahrain	No	Yes MLI	PPT
7	Belarus	No	No	PPT
8	Belgium	No	Yes MLI	PPT
9	Canada	No	Yes MLI	PPT

[28] Bulgaria indicated that the new agreement with Netherlands, which is compliant with the minimum standard, has been signed and is expected to enter into force later in 2021.

[29] While Bulgaria had chosen to apply the PPT and LOB at the time of signature of the MLI, it indicated in its response to the Peer Review questionnaire that it intends to change its MLI position to implement the minimum standard through the inclusion of the preamble statement (Article 6 of the MLI) and PPT (Article 7 of the MLI) only. Bulgaria has made a reservation pursuant to Article 6(4) of the MLI (covering two agreements).

10	China (People's Republic of)	No	Yes MLI	PPT
11	Croatia	No	Yes MLI	PPT
12	Cyprus*	No	Yes MLI	PPT
13	Czech Republic	No	Yes MLI	PPT
14	Denmark	No	Yes MLI	PPT
15	Egypt	No	Yes MLI	PPT
16	Estonia	No	Yes MLI	PPT
17	Finland	No	No	
18	France	No	Yes MLI	PPT
19	Georgia	No	Yes MLI	PPT
20	Germany	No	No	PPT
21	Greece	No	Yes MLI	PPT
22	Hungary	No	Yes MLI	PPT
23	India	No	Yes MLI	PPT
24	Indonesia	No	Yes MLI	PPT
25	Iran*	No	No	PPT
26	Ireland	No	Yes MLI	PPT
27	Israel	No	Yes MLI	PPT
28	Italy	No	Yes MLI	PPT
29	Japan	No	Yes MLI	PPT
30	Jordan	No	Yes MLI	PPT
31	Kazakhstan	No	Yes MLI	PPT
32	Democratic People's Republic of Korea*	No	No	PPT
33	Korea	No	Yes MLI	PPT
34	Kuwait*	No	Yes MLI	PPT
35	Latvia	No	Yes MLI	PPT
36	Lebanon*	No	No	PPT
37	Lithuania	No	Yes MLI	PPT
38	Luxembourg	No	Yes MLI	PPT
39	Malta	No	No	
40	Moldova*	No	No	PPT
41	Mongolia	No	No	PPT
42	Montenegro	No	No	PPT
43	Morocco	No	Yes MLI	PPT
44	Netherlands	No	Yes other	PPT
45	North Macedonia	No	Yes MLI	PPT
46	Norway	No	Yes MLI	PPT
47	Pakistan	Yes other		PPT
48	Poland	No	Yes MLI	PPT
49	Portugal	No	Yes MLI	PPT
50	Qatar	No	Yes MLI	PPT
51	Romania	No	Yes MLI	PPT
52	Russian Federation	No	Yes MLI	PPT
53	Saudi Arabia	Yes other		PPT
54	Serbia	No	Yes MLI	PPT
55	Singapore	No	Yes MLI	PPT
56	Slovak Republic	No	Yes MLI	PPT
57	Slovenia	No	Yes MLI	PPT
58	South Africa	No	Yes MLI	PPT
59	Spain	No	Yes MLI	PPT
60	Sweden	No	Yes MLI	PPT
61	Switzerland	No	No	
62	Syrian Arab Republic*	No	No	PPT

63	Thailand	No	No	PPT
64	Turkey	No	Yes MLI	PPT
65	Ukraine	No	Yes MLI	PPT
66	United Arab Emirates	No	Yes MLI	PPT
67	United Kingdom	No	Yes MLI	PPT
68	United States	No	No	PPT+LOB
69	Uzbekistan*	No	No	
70	Viet Nam	No	No	PPT
71	Zimbabwe*	No	No	PPT

Burkina Faso

A. Progress in the implementation of the minimum standard

Burkina Faso has three tax agreements in force, as reported in its response to the Peer Review questionnaire, including the multilateral Regulation 08/2008/COM adopting the rules for the avoidance of double taxation within the West African Economic and Monetary Union and the rule for assistance in tax matters (the UEMOA) concluded with seven partners.[30] None of those agreements comply with the minimum standard.

Burkina Faso signed the MLI in 2017 and deposited its instrument of ratification on 30 October 2020, listing its non-compliant bilateral agreements. The MLI entered into force for Burkina Faso on 1 February 2021. The agreements modified by the MLI will come into compliance with the minimum standard once the provisions of the MLI take effect.

Burkina Faso is implementing the minimum standard through the inclusion of the preamble statement and the PPT.[31]

B. Conclusion

The UEMOA does not at this stage comply with the minimum standard and discussions to bring this agreement up to date should be contemplated.[32]

Summary of the jurisdiction response – Burkina Faso

	1.Treaty partners	2. Compliance with the standard	3. Signature of a complying instrument	4. Minimum standard provision used
1	France	No	Yes MLI	PPT
2	Tunisia	No	Yes MLI	PPT

Other agreements

	1.Treaty partners	2. Inclusive Framework member
1	Benin	Yes
2	Côte d'Ivoire	Yes

[30] Règlement n°08/2008/CM des pays de l'Union économique et monétaire Ouest Africaine (UEMOA) du 26 septembre 2008 portant adoption des règles visant à éviter la double imposition au sein de l'UEMOA et des règles d'assistance en matière fiscale. In total, Burkina Faso identified nine "agreements" in its List of Tax agreements: two bilateral agreements and the UEMOA concluded with seven of its treaty partners.

[31] For its agreements listed under the MLI, Burkina Faso is implementing the preamble statement (Article 6 of the MLI) and the PPT (Article 7 of the MLI).

[32] Revisions to the UEMOA require an agreement from its eight treaty partners.

3	Guinea-Bissau*	No
4	Mali*	No
5	Niger*	No
6	Senegal	Yes
7	Togo*	No

Cabo Verde

A. Progress in the implementation of the minimum standard

Cabo Verde has five tax agreements in force, as reported in its response to the Peer Review questionnaire. One of those agreements, the agreement with Senegal, complies with the minimum standard.

Cabo Verde has not signed the MLI.

Cabo Verde indicated in its response to the Peer Review questionnaire that steps have been taken (other than under the MLI) to implement the minimum standard in its agreements with Macau (China) and Portugal.

Cabo Verde is implementing the minimum standard through the inclusion of the preamble statement and the PPT.

B. Conclusion

Cabo Verde has developed a plan for the implementation of the minimum standard in its agreements with Mauritius and Spain. Cabo Verde indicated in its response to the Peer Review questionnaire that bilateral negotiations would be pursued with respect to those agreements.

Summary of the jurisdiction response – Cabo Verde

	1.Treaty partners	2. Compliance with the standard	3. Signature of a complying instrument	4. Minimum standard provision used
1	Macau (China)	No	No	PPT
2	Portugal	No	No	PPT
3	Senegal	Yes other		PPT

Other agreements

	1.Treaty partners	2. Inclusive Framework member
1	Mauritius	Yes
2	Spain	Yes

Cameroon

A. Progress in the implementation of the minimum standard

Cameroon has six tax agreements in force, as reported in its response to the Peer Review questionnaire. None of those agreements comply with the minimum standard.

Cameroon signed the MLI in 2017 and listed its non-compliant agreements.[33] The agreements modified by the MLI will come into compliance with the minimum standard once the provisions of the MLI take effect.

Cameroon is implementing the minimum standard through the inclusion of the preamble statement and the PPT.[34]

B. Conclusion

Recommendation

It is recommended that Cameroon completes the steps to have the MLI take effect with respect to its agreements listed under the MLI as those agreements will only be modified by the MLI (and come into compliance with the minimum standard) once the provisions of the MLI take effect.

Summary of the jurisdiction response - Cameroon

	1.Treaty partners	2. Compliance with the standard	3. Signature of a complying instrument	4. Minimum standard provision used
1	Canada	No	Yes MLI	PPT
2	France	No	Yes MLI	PPT
3	Morocco	No	Yes MLI	PPT
4	South Africa	No	Yes MLI	PPT
5	Tunisia	No	Yes MLI	PPT
6	United Arab Emirates	No	Yes MLI	PPT

[33] The agreement with the United Arab Emirates is included in Cameroon's draft definitive list of reservations and notifications under the MLI, to be deposited upon the deposit of Cameroon's instrument of ratification of the MLI.

[34] For its agreements listed under the MLI, Cameroon is implementing the preamble statement (Article 6 of the MLI) and the PPT (Article 7 of the MLI).

Canada

A. Progress in the implementation of the minimum standard

Canada has 94 tax agreements in force,[35] as reported in its response to the Peer Review questionnaire. Thirty-six of those agreements comply with the minimum standard.

Canada signed the MLI in 2017 and deposited its instrument of ratification on 29 August 2019. The MLI entered into force for Canada on 1 December 2019. The agreements modified by the MLI come into compliance with the minimum standard once the provisions of the MLI take effect.

Canada indicated in its response to the Peer Review questionnaire that steps have been taken (other than under the MLI) to implement the minimum standard in the agreements with Brazil, Germany, Norway, Switzerland and the United States.

Canada is implementing the minimum standard through the inclusion of the preamble statement and the PPT.[36]

B. Conclusion

No jurisdiction has raised any concerns about their agreements with Canada.

Summary of the jurisdiction response - Canada

	1.Treaty partners	2. Compliance with the standard	3. Signature of a complying instrument	4. Minimum standard provision used
1	Algeria*	No	No	PPT
2	Argentina	No	Yes MLI	PPT
3	Armenia	No	Yes MLI	PPT
4	Australia	Yes MLI		PPT
5	Austria	Yes MLI		PPT
6	Azerbaijan*	No	No	PPT
7	Bangladesh*	No	No	PPT
8	Barbados	No	Yes MLI	PPT
9	Belgium	Yes MLI		PPT
10	Brazil	No	No	
11	Bulgaria	No	Yes MLI	PPT
12	Cameroon	No	Yes MLI	PPT
13	Chile	No	Yes MLI	PPT
14	China (People's Republic of)	No	Yes MLI	PPT
15	Colombia	No	Yes MLI	PPT

[35] This includes an Arrangement for the Avoidance of Double Taxation and the Prevention of Fiscal Evasion with Respect to Taxes on Income between the Canadian Trade Office in Taipei and the Taipei Economic and Cultural Office in Canada.

[36] For its agreements listed under the MLI, Canada is implementing the preamble statement (Article 6 of the MLI) and the PPT (Article 7 of the MLI). Canada expressed a statement, in accordance with Article 7(17)(a) of the MLI, that while it accepts the application of PPT alone as an interim measure, it intends where possible to adopt an LOB provision in addition to or in replacement of the PPT through bilateral negotiation.

16	Côte d'Ivoire	No	Yes MLI	PPT
17	Croatia	No	Yes MLI	PPT
18	Cyprus*	Yes MLI		PPT
19	Czech Republic	Yes MLI		PPT
20	Denmark	Yes MLI		PPT
21	Dominican Republic	No	No	PPT
22	Egypt	Yes MLI		PPT
23	Estonia	No	Yes MLI	PPT
24	Finland	Yes MLI		PPT
25	France	Yes MLI		PPT
26	Gabon	No	Yes MLI	PPT
27	Germany	No	No	
28	Greece	No	Yes MLI	PPT
29	Hong Kong (China)	No	Yes MLI	PPT
30	Hungary	No	Yes MLI	PPT
31	Iceland	Yes MLI		PPT
32	India	Yes MLI		PPT
33	Indonesia	Yes MLI		PPT
34	Ireland	Yes MLI		PPT
35	Israel	Yes MLI		PPT
36	Italy	No	Yes MLI	PPT
37	Jamaica	No	Yes MLI	PPT
38	Japan	Yes MLI		PPT
39	Jordan	Yes MLI		PPT
40	Kazakhstan	Yes MLI		PPT
41	Kenya	No	Yes MLI	PPT
42	Korea	Yes MLI		PPT
43	Kuwait*	No	Yes MLI	PPT
44	Latvia	Yes MLI		PPT
45	Lithuania	Yes MLI		PPT
46	Luxembourg	Yes MLI		PPT
47	Malaysia	No	Yes MLI	PPT
48	Malta	Yes MLI		PPT
49	Mexico	No	Yes MLI	PPT
50	Moldova*	No	No	PPT
51	Mongolia	No	No	PPT
52	Morocco	No	Yes MLI	PPT
53	Netherlands	Yes MLI		PPT
54	New Zealand	Yes MLI		PPT
55	Nigeria	No	Yes MLI	PPT
56	Norway	No	No	n/a
57	Oman	Yes MLI		PPT
58	Pakistan	Yes MLI		PPT
59	Papua New Guinea	No	Yes MLI	PPT
60	Peru	No	Yes MLI	PPT
61	Philippines*	No	No	PPT
62	Poland	Yes MLI		PPT
63	Portugal	Yes MLI		PPT
64	Romania	No	Yes MLI	PPT
65	Russian Federation	Yes MLI		PPT
66	Senegal	No	Yes MLI	PPT
67	Serbia	Yes MLI		PPT
68	Singapore	Yes MLI		PPT

69	Slovak Republic	Yes MLI		PPT
70	Slovenia	Yes MLI		PPT
71	South Africa	No	Yes MLI	PPT
72	Spain	No	Yes MLI	PPT
73	Sri Lanka	No	No	PPT
74	Sweden	No	Yes MLI	PPT
75	Switzerland	No	No	n/a
76	Tanzania*	No	No	PPT
77	Thailand	No	No	PPT
78	Trinidad and Tobago	No	No	PPT
79	Tunisia	No	Yes MLI	PPT
80	Turkey	No	Yes MLI	PPT
81	Ukraine	Yes MLI		PPT
82	United Arab Emirates	Yes MLI		PPT
83	United Kingdom	Yes MLI		PPT
84	United States	No	No	
85	Viet Nam	No	No	PPT
86	Zambia	No	No	PPT
87	Zimbabwe*	No	No	PPT

Other agreements

	1.Treaty partners	2. Inclusive Framework member
1	Chinese Taipei*	No
2	Ecuador*	No
3	Guyana*	No
4	Kyrgyzstan*	No
5	Madagascar*	No
6	Uzbekistan*	No
7	Venezuela*	No

Cayman Islands

A. Progress in the implementation of the minimum standard

The Cayman Islands has no tax agreements, as reported in its response to the Peer Review questionnaire.

B. Conclusion

No jurisdiction has raised any concerns about the Cayman Islands.

Chile

A. Progress in the implementation of the minimum standard

Chile has 33 tax agreements in force, as reported in its response to the Peer Review questionnaire. Five of those agreements comply with the minimum standard.

Chile signed the MLI in 2017 and deposited its instrument of ratification on 26 November 2020, listing its non-compliant agreements. The MLI entered into force for Chile on 1 March 2021. The agreements modified by the MLI come into compliance with the minimum standard once the provisions of the MLI take effect.

Chile indicated in its response to the Peer Review questionnaire that steps had been taken (other than under the MLI) to implement the minimum standard in the agreements with Brazil, Ecuador* and Paraguay.

Chile is implementing the minimum standard through the inclusion of the preamble statement and the PPT combined with the LOB. For its compliant agreements with Italy and Japan, the minimum standard is implemented through the inclusion of the preamble statement and the PPT. [37]

B. Conclusion

No jurisdiction has raised any concerns about their agreements with Chile.

Summary of the jurisdiction response - Chile

	1.Treaty partners	2. Compliance with the standard	3. Signature of a complying instrument	4. Minimum standard provision used
1	Argentina	Yes other		PPT+LOB
2	Australia	No	Yes MLI	PPT
3	Austria	No	Yes MLI	PPT
4	Belgium	No	Yes MLI	PPT
5	Brazil	No	No	PPT+LOB
6	Canada	No	Yes MLI	PPT
7	China (People's Republic of)	Yes other		PPT+LOB
8	Colombia	No	Yes MLI	PPT+LOB
9	Croatia	No	Yes MLI	PPT
10	Czech Republic	No	Yes MLI	PPT
11	Denmark	No	Yes MLI	PPT+LOB
12	Ecuador*	No	No	PPT+LOB
13	France	No	Yes MLI	PPT
14	Ireland	No	Yes MLI	PPT

[37] For its agreements listed under the MLI, Chile is implementing the preamble statement (Article 6 of the MLI) and the PPT (Article 7 of the MLI). Chile has also adopted the simplified LOB under Article 7(6) of the MLI and expressed a statement, in accordance with Article 7(17)(a) of the MLI, that while Chile accepts the application of the PPT under the MLI, it intends where possible to adopt an LOB provision through bilateral negotiation. Chile has made a reservation pursuant to Article 6(4) of the MLI not to apply Article 6(1) of the MLI with respect to agreements, which already contain the relevant preamble language (covering four agreements). Chile has also made a reservation pursuant to Article 7(15)(b) of the MLI not to apply Article 7(1) of the MLI with respect to agreements which already contain a PPT (covering four agreements).

15	Italy	Yes other		PPT
16	Japan	Yes other		PPT
17	Korea	No	Yes MLI	PPT
18	Malaysia	No	Yes MLI	PP
19	Mexico	No	Yes MLI	PPT+LOB
20	New Zealand	No	Yes MLI	PPT
21	Norway	No	Yes MLI	PPT+LOB
22	Paraguay	No	No	PPT+LOB
23	Peru	No	Yes MLI	PPT
24	Poland	No	Yes MLI	PPT
25	Portugal	No	Yes MLI	PPT
26	Russian Federation	No	Yes MLI	PPT+LOB
27	South Africa	No	Yes MLI	PPT
28	Spain	No	Yes MLI	PPT
29	Sweden	No	Yes MLI	PPT
30	Switzerland	No	Yes MLI	PPT
31	Thailand	No	No	PPT+LOB
32	United Kingdom	No	Yes MLI	PPT
33	Uruguay	Yes other		PPT+LOB

China (People's Republic of)

A. Progress in the implementation of the minimum standard

China has 102 tax agreements in force as reported in its response to the Peer Review questionnaire. Four of those agreements comply with the minimum standard.

China signed the MLI in 2017 and listed its non-compliant agreements. The agreements modified by the MLI come into compliance with the minimum standard once the provisions of the MLI take effect.

China indicated in its response to the Peer Review questionnaire that steps have been taken (other than under the MLI) to implement the minimum standard in its agreements with Brazil, Germany and Switzerland.

China is generally implementing the minimum standard through the inclusion of the preamble statement and PPT.[38]

B. Conclusion

Recommendation

It is recommended that China completes the steps to have the MLI take effect with respect to its agreements listed under the MLI as those agreements will only be modified by the MLI (and come into compliance with the minimum standard) once the provisions of the MLI take effect.

Summary of the jurisdiction response – China (People's Republic of)

	1.Treaty partners	2. Compliance with the standard	3. Signature of a complying instrument	4. Minimum standard provision used
1	Albania	No	Yes MLI	PPT
2	Algeria*	No	No	PPT
3	Armenia	No	Yes MLI	PPT
4	Australia	No	Yes MLI	PPT
5	Austria	No	Yes MLI	PPT
6	Azerbaijan*	No	No	PPT
7	Bahrain	No	Yes MLI	PPT
8	Bangladesh*	No	No	PPT
9	Barbados	No	Yes MLI	PPT
10	Belarus	No	No	PPT
11	Belgium	No	Yes MLI	PPT
12	Bosnia-Herzegovina	No	Yes MLI	PPT
13	Botswana	No	No	PPT
14	Brazil	No	No	PPT

[38] For its agreements listed under the MLI, China is implementing the preamble statement (Article 6 of the MLI) and the PPT (Article 7 of the MLI).

15	Brunei Darussalam	No	No	PPT
16	Bulgaria	No	Yes MLI	PPT
17	Cambodia*	No	No	PPT
18	Canada	No	Yes MLI	PPT
19	Chile	Yes other		PPT+LOB
20	Croatia	No	Yes MLI	PPT
21	Cuba*	No	No	PPT
22	Cyprus*	No	Yes MLI	PPT
23	Czech Republic	No	Yes MLI	PPT
24	Denmark	No	Yes MLI	PPT
25	Ecuador*	No	No	PPT+LOB
26	Egypt	No	Yes MLI	PPT
27	Estonia	No	Yes MLI	PPT
28	Ethiopia*	No	No	PPT
29	Finland	No	Yes MLI	PPT
30	France	No	Yes MLI	PPT
31	Georgia	No	Yes MLI	PPT
32	Germany	No	No	PPT
33	Greece	No	Yes MLI	PPT
34	Hungary	No	Yes MLI	PPT
35	Iceland	No	Yes MLI	PPT
36	India	Yes other		PPT
37	Indonesia	No	Yes MLI	PPT
38	Iran*	No	No	PPT
39	Ireland	No	Yes MLI	PPT
40	Israel	No	Yes MLI	PPT
41	Italy	No	Yes MLI	PPT
42	Jamaica	No	Yes MLI	PPT
43	Japan	No	Yes MLI	PPT
44	Kazakhstan	No	Yes MLI	PPT
45	Korea	No	Yes MLI	PPT
46	Kuwait*	No	Yes MLI	PPT
47	Kyrgyzstan*	No	No	PPT
48	Lao People's Democratic Republic*	No	No	PPT
49	Latvia	No	Yes MLI	PPT
50	Lithuania	No	Yes MLI	PPT
51	Luxembourg	No	Yes MLI	PPT
52	Malaysia	No	Yes MLI	PPT
53	Malta	No	Yes MLI	PPT
54	Mauritius	No	Yes MLI	PPT
55	Mexico	No	Yes MLI	PPT+LOB
56	Moldova*	No	No	PPT
57	Mongolia	No	No	PPT
58	Montenegro	No	No	PPT
59	Morocco	No	Yes MLI	PPT
60	Nepal*	No	No	PPT
61	Netherlands	No	Yes MLI	PPT
62	New Zealand	Yes other		PPT
63	Nigeria	No	Yes MLI	PPT
64	North Macedonia	No	Yes MLI	PPT
65	Norway	No	Yes MLI	PPT
66	Oman	No	Yes MLI	PPT
67	Pakistan	No	Yes MLI	PPT

68	Papua New Guinea	No	Yes MLI	PPT
69	Philippines*	No	No	PPT
70	Poland	No	Yes MLI	PPT
71	Portugal	No	Yes MLI	PPT
72	Qatar	No	Yes MLI	PPT
73	Romania	No	Yes MLI	PPT
74	Russian Federation	No	Yes MLI	PPT+LOB
75	Saudi Arabia	No	Yes MLI	PPT
76	Serbia	No	Yes MLI	PPT
77	Seychelles	No	Yes MLI	PPT
78	Singapore	No	Yes MLI	PPT
79	Slovak Republic	No	Yes MLI	PPT
80	Slovenia	No	Yes MLI	PPT
81	South Africa	No	Yes MLI	PPT
82	Spain	Yes other		PPT
83	Sri Lanka	No	No	PPT
84	Sudan*	No	No	PPT
85	Sweden	No	Yes MLI	PPT
86	Switzerland	No	No	PPT
87	Syrian Arab Republic*	No	No	PPT
88	Tajikistan*	No	No	PPT
89	Thailand	No	No	PPT
90	Trinidad and Tobago	No	No	PPT
91	Tunisia	No	Yes MLI	PPT
92	Turkey	No	Yes MLI	PPT
93	Turkmenistan*	No	No	PPT
94	Ukraine	No	Yes MLI	PPT
95	United Arab Emirates	No	Yes MLI	PPT
96	United Kingdom	No	Yes MLI	PPT
97	United States	No	No	PPT+LOB
98	Uzbekistan*	No	No	PPT
99	Venezuela*	No	No	PPT
100	Viet Nam	No	No	PPT
101	Zambia	No	No	PPT
102	Zimbabwe*	No	No	PPT

Colombia

A. Progress in the implementation of the minimum standard

Colombia has eleven tax agreements in force[39] as reported in its response to the Peer Review questionnaire, including the Decision 578 of the Andean Community Commission (Decision 578) for the members of the Andean Community (the Andean Community Agreement).[40] One of those agreements, the agreement with the United Kingdom, complies with the minimum standard.

Colombia signed the MLI in 2017 and listed its non-compliant bilateral agreements. The agreements modified by the MLI come into compliance with the minimum standard once the provisions of the MLI take effect.

Colombia indicated in its response to the Peer Review questionnaire that steps have been taken (other than under the MLI) to implement the minimum standard in the Andean Community Agreement and the agreement with Switzerland.

Colombia is implementing the minimum standard through the inclusion of the preamble statement and the PPT combined with the LOB.[41]

[39] Colombia has also concluded an agreement with Italy, which entered into force on 6 October 2021. Therefore, as of that date, Colombia has twelve tax agreements in force. The agreement with Italy complies with the minimum standard.

[40] The Decision of the Commission of the Andean Community 578 on the regime for the avoidance of double taxation and the prevention of fiscal evasion, adopted on 4 May 2004. The current members of the Andean Community are Bolivia*, Colombia, Ecuador* and Peru. In total, Colombia identified thirteen "agreements" in its List of Tax agreements: ten bilateral agreements and the Andean Community Agreement.

[41] For its agreements listed under the MLI, Colombia is implementing the preamble statement (Article 6 of the MLI) and the PPT (Article 7 of the MLI). Colombia has also adopted the simplified LOB under Article 7(6) of the MLI and expressed a statement, in accordance with Article 7(17)(a) of the MLI, that while it accepts the application of PPT alone as an interim measure, it intends where possible to adopt an LOB provision in addition to or in replacement of the PPT through bilateral negotiation. Colombia has made a reservation pursuant to Article 6(4) of the MLI not to apply Article 6(1) of the MLI with respect to agreements that already contain the relevant preamble language (covering one agreement).

B. Conclusion

Recommendation

It is recommended that Colombia completes the steps to have the MLI take effect with respect to its agreements listed under the MLI as those agreements will only be modified by the MLI (and come into compliance with the minimum standard) once the provisions of the MLI take effect.

Summary of the jurisdiction response - Colombia

	1.Treaty partners	2. Compliance with the standard	3. Signature of a complying instrument	4. Minimum standard provision used
1	Bolivia*	No	No	PPT + LOB
2	Canada	No	Yes MLI	PPT
3	Chile	No	Yes MLI	PPT
4	Czech Republic	No	Yes MLI	PPT
5	Ecuador*	No	No	PPT + LOB
6	India	No	Yes MLI	PPT + LOB
7	Korea	No	Yes MLI	PPT
8	Mexico	No	Yes MLI	PPT
9	Peru	No	No	PPT + LOB
10	Portugal	No	Yes MLI	PPT
11	Spain	No	Yes MLI	PPT
12	Switzerland	No	No	PPT
13	United Kingdom	Yes other		PPT

Congo

A. Progress in the implementation of the minimum standard

Congo has three tax agreements in force as reported in its response to the Peer Review questionnaire. None of those agreements, comply with the minimum standard.

Congo has not signed the MLI.

In its response to the Peer Review Questionnaire, Italy indicated that its agreement with Congo did not give rise to material treaty shopping concerns for Italy.

B. Conclusion

Recommendation

It is recommended that Congo formulates a plan for the implementation of the minimum standard in its agreements for which no steps have yet been taken and that were concluded with members of the BEPS Inclusive Framework (France and Mauritius).

Other agreements

This Table shows the agreements that are not compliant, not subject to a complying instrument, not covered by a general statement on the implementation of the detailed LOB and for which no steps have been taken to implement the minimum standard.

	1.Treaty partners	2. Inclusive Framework member
1	France	Yes
2	Italy	Yes
3	Mauritius	Yes

Cook Islands

A. Progress in the implementation of the minimum standard

The Cook Islands has no tax agreements in force as reported in its response to the Peer Review questionnaire.

B. Conclusion

No jurisdiction has raised any concerns about the Cook Islands.

Costa Rica

A. Progress in the implementation of the minimum standard

Costa Rica has three tax agreements in force as reported in its response to the Peer Review questionnaire. None of those agreements comply with the minimum standard.

Costa Rica signed the MLI in 2017 and deposited its instrument of ratification on 22 September 2020. The MLI entered into force for Costa Rica on 1 January 2021. The agreements modified by the MLI come into compliance with the minimum standard once the provisions of the MLI take effect.

Costa Rica has not listed its agreement with Germany under the MLI but indicated in its response to the Peer Review questionnaire that steps have been taken (other than under the MLI) to implement the minimum standard in that agreement.

Costa Rica is implementing the minimum standard through the inclusion of the preamble statement and the PPT.[42]

B. Conclusion

No jurisdiction has raised any concerns about their agreements with Costa Rica.

Summary of the jurisdiction response – Costa Rica

	1.Treaty partners	2. Compliance with the standard	3. Signature of a complying instrument	4. Minimum standard provision used
1	Germany	No	No	PPT
2	Mexico	No	Yes MLI	
3	Spain	No	Yes MLI	

[42] For its agreements listed under the MLI, Costa Rica is implementing the preamble statement (Article 6 of the MLI) and the PPT (Article 7 of the MLI).

Côte d'Ivoire

A. Progress in the implementation of the minimum standard

Côte d'Ivoire has twelve tax agreements in force as reported in its response to the Peer Review questionnaire, including the multilateral Regulation 08/2008/COM adopting the rules for the avoidance of double taxation within the West African Economic and Monetary Union and the rule for assistance in tax matters (the UEMOA) concluded with seven partners.[43]

Côte d'Ivoire signed the MLI in 2018. The agreements modified by the MLI come into compliance with the minimum standard once the provisions of the MLI take effect.

Côte d'Ivoire has not listed its agreement with Switzerland under the MLI, but indicated in its response to the Peer Review questionnaire that steps had been taken (other than under the MLI) to implement the minimum standard in this agreement.

Côte d'Ivoire is implementing the minimum standard through the inclusion of the preamble statement and the PPT.[44]

B. Conclusion

The UEMOA does not at this stage comply with the minimum standard and discussions to bring this agreement up to date should be contemplated.[45]

[43] Règlement n°08/2008/CM des pays de l'Union économique et monétaire Ouest Africaine (UEMOA) du 26 septembre 2008 portant adoption des règles visant à éviter la double imposition au sein de l'UEMOA et des règles d'assistance en matière fiscale. In total, Côte d'Ivoire identified 18 "agreements" in its List of Tax agreements: eleven bilateral agreements and the UEMOA.

[44] For its agreements listed under the MLI, Côte d'Ivoire is implementing the preamble statement (Article 6 of the MLI) and the PPT (Article 7 of the MLI). Côte d'Ivoire has also adopted the asymmetrical application of the simplified LOB under Article 7(7)(b) of the MLI.

[45] Revisions to the UEMOA require an agreement from its eight treaty partners.

Recommendation

It is recommended that Côte d'Ivoire completes the steps to have the MLI take effect with respect to its agreements listed under the MLI as those agreements will only be modified by the MLI (and come into compliance with the minimum standard) once the provisions of the MLI take effect.

Summary of the jurisdiction response – Côte d'Ivoire

	1.Treaty partners	2. Compliance with the standard	3. Signature of a complying instrument	4. Minimum standard provision used
1	Belgium	No	Yes MLI	PPT
2	Canada	No	Yes MLI	PPT
3	France	No	Yes MLI	PPT
4	Germany	No	No	PPT
5	Italy	No	Yes MLI	PPT
6	Morocco	No	Yes MLI	PPT
7	Norway	No	No	PPT
8	Portugal	No	Yes MLI	PPT
9	Switzerland	No	No	PPT
10	Tunisia	No	Yes MLI	PPT
11	United Kingdom	No	Yes MLI	PPT

Other agreements

	1.Treaty partners	2. Inclusive Framework member
1	Benin	Yes
2	Burkina Faso	Yes
3	Guinea-Bissau*	No
4	Mali*	No
5	Niger*	No
6	Senegal	Yes
7	Togo*	No

Croatia

A. Progress in the implementation of the minimum standard

Croatia has 66 tax agreements in force as reported in its response to the Peer Review questionnaire. One of those agreements, the agreement with Japan, complies with the minimum standard.

Croatia signed the MLI in 2017 and deposited its instrument of ratification on 18 February 2021, listing its non-compliant agreements. The MLI entered into force for Croatia on 1 June 2021. The agreements modified by the MLI come into compliance with the minimum standard once the provisions of the MLI take effect.

Croatia is implementing the minimum standard through the inclusion of the preamble statement and the PPT.[46]

B. Conclusion

No jurisdiction has raised any concerns about their agreements with Croatia.

Summary of the jurisdiction response - Croatia

	1.Treaty partners	2. Compliance with the standard	3. Signature of a complying instrument	4. Minimum standard provision used
1	Albania	No	Yes MLI	PPT
2	Armenia	No	Yes MLI	PPT
3	Austria	No	Yes MLI	PPT
4	Azerbaijan*	No	No	PPT
5	Belarus	No	No	PPT
6	Belgium	No	Yes MLI	PPT
7	Bosnia-Herzegovina	No	Yes MLI	PPT
8	Bulgaria	No	Yes MLI	PPT
9	Canada	No	Yes, MLI	PPT
10	Chile	No	Yes MLI	PPT
11	China (People's Republic of)	No	Yes MLI	PPT
12	Czech Republic	No	Yes MLI	PPT
13	Denmark	No	Yes MLI	PPT
14	Estonia	No	Yes MLI	PPT
15	Finland	No	Yes MLI	PPT
16	France	No	Yes MLI	PPT
17	Georgia	No	Yes MLI	PPT
18	Germany	No	Yes MLI	PPT
19	Greece	No	Yes MLI	PPT
20	Hungary	No	Yes MLI	PPT
21	Iceland	No	Yes MLI	PPT
22	India	No	Yes MLI	PPT
23	Indonesia	No	Yes MLI	PPT

[46] For its agreements listed under the MLI, Croatia is implementing the preamble statement (Article 6 of the MLI) and the PPT (Article 7 of the MLI).

24	Iran*	No	No	PPT
25	Ireland	No	Yes MLI	PPT
26	Israel	No	Yes MLI	PPT
27	Italy	No	Yes MLI	PPT
28	Japan	Yes other		PPT and LOB
29	Jordan	No	Yes MLI	PPT
30	Kazakhstan	No	Yes MLI	PPT
31	Korea	No	Yes MLI	PPT
32	Kosovo*	No	No	PPT
33	Kuwait*	No	Yes MLI	PPT
34	Latvia	No	Yes MLI	PPT
35	Lithuania	No	Yes MLI	PPT
36	Luxembourg	No	Yes MLI	PPT
37	Malaysia	No	Yes MLI	PPT
38	Malta	No	Yes MLI	PPT
39	Mauritius	No	Yes MLI	PPT
40	Moldova*	No	No	PPT
41	Montenegro	No	No	PPT
42	Morocco	No	Yes MLI	PPT
43	Netherlands	No	Yes MLI	PPT
44	North Macedonia	No	Yes MLI	PPT
45	Norway	No	No	PPT
46	Oman	No	Yes MLI	PPT
47	Poland	No	Yes MLI	PPT
48	Portugal	No	Yes MLI	PPT
49	Qatar	No	Yes MLI	PPT
50	Romania	No	Yes MLI	PPT
51	Russian Federation	No	Yes MLI	PPT
52	San Marino	No	Yes MLI	PPT
53	Serbia	No	Yes MLI	PPT
54	Slovak Republic	No	Yes MLI	PPT
55	Slovenia	No	Yes MLI	PPT
56	South Africa	No	Yes MLI	PPT
57	Spain	No	Yes MLI	PPT
58	Sweden	No	No	PPT
59	Switzerland	No	No	PPT
60	Syrian Arab Republic*	No	No	PPT
61	Turkey	No	Yes MLI	PPT
62	Turkmenistan*	No	No	PPT
63	Ukraine	No	Yes MLI	PPT
64	United Arab Emirates	No	Yes MLI	PPT
65	United Kingdom	No	Yes MLI	PPT
66	Viet Nam	No	No	PPT

Curaçao

A. Progress in the implementation of the minimum standard

Curaçao has four tax agreements in force as reported in its response to the Peer Review Questionnaire. One of those agreements, the agreement with Malta, complies with the minimum standard.

Curaçao joined the MLI in 2017 and the Kingdom of Netherlands deposited its instrument of acceptance on 29 March 2019, listing its non-compliant agreements. The MLI entered into force for Curaçao on 1 July 2019. The agreements modified by the MLI come into compliance with the minimum standard once the provisions of the MLI take effect.

Curaçao indicated in its response to the Peer Review questionnaire that steps have been taken (other than under the MLI) to implement the minimum standard in the arrangement for the Kingdom of Netherlands (applicable between Curaçao, Aruba and Sint Maarten*) and the arrangement between Curaçao and Netherlands, that are governed by the domestic law of the Kingdom of Netherlands.[47]

Curaçao is implementing the minimum standard through the inclusion of the preamble statement and the PPT.[48]

B. Conclusion

No jurisdiction has raised any concerns about their agreements with Curaçao.

Summary of the jurisdiction response – Curaçao

	1.Treaty partners	2. Compliance with the standard	3. Signature of a complying instrument	4. Minimum standard provision used
1	Aruba / Sint Maarten*	No	No	
2	Malta	Yes MLI		PPT
3	Netherlands	No	No	PPT
4	Norway	No	No	PPT

[47] Curaçao indicated in its response that the tax arrangement for the Kingdom of Netherlands governs the relationship between Aruba, Curaçao, Sint Maarten* and Netherlands. This arrangement is similar to the agreement Curaçao has with Netherlands. The MLI cannot be applicable to those arrangements, since they are arrangements governed by the domestic law of the Kingdom of Netherlands.

[48] For its agreements listed under the MLI, Curaçao is implementing the preamble statement (Article 6 of the MLI) and the PPT (Article 7 of the MLI).

Czech Republic

A. Progress in the implementation of the minimum standard

The Czech Republic has 92 tax agreements in force[49] as reported in its response to the Peer Review questionnaire. Thirty-five of those agreements[50] comply with the minimum standard.

The Czech Republic signed the MLI in 2017 and deposited its instrument of ratification on 13 May 2020. The MLI entered into force for the Czech Republic on 1 September 2020. The agreements modified by the MLI come into compliance with the minimum standard once the provisions of the MLI take effect.

The Czech Republic has not listed its agreements with Albania, Bahrain, Barbados, Belarus, Bosnia-Herzegovina, Botswana, Brazil, Estonia, Indonesia, Jordan, Kazakhstan, Malaysia, Mongolia, Montenegro[51], Morocco, North Macedonia, Panama, Saudi Arabia, Sri Lanka, Thailand, Tunisia, Ukraine, the United Arab Emirates, the United States and Viet Nam. These agreements will therefore not, at this stage, be modified by the MLI. Albania, Bahrain, Barbados, Bosnia-Herzegovina, Estonia, Indonesia, Jordan, Kazakhstan, Malaysia, Morocco, North Macedonia, Panama, Saudi Arabia, Tunisia, Ukraine, the United Arab Emirates and Viet Nam have listed their agreements with the Czech Republic under the MLI.

The Czech republic indicated in its response to the Peer Review questionnaire that steps have been taken (other than under the MLI) to implement the minimum standard in its agreements with Brazil, Montenegro and Sri Lanka.

The Czech Republic is implementing the minimum standard through the inclusion of the preamble statement and the PPT.[52]

B. Conclusion

Albania, Bahrain, Barbados, Bosnia-Herzegovina, Estonia, Indonesia, Jordan, Kazakhstan, Malaysia, Morocco, North Macedonia, Panama, Saudi Arabia, Tunisia, Ukraine, the United Arab Emirates and Viet Nam have listed their agreements with the Czech Republic under the MLI, which amount to requests to implement the minimum standard.

The Czech Republic has developed a plan for the implementation of the minimum standard in its agreements with Albania, Bahrain, Barbados, Belarus, Bosnia-Herzegovina, Botswana, Estonia, Indonesia, Jordan, Kazakhstan, Malaysia, Mongolia, Morocco, North Macedonia, Panama, Saudi Arabia, Thailand, Tunisia, Ukraine, the United Arab Emirates, the United States and Viet Nam.

The Czech Republic indicated in its response to the Peer Review questionnaire that over the next two years, it intends to expand its list of agreements to be covered under the MLI to include the agreements

[49] The Czech Republic continues to apply the agreement with former Serbia and Montenegro to both Serbia and Montenegro.

[50] One of these agreements, the agreement with former Serbia and Montenegro complies with the minimum standard only in relation to Serbia. The Czech Republic has indicated that discussions are ongoing to implement the minimum standard in the agreement with Montenegro.

[51] The Czech Republic has listed the agreement with former Serbia and Montenegro under the MLI only in relation to Serbia.

[52] For its agreements listed under the MLI, the Czech Republic is implementing the preamble statement (Article 6 of the MLI) and the PPT (Article 7 of the MLI).

concluded with jurisdictions that have signed the MLI and have listed their agreements with the Czech Republic. The Czech Republic has indicated that to avoid doubts and misunderstandings in the future, the Czech Republic will list only such jurisdictions with which it bilaterally confirms the changes that the MLI would bring to the treaty. After finishing this procedure, the Czech Republic indicated that it would pursue bilateral renegotiations or negotiations of amending protocols to implement the minimum standard in its remaining agreements.

Summary of the jurisdiction response – Czech Republic

	1.Treaty partners	2. Compliance with the standard	3. Signature of a complying instrument	4. Minimum standard provision used
1	Armenia	No	Yes MLI	PPT
2	Australia	Yes MLI		PPT
3	Austria	Yes MLI		PPT
4	Bangladesh*	Yes other		PPT
5	Belgium	Yes MLI		PPT
6	Brazil	No	No	N/A
7	Bulgaria	No	Yes MLI	PPT
8	Canada	Yes MLI		PPT
9	Chile	No	Yes MLI	PPT
10	China (People's Republic of)	No	Yes MLI	PPT
11	Colombia	No	Yes MLI	PPT
12	Croatia	No	Yes MLI	PPT
13	Cyprus*	Yes MLI		PPT
14	Denmark	Yes MLI		PPT
15	Egypt	Yes MLI		PPT
16	Finland	Yes MLI		PPT
17	France	Yes MLI		PPT
18	Georgia	Yes MLI		PPT
19	Germany	No	Yes MLI	PPT
20	Greece	No	Yes MLI	PPT
21	Hong Kong (China)	No	Yes MLI	PPT
22	Hungary	No	Yes MLI	PPT
23	Iceland	Yes MLI		PPT
24	India	Yes MLI		PPT
25	Ireland	Yes MLI		PPT
26	Israel	Yes MLI		PPT
27	Italy	No	Yes MLI	PPT
28	Japan	Yes MLI		PPT
29	Korea	Yes other		PPT
30	Kuwait*	No	Yes MLI	PPT
31	Kyrgyzstan*	Yes other		PPT
32	Latvia	Yes MLI		PPT
33	Liechtenstein	Yes MLI		PPT
34	Lithuania	Yes MLI		PPT
35	Luxembourg	Yes MLI		PPT
36	Malta	Yes MLI		PPT
37	Mexico	No	Yes MLI	PPT
38	Montenegro	No	No	N/A
39	Netherlands	Yes MLI		PPT
40	New Zealand	Yes MLI		PPT
41	Nigeria	No	Yes MLI	PPT

42	Norway	Yes MLI		PPT
43	Pakistan	Yes MLI		PPT
44	Poland	Yes MLI		PPT
45	Portugal	Yes MLI		PPT
46	Romania	No	Yes MLI	PPT
47	Russian Federation	Yes MLI		PPT
48	Serbia	Yes MLI		PPT
49	Singapore	Yes MLI		PPT
50	Slovak Republic	Yes MLI		PPT
51	Slovenia	Yes MLI		PPT
52	South Africa	No	Yes MLI	PPT
53	Spain	No	Yes MLI	PPT
54	Sri Lanka	No	No	N/A
55	Sweden	No	Yes MLI	PPT
56	Switzerland	No	Yes MLI	PPT
57	Turkey	No	Yes MLI	PPT
58	United Kingdom	Yes MLI		PPT
59	United States	No	No	N/A

Other Agreements

	1.Treaty partners	2. Inclusive Framework member
1	Albania	Yes
2	Azerbaijan*	No
3	Bahrain	Yes
4	Barbados	Yes
5	Belarus	Yes
6	Bosnia-Herzegovina	Yes
7	Botswana	Yes
8	Democratic People's Republic of Korea*	No
9	Estonia	Yes
10	Ethiopia*	No
11	Ghana*	No
12	Indonesia	Yes
13	Iran*	No
14	Jordan	Yes
15	Kazakhstan	Yes
16	Lebanon*	No
17	North Macedonia	Yes
18	Malaysia	Yes
19	Moldova*	No
20	Mongolia	Yes
21	Morocco	Yes
22	Panama	Yes
23	Philippines*	No
24	Saudi Arabia	Yes
25	Syrian Arab Republic*	No
26	Tajikistan*	No
27	Thailand	Yes
28	Tunisia	Yes
29	Turkmenistan*	No
30	Ukraine	Yes

31	United Arab Emirates	Yes
32	Uzbekistan*	No
33	Venezuela*	No
34	Viet Nam	Yes

Democratic Republic of the Congo

A. Progress in the implementation of the minimum standard

The Democratic Republic of the Congo has two tax agreements in force as reported in its response to the Peer Review questionnaire. Neither of those agreements comply with the minimum standard.

The Democratic Republic of the Congo has not signed the MLI.

B. Conclusion

Recommendation

It is recommended that the Democratic Republic of Congo formulates a plan for the implementation of the minimum standard in its agreements for which no steps have yet been taken and that were concluded with members of the BEPS Inclusive Framework (Belgium and South Africa).[53]

Other agreements

This Table shows the agreements that are not compliant, not subject to a complying instrument, not covered by a general statement on the implementation of the detailed LOB and for which no steps have been taken to implement the minimum standard.

	1.Treaty partners	2. Inclusive Framework member
1	Belgium	Yes
2	South Africa	Yes

[53] It is noted that the Democratic Republic of Congo has worked with the Secretariat towards signature of the MLI and has prepared a draft list of reservations and notifications under the MLI.

Denmark

A. Progress in the implementation of the minimum standard

Denmark has 72 tax agreements in force as reported in its response to the Peer Review questionnaire, including the multilateral Nordic Convention concluded with the Faroe Islands, Finland, Iceland, Norway and Sweden (the Nordic Convention).[54] Thirty of those agreements, including the Nordic Convention, comply with the minimum standard.

Denmark signed the MLI in 2017 and deposited its instrument of ratification on 30 September 2019. The MLI entered into force for Denmark on 1 January 2020. The agreements modified by the MLI come into compliance with the minimum standard once the provisions of the MLI take effect.

Denmark has not listed its agreements with Germany and Switzerland under the MLI. These agreements will therefore not, at this stage, be modified by the MLI. Denmark has signed a bilateral complying instrument with respect to its agreements with Germany and Sri Lanka, and indicated in its response to the Peer Review questionnaire that steps have been taken (other than under the MLI) to implement the minimum standard in its agreements with Greenland and Switzerland.

Denmark is implementing the minimum standard through the inclusion of the preamble statement and the PPT.[55]

B. Conclusion

No jurisdiction has raised any concerns about their agreements with Denmark.

Summary of the jurisdiction response - Denmark

	1.Treaty partners	2. Compliance with the standard	3. Signature of a complying instrument	4. Minimum standard provision used
1	Argentina	No	Yes MLI	PPT+LOB
2	Armenia	Yes other		PPT
3	Australia	Yes MLI		PPT
4	Austria	No	No	PPT+LOB
5	Azerbaijan*	No	No	PPT+LOB
6	Bangladesh*	No	No	PPT+LOB
7	Belgium	Yes MLI		PPT
8	Brazil	No	No	PPT+LOB
9	Bulgaria	No	Yes MLI	PPT

[54] See the Multilateral convention concluded by Denmark, Finland, the Faroe Islands, Iceland, Norway and Sweden: for the avoidance of double taxation with respect to taxes on income and on capital (1996, 1997, 2008 and 2018). In total, Denmark identified 76 "agreements" in its List of Tax agreements: 71 bilateral agreements and the Nordic Convention concluded with five treaty partners.

[55] For its agreements listed under the MLI, Denmark is implementing the preamble statement (Article 6 of the MLI) and the PPT (Article 7 of the MLI). Under Article 7(7)(a) of the MLI, Denmark is also implementing the simplified LOB (Article 7(8 to 13) of the MLI) in agreements concluded with treaty partners that have adopted the simplified LOB.

10	Canada	Yes MLI		PPT
11	Chile	No	Yes MLI	PPT+LOB
12	China (People's Republic of)	No	Yes MLI	PPT
13	Chinese Taipei*	No	No	PPT+LOB
14	Croatia	No	Yes MLI	PPT
15	Cyprus*	Yes MLI		PPT
16	Czech Republic	Yes MLI		PPT
17	Egypt	Yes MLI		PPT
18	Estonia	No	Yes MLI	PPT
19	Faroe Islands	Yes other		PPT
20	Finland	Yes other		PPT
21	Georgia	No	No	PPT+LOB
22	Germany	No	Yes other	PPT
23	Ghana*	No	No	PPT+LOB
24	Greece	No	Yes MLI	
25	Greenland	No	No	
26	Hungary	No	Yes MLI	
27	Iceland	Yes other		PPT
28	India	Yes MLI		PPT+LOB
29	Indonesia	Yes MLI		PPT
30	Ireland	Yes MLI		PPT
31	Israel	Yes MLI		PPT
32	Italy	No	Yes MLI	PPT
33	Jamaica	No	Yes MLI	PPT
34	Japan	Yes other		PPT+LOB
35	Kenya	No	Yes MLI	PPT+LOB
36	Korea	Yes MLI		PPT
37	Kuwait*	No	Yes MLI	PPT
38	Latvia	Yes MLI		PPT
39	Lithuania	Yes MLI		PPT
40	Luxembourg	Yes MLI		PPT
41	Malaysia	No	Yes MLI	PPT
42	Malta	Yes MLI		PPT
43	Mexico	No	Yes MLI	PPT+LOB
44	Montenegro	No	No	PPT+LOB
45	Morocco	No	Yes MLI	PPT
46	Netherlands	Yes other		PPT
47	New Zealand	Yes MLI		PPT
48	North Macedonia	No	Yes MLI	PPT
49	Norway	Yes other		PPT
50	Pakistan	Yes MLI		PPT+LOB
51	Philippines*	No	No	PPT+LOB
52	Poland	Yes MLI		PPT
53	Portugal	Yes MLI		PPT
54	Romania	No	Yes MLI	PPT
55	Russian Federation	Yes MLI		PPT+LOB
56	Serbia	Yes MLI		PPT
57	Singapore	Yes MLI		PPT
58	Slovak Republic	Yes MLI		PPT+LOB
59	Slovenia	Yes MLI		PPT
60	South Africa	No	Yes MLI	PPT
61	Sri Lanka	No	Yes other	PPT

62	Sweden	Yes other		PPT
63	Switzerland	No	No	PPT
64	Tanzania*	No	No	PPT+LOB
65	Thailand	No	No	PPT+LOB
66	Trinidad and Tobago	No	No	PPT+LOB
67	Tunisia	No	Yes MLI	PPT
68	Turkey	No	Yes MLI	PPT
69	Uganda*	No	No	PPT+LOB
70	Ukraine	Yes MLI		PPT
71	United Kingdom	Yes MLI		PTT
72	United States	No	No	PPT+LOB
73	Venezuela*	No	No	PPT+LOB
74	Viet Nam	No	No	PPT+LOB
75	Zambia	No	No	PPT+LOB

Other agreements

	1.Treaty partners	2. Inclusive Framework member
1	Belarus	Yes

Djibouti

A. Progress in the implementation of the minimum standard

Djibouti has no tax agreements in force as reported in its response to the Peer Review questionnaire.

B. Conclusion

No jurisdiction has raised any concerns about Djibouti.

Dominica

A. Progress in the implementation of the minimum standard

Dominica has two tax agreements in force as reported in its response to the Peer Review questionnaire, including the multilateral agreement among the members of the CARICOM concluded with ten treaty partners (the CARICOM Agreement).[56] Neither of those agreements comply with the minimum standard.

Dominica has not signed the MLI.

In its response to the Peer Review questionnaire, Switzerland indicated that its agreement with Dominica did not give rise to material treaty shopping concerns for Switzerland.

B. Conclusion

Dominica acknowledges that the CARICOM Agreement does not at this stage comply with the minimum standard and that discussions to bring this agreement up to date would be contemplated.[57]

Other agreements

This Table shows the agreements that are not compliant, not subject to a complying instrument, not covered by a general statement on the implementation of the detailed LOB and for which no steps have been taken to implement the minimum standard.

	1.Treaty partners	2. Inclusive Framework member
1	Antigua and Barbuda	Yes
2	Barbados	Yes
3	Belize	Yes
4	Grenada	Yes
5	Guyana*	No
6	Jamaica	Yes
7	Saint Kitts and Nevis	Yes
8	Saint Lucia	Yes
9	Saint Vincent and the Grenadines	Yes
10	Switzerland	Yes
11	Trinidad and Tobago	Yes

[56] Agreement Among the Governments of the Member States of the Caribbean Community for the Avoidance of Double Taxation and the Prevention of Fiscal Evasion with Respect to Taxes on Income, Profits or Gains and Capital Gains and for the Encouragement of Regional Trade and Investment, St. Michael Barbados, 6 July 1994; between: Antigua and Barbuda (18 February 1998), Barbados (7 July 1995), Belize (30 November 1994), Dominica (19 June 1996), Grenada (1 March 1996), Guyana* (26 November 1997), Jamaica (16 February 1995), St. Kitts/Nevis (8 May 1997), St. Lucia (22 May 1995) St. Vincent (12 February 1998) and Trinidad & Tobago (29 November 1994). In total, Dominica identified twelve "agreements" in its List of Tax agreements: two bilateral agreements and the CARICOM Agreement.

[57] Revisions to the CARICOM Agreement require an agreement from its eleven treaty partners.

Dominican Republic

A. Progress in the implementation of the minimum standard

The Dominican Republic has two tax agreements in force as reported in its response to the Peer Review questionnaire. Neither of those agreements comply with the minimum standard.

The Dominican Republic has not signed the MLI.

B. Conclusion

The Dominican Republic has developed a plan for the implementation of the minimum standard in its agreements with Canada and Spain. The Dominic Republic indicated in its response to the Peer Review questionnaire that bilateral negotiations would be pursued with respect to those agreements.

Other agreements

This Table shows the agreements that are not compliant, not subject to a complying instrument, not covered by a general statement on the implementation of the detailed LOB and for which no steps have been taken to implement the minimum standard.

	1.Treaty partners	2. Inclusive Framework member
1	Canada	Yes
2	Spain	Yes

Egypt

A. Progress in the implementation of the minimum standard

Egypt has 59[58] tax agreements in force as reported in its response to the Peer Review questionnaire. Twenty-four of those agreements comply with the minimum standard.

Egypt signed the MLI in 2017 and deposited its instrument of ratification on 30 September 2020, listing its non-compliant agreements concluded with other members of the Inclusive Framework. The MLI entered into force for Egypt on 1 January 2021. The agreements modified by the MLI come into compliance with the minimum standard once the provisions of the MLI take effect.

Egypt is implementing the minimum standard through the inclusion of the preamble statement and the PPT.[59]

B. Conclusion

No jurisdiction has raised any concerns about their agreements with Egypt.

Summary of the jurisdiction response - Egypt

	1.Treaty partners	2. Compliance with the standard	3. Signature of a complying instrument	4. Minimum standard provision used
1	Albania	Yes MLI		PPT
2	Algeria*	No	No	PPT
3	Austria	No	No	PPT
4	Bahrain	No	Yes MLI	PPT
5	Belarus	No	No	PPT
6	Belgium	Yes MLI		PPT
7	Bulgaria	No	Yes MLI	PPT
8	Canada	Yes MLI		PPT
9	China (People's Republic of)	No	Yes MLI	PPT
10	Cyprus*	Yes other		PPT
11	Czech Republic	Yes MLI		PPT
12	Denmark	Yes MLI		PPT
13	Ethiopia*	No	No	PPT
14	Finland	Yes MLI		PPT
15	France	Yes MLI		PPT
16	Georgia	No	No	PPT
17	Germany	No	No	PPT
18	Greece	No	Yes MLI	PPT
19	Hungary	No	Yes MLI	PPT

58 Egypt indicated in its response to the Peer Review questionnaire that the agreement between the Arab Republic of Egypt and the Council of Ministers of Serbia and Montenegro was inherited between Serbia and has been counted as two separate agreements.

59 For its agreements listed under the MLI, Egypt is implementing the preamble statement (Article 6 of the MLI) and the PPT (Article 7 of the MLI).

20	India	Yes MLI		PPT
21	Indonesia	No	Yes MLI	PPT
22	Iraq	No	No	PPT
23	Ireland	Yes MLI		PPT
24	Italy	No	Yes MLI	PPT
25	Japan	Yes MLI		PPT
26	Jordan	Yes MLI		PPT
27	Korea	Yes MLI		PPT
28	Kuwait*	No	Yes MLI	PPT
29	Lebanon*	No	No	PPT
30	Libya*	No	No	PPT
31	Malaysia	No	Yes MLI	PPT
32	Malta	Yes MLI		PPT
33	Mauritius	Yes MLI		PPT
34	Montenegro	No	No	PPT
35	Morocco	No	Yes MLI	PPT
36	Netherlands	Yes MLI		PPT
37	Norway	No	No	PPT
38	Pakistan	Yes MLI		PPT
39	Palestine*	No	No	PPT
40	Poland	Yes MLI		PPT
41	Romania	No	Yes MLI	PPT
42	Russian Federation	No	Yes MLI	PPT
43	Saudi Arabia	Yes MLI		PPT
44	Serbia	Yes MLI		PPT
45	Singapore	Yes MLI		PPT
46	South Africa	No	Yes MLI	PPT
47	Spain	No	Yes MLI	PPT
48	Sudan*	No	No	PPT
49	Sweden	No	Yes MLI	PPT
50	Switzerland	No	No	PPT
51	Syria*	No	No	PPT
52	Tunisia	No	Yes MLI	PPT
53	Turkey	No	Yes MLI	PPT
54	Ukraine	Yes MLI		PPT
55	United Arab Emirates	Yes other		PPT
56	United Kingdom	Yes MLI		PPT
57	United States	No	No	D-LOB
58	Yemen*	No	No	PPT

Other agreements

	1.Treaty partners	2. Inclusive Framework member
1	Uzbekistan*	No

Estonia

A. Progress in the implementation of the minimum standard

Estonia has 61 tax agreements in force as reported in its response to the Peer Review questionnaire. Three of those agreements comply with the minimum standard.

Estonia signed the MLI in 2018 and deposited its instrument of ratification on 15 January 2021. The MLI entered into force for Estonia on 1 May 2021. The agreements modified by the MLI come into compliance with the minimum standard once the provisions of the MLI take effect.

Estonia reserved the right to delay the entry into effect of the provisions of the MLI until Estonia has completed its internal procedures for this purpose with respect to each of its listed agreements.[60] Estonia notified that it completed its internal procedures for the entry into effect of the MLI with respect to its agreements with Austria, Cyprus*, Finland, Latvia, Poland, the Slovak Republic and Ukraine on 25 November 2021.

Estonia has not listed its agreements with Germany and Switzerland under the MLI but has signed a bilateral complying instrument with respect to its agreement with Germany, and indicated in its response to the Peer Review questionnaire that steps have been taken (other than under the MLI) to implement the minimum standard in its agreement with Switzerland.

Estonia is generally implementing the minimum standard through the inclusion of the preamble statement and the PPT.[61]

B. Conclusion

Estonia is encouraged to complete (and notify that is has completed) its internal procedures for the entry into effect of the MLI with respect to its agreements that are covered tax agreements under the MLI and for which no such notification has yet been made.

Summary of the jurisdiction response - Estonia

	1.Treaty partners	2. Compliance with the standard	3. Signature of a complying instrument	4. Minimum standard provision used
1	Albania	No	Yes MLI	PPT
2	Armenia	No	Yes MLI	PPT
3	Austria	No	Yes MLI	PPT
4	Azerbaijan*	No	No	PPT
5	Bahrain	No	Yes MLI	PPT
6	Belarus	No	No	PPT
7	Belgium	No	Yes MLI	PPT
8	Bulgaria	No	Yes MLI	PPT
9	Canada	No	Yes MLI	PPT
10	China (People's Republic of)	No	Yes MLI	PPT

60 The reservation was made under Article 35(7)(a) of the MLI.

61 For its agreements listed under the MLI, Estonia is implementing the preamble statement (Article 6 of the MLI) and the PPT (Article 7 of the MLI).

11	Croatia	No	Yes MLI	PPT
12	Cyprus*	No	Yes MLI	PPT
13	Czech Republic	No	No	PPT
14	Denmark	No	Yes MLI	PPT
15	Finland	No	Yes MLI	PPT
16	France	No	Yes MLI	PPT
17	Georgia	No	Yes MLI	PPT
18	Germany	No	Yes other	PPT
19	Greece	No	Yes MLI	PPT
20	Guernsey	Yes other		PPT
21	Hong Kong (China)	Yes other		PPT
22	Hungary	No	Yes MLI	PPT
23	Iceland	No	Yes MLI	PPT
24	India	No	Yes MLI	PPT
25	Ireland	No	Yes MLI	PPT
26	Isle of Man	No	Yes MLI	PPT
27	Israel	No	Yes MLI	PPT
28	Italy	No	Yes MLI	PPT
29	Japan	Yes other		PPT+LOB
30	Jersey	No	Yes MLI	PPT
31	Kazakhstan	No	Yes MLI	PPT
32	Korea	No	Yes MLI	PPT
33	Kyrgyzstan*	No	No	PPT
34	Latvia	No	Yes MLI	PPT
35	Lithuania	No	Yes MLI	PPT
36	Luxembourg	No	Yes MLI	PPT
37	Malta	No	Yes MLI	PPT
38	Mexico	No	Yes MLI	PPT
39	Moldova*	No	No	PPT
40	Netherlands	No	Yes MLI	PPT
41	North Macedonia	No	Yes MLI	PPT
42	Norway	No	Yes MLI	PPT
43	Poland	No	Yes MLI	PPT
44	Portugal	No	Yes MLI	PPT
45	Romania	No	Yes MLI	PPT
46	Serbia	No	Yes MLI	PPT
47	Singapore	No	Yes MLI	PPT
48	Slovak Republic	No	Yes MLI	PPT
49	Slovenia	No	Yes MLI	PPT
50	Spain	No	Yes MLI	PPT
51	Sweden	No	Yes MLI	PPT
52	Switzerland	No	No	PPT
53	Thailand	No	No	PPT
54	Turkey	No	Yes MLI	PPT
55	Turkmenistan*	No	No	PPT
56	Ukraine	No	Yes MLI	PPT
57	United Arab Emirates	No	Yes MLI	PPT
58	United Kingdom	No	Yes MLI	PPT
59	United States	No	No	PPT+LOB
60	Uzbekistan*	No	No	PPT
61	Viet Nam	No	No	PPT

Eswatini

A. Progress in the implementation of the minimum standard

Eswatini has seven tax agreements in force as reported in its response to the Peer Review questionnaire. One of those agreements, the agreement with Lesotho*, complies with the minimum standard.

Eswatini has not signed the MLI.

Eswatini is implementing the minimum standard through the inclusion of the preamble statement and the PPT.

B. Conclusion

Eswatini is currently developing a plan, in consultation with the Secretariat, for the implementation of the minimum standard in its agreements with Botswana, Mauritius, Seychelles, South Africa and the United Kingdom.

Summary of the jurisdiction response - Eswatini

	1.Treaty partners	2. Compliance with the standard	3. Signature of a complying instrument	4. Minimum standard provision used
1	Lesotho*	Yes other		PPT

Other agreements

	1.Treaty partners	2. Inclusive Framework member
1	Botswana	Yes
2	Chinese Taipei*	No
3	Mauritius	Yes
4	Seychelles	Yes
5	South Africa	Yes
6	United Kingdom	Yes

Faroe Islands

A. Progress in the implementation of the minimum standard

The Faroe Islands has five tax agreements in force as reported in its response to the Peer Review questionnaire, including the multilateral Nordic Convention concluded with Denmark, Finland, Iceland, Norway and Sweden (the Nordic Convention).[62] Three of those agreements, including the Nordic Convention, comply with the minimum standard.

The Faroe Islands has not joined the MLI.

The Faroe Islands indicated in its response to the Peer Review questionnaire that steps have been taken (other than under the MLI) to implement the minimum standard in its agreements with Switzerland.

The Faroe Islands is implementing the minimum standard through the inclusion of the preamble statement and the PPT.

B. Conclusion

The Faroe Islands has developed a plan for the implementation of the minimum standard in its agreement with the United Kingdom. The Faroe Islands indicated in its response to the Peer Review questionnaire that bilateral negotiations would be pursued with respect to that agreement.

Summary of the jurisdiction response – Faroe Islands

	1.Treaty partners	2. Compliance with the standard	3. Signature of a complying instrument	4. Minimum standard provision used
1	Denmark	Yes other		PPT
2	Finland	Yes other		PPT
3	Greenland	Yes other		PPT
4	Iceland	Yes other		PPT
5	India	Yes other		PPT + LOB
6	Norway	Yes other		PPT
7	Sweden	Yes other		PPT
8	Switzerland	No	No	

Other agreements

	1.Treaty partners	2. Inclusive Framework member
1	United Kingdom	Yes

[62] See the Multilateral convention concluded by Denmark, Finland, the Faroe Islands, Iceland, Norway and Sweden: for the avoidance of double taxation with respect to taxes on income and on capital (1996, 1997, 2008 and 2018). In total, the Faroe Islands identified nine "agreements" in its List of Tax agreements: four bilateral agreements and the Nordic Convention concluded with five treaty partners.

Finland

A. Progress in the implementation of the minimum standard

Finland has 73 tax agreements in force as reported in its response to the Peer Review questionnaire, including the multilateral Nordic Convention concluded with Denmark, the Faroe Islands, Iceland, Norway and Sweden (the Nordic Convention).[63] Thirty-six of those agreements, including the Nordic Convention, comply with the minimum standard.

Finland signed the MLI in 2017 and deposited its instrument of ratification on 25 February 2019. The MLI entered into force for Finland on 1 June 2019. The agreements modified by the MLI come into compliance with the minimum standard once the provisions of the MLI take effect.

Finland has not listed its agreement with Bulgaria under the MLI but indicated in its response to the Peer Review questionnaire that steps have been taken (other than under the MLI) to implement the minimum standard in that agreement.

Finland is implementing the minimum standard through the inclusion of the preamble statement and the PPT.[64]

B. Conclusion

No jurisdiction has raised any concerns about their agreements with Finland.

Summary of the jurisdiction response - Finland

	1.Treaty partners	2. Compliance with the standard	3. Signature of a complying instrument	4. Minimum standard provision used
1	Argentina	No	Yes MLI	PPT
2	Armenia	No	Yes MLI	PPT
3	Australia	Yes MLI		PPT
4	Austria	Yes MLI		PPT
5	Azerbaijan*	No	No	PPT
6	Barbados	No	Yes MLI	PPT
7	Belarus	No	No	PPT
8	Belgium	Yes MLI		PPT
9	Bosnia-Herzegovina	No	Yes MLI	PPT
10	Brazil	No	No	
11	Bulgaria	No	No	
12	Canada	Yes MLI		PPT
13	China (People's Republic of)	No	Yes MLI	PPT
14	Croatia	No	Yes MLI	PPT

[63] See the Multilateral convention concluded by Denmark, Finland, the Faroe Islands, Iceland, Norway and Sweden: for the avoidance of double taxation with respect to taxes on income and on capital (1996, 1997, 2008 and 2018). In total, Finland identified 77 "agreements" in its List of Tax agreements: 72 bilateral agreements and the Nordic Convention concluded with five treaty partners.

[64] For its agreements listed under the MLI, Finland is implementing the preamble statement (Article 6 of the MLI) and the PPT (Article 7 of the MLI).

15	Cyprus*	Yes MLI		PPT
16	Czech Republic	Yes MLI		PPT
17	Denmark	Yes other		PPT
18	Egypt	Yes MLI		PPT
19	Estonia	No	Yes MLI	PPT
20	Faroe Islands	Yes other		PPT
21	France	Yes MLI		PPT
22	Georgia	Yes MLI		PPT
23	Germany	Yes other		PPT
24	Greece	No	Yes MLI	PPT
25	Hong Kong (China)	Yes other		PPT
26	Hungary	No	Yes MLI	PPT
27	Iceland	Yes other		PPT
28	India	Yes MLI		PPT
29	Indonesia	Yes MLI		PPT
30	Ireland	Yes MLI		PPT
31	Israel	Yes MLI		PPT
32	Italy	No	Yes MLI	PPT
33	Japan	Yes MLI		PPT
34	Kazakhstan	Yes MLI		PPT
35	Korea	Yes MLI		PPT
36	Kosovo*	No	No	PPT
37	Kyrgyzstan*	No	No	PPT
38	Latvia	Yes MLI		PPT
39	Lithuania	Yes MLI		PPT
40	Luxembourg	Yes MLI		PPT
41	North Macedonia	No	Yes MLI	PPT
42	Malaysia	No	Yes MLI	PPT
43	Malta	Yes MLI		PPT
44	Mexico	No	Yes MLI	PPT
45	Moldova*	No	No	PPT
46	Montenegro	No	No	PPT
47	Morocco	No	Yes MLI	PPT
48	Netherlands	Yes MLI		PPT
49	New Zealand	Yes MLI		PPT
50	Norway	Yes other		PPT
51	Pakistan	Yes MLI		PPT
52	Philippines*	No	No	PPT
53	Poland	Yes MLI		PPT
54	Romania	No	Yes MLI	PPT
55	Russian Federation	Yes MLI		PPT
56	Serbia	Yes MLI		PPT
57	Singapore	Yes MLI		PPT
58	Slovak Republic	Yes MLI		PPT
59	Slovenia	Yes MLI		PPT
60	South Africa	No	Yes MLI	PPT
61	Spain	No	Yes MLI	PPT
62	Sri Lanka	No	No	PPT
63	Sweden	Yes other		PPT
64	Switzerland	No	No	PPT
65	Tajikistan*	No	No	PPT
66	Tanzania*	No	No	PPT
67	Thailand	No	No	PPT

68	Turkey	No	Yes MLI	PPT
69	Turkmenistan*	No	No	PPT
70	Ukraine	Yes MLI		PPT
71	United Arab Emirates	Yes MLI		PPT
72	United Kingdom	Yes MLI		PPT
73	United States	No	No	PPT
74	Uruguay	Yes MLI		PPT
75	Uzbekistan*	No	No	PPT
76	Viet Nam	No	No	PPT
77	Zambia	No	No	PPT

France

A. Progress in the implementation of the minimum standard

France has 119 tax agreements in force as reported in its response to the Peer Review questionnaire. Forty-one of those agreements comply with the minimum standard.

France signed the MLI in 2017 and deposited its instrument of ratification on 26 September 2018. The MLI entered into force for France on 1 January 2019. On 22 September 2020, France made an additional notification to expand its list of agreements to be covered under the MLI. The agreements modified by the MLI come into compliance with the minimum standard once the provisions of the MLI take effect.

France is implementing the minimum standard through the inclusion of the preamble statement and the PPT.[65]

B. Conclusion

No jurisdiction has raised any concerns about their agreements with France.

Summary of the jurisdiction response – France

	1.Treaty partners	2. Compliance with the standard	3. Signature of a complying instrument	4. Minimum standard provision used
1	Albania	Yes MLI		PPT
2	Algeria*	No	No	PPT
3	Andorra	No	Yes MLI	PPT
4	Argentina	No	Yes MLI	PPT
5	Armenia	No	Yes MLI	PPT
6	Australia	Yes MLI		PPT
7	Austria	Yes MLI		PPT
8	Azerbaijan*	No	No	PPT
9	Bahrain	No	Yes MLI	PPT
10	Bangladesh*	No	No	PPT
11	Belarus	No	No	PPT
12	Belgium	Yes MLI		PPT
13	Benin	No	No	PPT
14	Bolivia*	No	No	PPT
15	Bosnia-Herzegovina	Yes MLI		PPT
16	Botswana	No	No	PPT
17	Brazil	No	No	PPT
18	Bulgaria	No	Yes MLI	PPT
19	Burkina Faso	No	Yes MLI	PPT
20	Cameroon	No	Yes MLI	PPT
21	Canada	Yes MLI		PPT
22	Central African Republic*	No	No	PPT
23	Chile	No	Yes MLI	PPT

65 For its agreements listed under the MLI, France is implementing the preamble statement (Article 6 of the MLI) and the PPT (Article 7 of the MLI).

24	China (People's Republic)	No	Yes MLI	PPT
25	Côte d'Ivoire	No	Yes MLI	PPT
26	Croatia	No	Yes MLI	PPT
27	Cyprus*	Yes MLI		PPT
28	Czech Republic	Yes MLI		PPT
29	Ecuador*	No	No	PPT
30	Egypt	Yes MLI		PPT
31	Estonia	No	Yes MLI	PPT
32	Ethiopia*	No	No	PPT
33	Finland	Yes MLI		PPT
34	Gabon	No	Yes MLI	PPT
35	Georgia	Yes MLI		PPT
36	Germany	No	Yes MLI	PPT
37	Ghana*	No	No	PPT
38	Greece	No	Yes MLI	PPT
39	Guinea*	No	No	PPT
40	Hong Kong (China)	No	Yes MLI	PPT
41	Hungary	No	Yes MLI	PPT
42	Iceland	Yes MLI		PPT
43	India	Yes MLI		PPT
44	Indonesia	Yes MLI		PPT
45	Iran*	No	No	PPT
46	Ireland	Yes MLI		PPT
47	Israel	Yes MLI		PPT
48	Italy	No	Yes MLI	PPT
49	Jamaica	No	Yes MLI	PPT
50	Japan	Yes MLI		PPT+LOB
51	Jordan	Yes MLI		PPT
52	Kazakhstan	Yes MLI		PPT
53	Kenya	No	Yes MLI	PPT
54	Korea	Yes MLI		PPT
55	Kosovo*	No	No	PPT
56	Kuwait*	No	Yes MLI	PPT
57	Kyrgyzstan*	No	No	PPT
58	Latvia	Yes MLI		PPT
59	Lebanon*	No	No	PPT
60	Libya*	No	No	PPT
61	Lithuania	Yes MLI		PPT
62	Luxembourg	Yes other		PPT
63	Madagascar*	No	No	PPT
64	Malawi*	No	No	PPT
65	Malaysia	No	Yes MLI	PPT
66	Mali*	No	No	PPT
67	Malta	Yes MLI		PPT
68	Mauritania*	No	No	PPT
69	Mauritius	Yes MLI		PPT
70	Mexico	No	Yes MLI	PPT
71	Monaco	Yes MLI		PPT
72	Mongolia	No	No	PPT
73	Montenegro	No	No	PPT
74	Morocco	No	Yes MLI	PPT
75	Namibia	No	No	PPT
76	Netherlands	Yes MLI		PPT

77	New Zealand	Yes MLI		PPT
78	Niger*	No	No	PPT
79	Nigeria	No	Yes MLI	PPT
80	North Macedonia	No	Yes MLI	PPT
81	Norway	No	No	PPT
82	Oman	Yes MLI		PPT
83	Pakistan	No	Yes MLI	PPT
84	Panama	No	Yes MLI	PPT
85	Philippines*	No	No	PPT
86	Poland	Yes MLI		PPT
87	Portugal	Yes MLI		PPT
88	Qatar	Yes MLI		PPT
89	Quebec*	No	No	PPT
90	Republic of the Congo	No	No	PPT
91	Romania	No	Yes MLI	PPT
92	Russian Federation	Yes MLI		PPT
93	Saudi Arabia	Yes MLI		PPT
94	Senegal	No	Yes MLI	PPT
95	Serbia	Yes MLI		PPT
96	Singapore	Yes MLI		PPT
97	Slovak Republic	Yes MLI		PPT
98	Slovenia	Yes MLI		PPT
99	South Africa	No	Yes MLI	PPT
100	Spain	No	Yes MLI	PPT
101	Sri Lanka	No	No	PPT
102	Sweden	No	No	PPT
103	Switzerland	No	No	PPT
104	Syrian Arab Republic*	No	No	PPT
105	Thailand	No	No	PPT
106	Togo*	No	No	PPT
107	Trinidad and Tobago	No	No	PPT
108	Tunisia	No	Yes MLI	PPT
109	Turkey	No	Yes MLI	PPT
110	Turkmenistan*	No	No	PPT
113	Ukraine	Yes MLI		PPT
111	United Arab Emirates	Yes MLI		PPT
112	United Kingdom	Yes MLI		PPT
114	United States	No	No	PPT
115	Uzbekistan*	No	No	PPT
116	Venezuela*	No	No	PPT
117	Viet Nam	No	No	PPT
118	Zambia	No	No	PPT
119	Zimbabwe*	No	No	PPT

Gabon

A. Progress in the implementation of the minimum standard

Gabon has six tax agreements in force as reported in its response to the Peer Review questionnaire. None of those agreements comply with the minimum standard.

Gabon signed the MLI in 2017. The agreements modified by the MLI come into compliance with the minimum standard once the provisions of the MLI take effect.

Gabon has not listed its agreements with Korea and Saudi Arabia. These agreements will therefore not, at this stage, be modified under the MLI. Korea and Saudi Arabia have both listed their agreements with Gabon under the MLI.

Gabon is implementing the minimum standard through the inclusion of the preamble statement and the PPT.[66]

B. Conclusion

Korea and Saudi Arabia have both listed their agreements with Gabon under the MLI, which amounts to requests to implement the minimum standard.

Gabon has developed a plan for the implementation of the minimum standard in its agreements with Korea and Saudi Arabia. Gabon indicated in its response to the Peer Review questionnaire that it intends expand its list of agreements to be covered under the MLI in to include those agreements.

Recommendation

It is recommended that Gabon completes the steps to have the MLI take effect with respect to its agreements listed under the MLI as those agreements will only be modified by the MLI (and come into compliance with the minimum standard) once the provisions of the MLI take effect.

Summary of the jurisdiction response - Gabon

	1.Treaty partners	2. Compliance with the standard	3. Signature of a complying instrument	4. Minimum standard provision used
1	Belgium	No	Yes MLI	PPT
2	Canada	No	Yes MLI	PPT
3	France	No	Yes MLI	PPT
4	Morocco	No	Yes MLI	PPT

[66] For its agreements listed under the MLI, Gabon is implementing the preamble statement (Article 6 of the MLI) and the PPT (Article 7 of the MLI).

Other agreements

	1.Treaty partners	2. Inclusive Framework member
1	Korea	Yes
2	Saudi Arabia	Yes

Georgia

A. Progress in the implementation of the minimum standard

Georgia has 56 tax agreements in force as reported in its response to the Peer Review questionnaire. Twenty-three of those agreements, comply with the minimum standard.

Georgia signed the MLI in 2017 and deposited its instrument of ratification on 29 March 2019, listing 34 of its agreements in force at that time. The MLI entered into force for Georgia on 1 July 2019. The agreements modified by the MLI come into compliance with the minimum standard once the provisions of the MLI take effect.

Georgia has not listed its agreements with Armenia, Austria, Bahrain, Belarus, Denmark, Egypt, Germany, Japan, Kazakhstan, Malta, Poland, Qatar, Saudi Arabia, Switzerland, Ukraine and the United Arab Emirates. These agreements will therefore not, at this stage, be modified under the MLI. Armenia, Bahrain, Denmark, Egypt, Kazakhstan, Malta, Saudi Arabia, Ukraine and the United Arab Emirates have listed their agreements with Georgia under the MLI.

Georgia has signed a bilateral complying instrument with respect to its agreement Japan.

Georgia indicated in its response to the Peer Review questionnaire that steps have been taken (other than under the MLI) to implement the minimum standard in its agreements with Malta and Poland.[67]

Georgia is implementing the minimum standard through the inclusion of the preamble statement and the PPT.[68]

In its response to the Peer Review questionnaire, Germany indicated that its agreement with Georgia did not give rise to material treaty shopping concerns for Germany.

B. Conclusion

Armenia, Bahrain, Denmark, Egypt, Kazakhstan, Malta, Saudi Arabia, Ukraine and the United Arab Emirates have listed their agreements with Georgia under the MLI, which amount to requests to implement the minimum standard.

Georgia has developed a plan for the implementation of the minimum standard in its agreements with Armenia, Austria, Bahrain, Belarus, Denmark, Egypt, Germany, Kazakhstan, Qatar, Saudi Arabia, Switzerland, Ukraine and the United Arab Emirates. Georgia indicated in its response to the Peer Review questionnaire that it intends to expand its list of agreements to be covered under the MLI to include these agreements, and that had intended to provide the revised list of agreements under the MLI before December 2021.

Georgia also indicated that bilateral negotiations would be pursued to implement the minimum standard in its agreements with Azerbaijan*, Iran*, Kuwait*, Moldova*, Turkmenistan* and Uzbekistan*.

---

[67] Georgia and Poland signed a new agreement on 7 July 2021, which will replace the current agreement once it enters into force.

[68] For its agreements listed under the MLI, Georgia is implementing the preamble statement (Article 6 of the MLI) and the PPT (Article 7 of the MLI).

Summary of the jurisdiction response - Georgia

	1.Treaty partners	2. Compliance with the standard	3. Signature of a complying instrument	4. Minimum standard provision used
1	Belgium	Yes MLI		PPT
2	Bulgaria	No	Yes MLI	PPT
3	China (People's Republic of)	No	Yes MLI	PPT
4	Croatia	No	Yes MLI	PPT
5	Cyprus*	Yes MLI		PPT
6	Czech Republic	Yes MLI		PPT
7	Estonia	No	Yes MLI	PPT
8	Finland	Yes MLI		PPT
9	France	Yes MLI		PPT
10	Greece	No	Yes MLI	PPT
11	Hungary	No	Yes MLI	PPT
12	Iceland	Yes MLI		PPT
13	India	Yes MLI		PPT
14	Ireland	Yes MLI		PPT
15	Israel	Yes MLI		PPT
16	Italy	No	Yes MLI	PPT
17	Japan	No	Yes other	PPT+LOB
18	Korea	Yes MLI		PPT
19	Latvia	Yes MLI		PPT
20	Liechtenstein	Yes MLI		PPT
21	Lithuania	Yes MLI		PPT
22	Luxembourg	Yes MLI		PPT
23	Malta	No	No	
24	Netherlands	Yes MLI		PPT
25	Norway	Yes MLI		PPT
26	Poland	No	No	
27	Portugal	Yes MLI		PPT
28	Romania	No	Yes MLI	
29	San Marino	Yes MLI		PPT
30	Serbia	Yes MLI		PPT
31	Singapore	Yes MLI		PPT
32	Slovak Republic	Yes MLI		PPT
33	Slovenia	Yes MLI		PPT
34	Spain	No	Yes MLI	PPT
35	Sweden	No	Yes MLI	PPT
36	Turkey	No	Yes MLI	PPT
37	United Kingdom	Yes MLI		PPT

Other agreements

	1.Treaty partners	2. Inclusive Framework member
1	Armenia	Yes
2	Austria	Yes
3	Azerbaijan*	No
4	Bahrain	Yes
5	Belarus	Yes
6	Denmark	Yes
7	Egypt	Yes

8	Germany	Yes
9	Iran*	No
10	Kazakhstan	Yes
11	Kuwait*	No
12	Moldova*	No
13	Qatar	Yes
14	Saudi Arabia	Yes
15	Switzerland	Yes
16	Turkmenistan*	No
17	Ukraine	Yes
18	United Arab Emirates	Yes
19	Uzbekistan*	No

Germany

A. Progress in the implementation of the minimum standard

Germany has 95 tax agreements in force as reported in its response to the Peer Review questionnaire. Four of those agreements[69], comply with the minimum standard.

Germany signed the MLI in 2017 and deposited its instrument of ratification on 18 December 2020, listing 14 of its agreements in force at that time. The MLI entered into force for Germany on 1 April 2021.The agreements modified by the MLI come into compliance with the minimum standard once the provisions of the MLI take effect.

Germany reserved the right to delay the entry into effect of the provisions of the MLI until Germany has completed its internal procedures for this purpose with respect to each of its listed agreements.[70] Germany has not yet notified that it completed its internal procedures for the entry into effect of the MLI with respect to any of its agreements.

Germany has not listed its agreements under the MLI with Albania, Argentina, Armenia, Belgium, Belarus, Bulgaria, Bosnia-Herzegovina, Canada, China (People's Republic of), Costa Rica, Côte d'Ivoire, Denmark, Egypt, Estonia[71], Georgia, Iceland, India, Indonesia, Ireland, Israel, Jamaica, Kazakhstan, Kenya, Korea, Latvia, Liberia, Liechtenstein[72], Lithuania, Malaysia, Mauritius, Mexico, Mongolia, Montenegro, Morocco, Namibia, New Zealand, the Netherlands, North Macedonia, Norway, Pakistan, Poland, Portugal, the Russian Federation, Serbia, Slovenia, South Africa, Sri Lanka, Sweden, Switzerland, Thailand, Tunisia, Ukraine, United Arab Emirates[73], the United Kingdom, Uruguay, Viet Nam and Zambia. These agreements will therefore not, at this stage, be modified under the MLI. Albania, Armenia, Bosnia-Herzegovina, China (People's Republic of), Côte d'Ivoire, Egypt, India, Jamaica, Kazakhstan, Liechtenstein[74], Lithuania, Malaysia, Mauritius, Mexico, Morocco, Namibia, the Netherlands, New Zealand, North Macedonia, Pakistan, Portugal, Serbia, Singapore, Tunisia, Ukraine, United Arab Emirates[75], and Uruguay have listed their agreement with Germany under the MLI.

Germany has signed a bilateral complying instrument with respect to its agreements with Cyprus*, Denmark, Estonia[76], Ireland, Liechtenstein[77], the Netherlands and the United Kingdom.[78]

---

[69] As of 29 June 2021, a fifth agreement (the agreement with Estonia) also complies with the minimum standard. As of 29 October 2021, a sixth agreement (the agreement with Liechtenstein) also complies with the minimum standard.

[70] The reservation was made under Article 35(7)(a) of the MLI.

[71] The complying instrument with respect to the agreement with Estonia entered into force on 29 June 2021. As of that date, the agreement with Estonia is compliant with the minimum standard.

[72] The complying instrument with respect to the agreement with Liechtenstein entered into force on 29 October 2021. As of that date, the agreement with Liechtenstein is compliant with the minimum standard.

[73] The agreement with the United Arab Emirates expires on 31 December 2021.

[74] See note above on the agreement with Liechtenstein.

[75] See note above on the agreement with the United Arab Emirates.

[76] See note above on the agreement with Estonia.

[77] See note above on the agreement with Liechtenstein.

[78] Germany signed a bilateral complying instrument with respect to its agreements with Mauritius and Mexico on 29 October 2021 and 8 October 2021, respectively.

Germany indicated in its response to the Peer Review questionnaire that steps have been taken (other than under the MLI) to implement the minimum standard in its agreement with Argentina, Belgium, Bolivia*, Bulgaria, Canada, China (People's Republic of), Costa Rica, Ecuador*, Egypt, Iceland, India, Indonesia, Iran*, Israel, Kazakhstan, Kenya, Korea, Kosovo*, Kuwait*, Latvia, Liberia, Lithuania, Mauritius[79], Mexico[80], Mongolia, Morocco, Namibia, New Zealand, Norway, Pakistan, Poland, Portugal, the Russian Federation, Serbia, Slovenia, South Africa, Sri Lanka, Sweden, Switzerland, Thailand, Trinidad and Tobago, Tunisia, Ukraine, Uruguay and Viet Nam.[81]

Germany indicated in its response to the Peer Review questionnaire that the agreements with Bosnia-Herzegovina, Montenegro and Zambia do not give rise to material treaty-shopping concerns for Germany, noting the application of German domestic anti-abuse provisions such as Section 42 of the German Fiscal Code (GAAR) or in Section 50d para. 3 of the German Income Tax Act (anti-conduit rule), which permits the proportionate denial of tax treaty benefits to companies with non-eligible shareholders. Germany further indicated that the agreements with Armenia, Belarus, Georgia, Malaysia, North Macedonia and the United Arab Emirates[82] do not give rise to material treaty-shopping concerns for Germany, because they contain a general reservation for the application of domestic anti-abuse provisions such as the two sections mentioned above and the CFC-legislation.

Germany is implementing the minimum standard through the inclusion of the preamble statement and the PPT.[83]

B. Conclusion

Albania, Armenia, Bosnia-Herzegovina, China (People's Republic of), Côte d'Ivoire, Egypt, India, Jamaica, Kazakhstan, Lithuania, Malaysia, Mauritius, Mexico, Morocco, Namibia, New Zealand, North Macedonia, Pakistan, Portugal, Serbia, Tunisia, Ukraine, United Arab Emirates[84] and Uruguay have listed their agreement with Germany under the MLI, which amount to requests to implement the minimum standard.

Germany gave effect to its plan to implement the minimum standard in its agreements with Albania, Côte d'Ivoire and Jamaica by pursuing bilateral negotiations to implement the minimum standard in those agreements.

Germany has developed a plan for the implementation of the minimum standard in its agreements with Armenia, Bosnia-Herzegovina and Malaysia. Germany indicated that bilateral negotiations would be pursued to implement the minimum standard with respect to those agreements.

---

79 See the note above on the agreement with Mauritius.

80 See the note above on the agreement with Mexico.

81 As described below, Germany has also started to give effect to its plan to implement the minimum standard in its agreements with Albania, Côte d'Ivoire and Jamaica.

82 See note above on the agreement with the United Arab Emirates.

83 For its agreements listed under the MLI, Germany is implementing the preamble statement (Article 6 of the MLI) and the PPT (Article 7 of the MLI). Germany has made a reservation pursuant to Article 6(4) of the MLI not to apply Article 6(1) of the MLI with respect to agreements that already contain the relevant preamble language (covering one agreement). Germany has also made a reservation pursuant to 7(15)(b) of the MLI not to apply Article 7(1) of the MLI with respect to agreements which already contain a PPT (covering one agreement).

84 See note above on the agreement with the United Arab Emirates.

Recommendations

It is recommended that Germany completes the steps to have the MLI take effect with respect to its agreements listed under the MLI as those agreements will only be modified by the MLI (and come into compliance with the minimum standard) once the provisions of the MLI take effect.

Summary of the jurisdiction response – Germany

	1.Treaty partners	2. Compliance with the standard	3. Signature of a complying instrument	4. Minimum standard provision used
1	Argentina	No	No	
2	Australia	Yes other		PPT
3	Austria	No	Yes MLI	PPT
4	Belgium	No	No	
5	Bolivia*	No	No	
6	Bulgaria	No	No	
7	Canada	No	No	
8	China (People's Republic of)	No	No	
9	Costa Rica	No	No	
10	Croatia	No	Yes MLI	PPT
11	Cyprus*	No	Yes other	PPT
12	Czech Republic	No	Yes MLI	PPT
13	Denmark	No	Yes other	PPT
14	Ecuador*	No	No	
15	Egypt	No	No	
16	Estonia	No	Yes other	PPT
17	Finland	Yes other		PPT
18	France	No	Yes MLI	PPT
19	Greece	No	Yes MLI	PPT
20	Hungary	No	Yes MLI	PPT
21	Iceland	No	No	
22	India	No	No	
23	Indonesia	No	No	
24	Iran*	No	No	
25	Ireland	No	Yes other	PPT
26	Israel	No	No	
27	Italy	No	Yes MLI	PPT
28	Japan	Yes other		PPT+LOB
29	Kazakhstan	No	No	
30	Kenya	No	No	
31	Korea	No	No	
32	Kosovo*	No	No	
33	Kuwait*	No	No	
34	Latvia	No	No	
35	Liberia	No	No	
36	Liechtenstein	No	Yes other	PPT
37	Lithuania	No	No	
38	Luxembourg	No	Yes MLI	PPT
39	Malta	No	Yes MLI	PPT

40	Mauritius	No	No	PPT
41	Mexico	No	No	PPT
42	Mongolia	No	No	
43	Morocco	No	No	
44	Namibia	No	No	
45	Netherlands	No	Yes other	PPT
46	New Zealand	No	No	
47	Norway	No	No	
48	Pakistan	No	No	
49	Poland	No	No	
50	Portugal	No	No	
51	Romania	No	Yes MLI	PPT
52	Russian Federation	No	No	
53	Serbia	No	No	
54	Singapore	Yes other		PPT
55	Slovak Republic	No	Yes MLI	PPT
56	Slovenia	No	No	
57	South Africa	No	No	
58	Spain	No	Yes MLI	PPT
59	Sri Lanka	No	No	
60	Sweden	No	No	
61	Switzerland	No	No	PPT
62	Thailand	No	No	
63	Trinidad and Tobago	No	No	
64	Tunisia	No	No	
65	Turkey	No	Yes MLI	PPT
66	Ukraine	No	No	
67	United Kingdom	No	Yes other	PPT
68	United States	No	No	D-LOB
69	Uruguay	No	No	
70	Viet Nam	No	No	

Other agreements

	1.Treaty partners	2. Inclusive Framework member
1	Albania	Yes
2	Algeria*	No
3	Armenia	Yes
4	Azerbaijan*	No
5	Bangladesh*	No
6	Belarus	Yes
7	Bosnia-Herzegovina	Yes
8	Côte d'Ivoire	Yes
9	Georgia	Yes
10	Ghana*	No
11	Jamaica	Yes
12	Kyrgyzstan*	No
13	Malaysia	Yes
14	Moldova*	No
15	Montenegro	Yes
16	North Macedonia	Yes
17	Philippines*	No

18	Syrian Arab Republic*	No
19	Tajikistan*	No
20	Turkmenistan*	No
21	United Arab Emirates	Yes
22	Uzbekistan*	No
23	Venezuela*	No
24	Zambia	Yes
25	Zimbabwe*	No

Gibraltar

A. Progress in the implementation of the minimum standard

Gibraltar has one tax agreement in force, the agreement with the United Kingdom, as reported in its response to the Peer Review questionnaire. This agreement complies with the minimum standard.

Gibraltar is implementing the minimum standard through the inclusion of the preamble statement and the PPT.

B. Conclusion

No jurisdiction has raised any concerns about Gibraltar.

Summary of the jurisdiction response - Gibraltar

	1.Treaty partners	2. Compliance with the standard	3. Signature of a complying instrument	4. Minimum standard provision used
1	United Kingdom	Yes other		PPT

Greece

A. Progress in the implementation of the minimum standard

Greece has 57 tax agreements in force as reported in its response to the Peer Review questionnaire. None of those agreements comply with the minimum standard.

Greece signed the MLI in 2017 and deposited its instrument of ratification on 30 March 2021, listing its non-compliant agreements. The MLI entered into force for Greece on 1 July 2021. The agreements modified by the MLI come into compliance with the minimum standard once the provisions of the MLI take effect.

Greece is implementing the minimum standard through the inclusion of the preamble statement and the PPT.[85]

B. Conclusion

No jurisdiction has raised any concerns about their agreements with Greece.

Summary of the jurisdiction response - Greece

	1.Treaty partners	2. Compliance with the standard	3. Signature of a complying instrument	4. Minimum standard provision used
1	Albania	No	Yes MLI	PPT
2	Armenia	No	Yes MLI	PPT
3	Austria	No	Yes MLI	PPT
4	Azerbaijan*	No	No	PPT
5	Belgium	No	Yes MLI	PPT
6	Bosnia-Herzegovina	No	Yes MLI	PPT
7	Bulgaria	No	Yes MLI	PPT
8	Canada	No	Yes MLI	PPT
9	China (People's Republic of)	No	Yes MLI	PPT
10	Croatia	No	Yes MLI	PPT
11	Cyprus*	No	Yes MLI	PPT
12	Czech Republic	No	Yes MLI	PPT
13	Denmark	No	Yes MLI	PPT
14	Egypt	No	Yes MLI	PPT
15	Estonia	No	Yes MLI	PPT
16	Finland	No	Yes MLI	PPT
17	France	No	Yes MLI	PPT
18	Georgia	No	Yes MLI	PPT
19	Germany	No	Yes MLI	PPT
20	Hungary	No	Yes MLI	PPT
21	Iceland	No	Yes MLI	PPT

85 For its agreements listed under the MLI, Greece is implementing the preamble statement (Article 6 of the MLI) and the PPT (Article 7 of the MLI). Greece has also adopted the asymmetrical application of the simplified LOB under Article 7(7)(b) of the MLI.

22	India	No	Yes MLI	PPT
23	Ireland	No	Yes MLI	PPT
24	Israel	No	Yes MLI	PPT
25	Italy	No	Yes MLI	PPT
26	Korea	No	Yes MLI	PPT
27	Kuwait*	No	Yes MLI	PPT
28	Latvia	No	Yes MLI	PPT
29	Lithuania	No	Yes MLI	PPT
30	Luxembourg	No	Yes MLI	PPT
31	Malta	No	Yes MLI	PPT
32	Mexico	No	Yes MLI	PPT
33	Moldova*	No	No	PPT
34	Morocco	No	Yes MLI	PPT
35	Netherlands	No	Yes MLI	PPT
36	Norway	No	Yes MLI	PPT
37	Poland	No	Yes MLI	PPT
38	Portugal	No	Yes MLI	PPT
39	Qatar	No	Yes MLI	PPT
40	Romania	No	Yes MLI	PPT
41	Russian Federation	No	Yes MLI	PPT
42	San Marino	No	Yes MLI	PPT
43	Saudi Arabia	No	Yes MLI	PPT
44	Serbia	No	Yes MLI	PPT
45	Slovak Republic	No	Yes MLI	PPT
46	Slovenia	No	Yes MLI	PPT
47	South Africa	No	Yes MLI	PPT
48	Spain	No	Yes MLI	PPT
49	Sweden	No	Yes MLI	PPT
50	Switzerland	No	No	PPT
51	Tunisia	No	Yes MLI	PPT
52	Turkey	No	Yes MLI	PPT
53	Ukraine	No	Yes MLI	PPT
54	United Arab Emirates	No	Yes MLI	PPT
55	United Kingdom	No	Yes MLI	PPT
56	United States	No	No	PPT
57	Uzbekistan*	No	No	PPT

Greenland

A. Progress in the implementation of the minimum standard

Greenland has four tax agreements in force as reported in its response to the Peer Review questionnaire. One of those agreements, the agreement with the Faroe Islands, complies with the minimum standard.

Greenland has not signed the MLI.

Greenland indicated in its response to the Peer Review questionnaire that steps have been taken (other than under the MLI) to implement the minimum standard in its agreements with Denmark, Iceland and Norway.

Greenland is implementing the minimum standard through the inclusion of the preamble statement and the PPT.

B. Conclusion

No jurisdiction has raised any concerns about their agreements with Greenland.

Summary of the jurisdiction response - Greenland

	1.Treaty partners	2. Compliance with the standard	3. Signature of a complying instrument	4. Minimum standard provision used
1	Denmark	No	No	
2	Faroe Islands	Yes other		PPT
3	Iceland	No	No	
4	Norway	No	No	

Grenada

A. Progress in the implementation of the minimum standard

Grenada has four tax agreements in force as reported in its response to the Peer Review questionnaire, including the multilateral agreement among the members of the CARICOM concluded with ten treaty partners (the CARICOM Agreement). [86] None of those agreements comply with the minimum standard.

Grenada has not signed the MLI. In its response to the Peer Review questionnaire, Switzerland indicated that its agreement with Grenada did not give rise to material treaty shopping concerns for Switzerland.

B. Conclusion

The CARICOM Agreement does not at this stage comply with the minimum standard and discussions to bring this agreement up to date should be contemplated.[87]

Recommendation

It is recommended that Grenada formulates a plan for the implementation of the minimum standard in its agreements for which no steps have yet been taken and that were concluded with members of the BEPS Inclusive Framework (South Africa and the United Kingdom).

Other agreements

This Table shows the agreements that are not compliant, not subject to a complying instrument, not covered by a general statement on the implementation of the detailed LOB and for which no steps have been taken to implement the minimum standard.

	1.Treaty partners	2. Inclusive Framework member
1	Antigua and Barbuda	Yes
2	Barbados	Yes
3	Belize	Yes

[86] Agreement Among the Governments of the Member States of the Caribbean Community for the Avoidance of Double Taxation and the Prevention of Fiscal Evasion with Respect to Taxes on Income, Profits or Gains and Capital Gains and for the Encouragement of Regional Trade and Investment, St. Michael Barbados, 6 July 1994; between: Antigua and Barbuda (18 February 1998), Barbados (7 July 1995), Belize (30 November 1994), Dominica (19 June 1996), Grenada (1 March 1996), Guyana* (26 November 1997), Jamaica (16 February 1995), St. Kitts/Nevis (8 May 1997), St. Lucia (22 May 1995) St. Vincent (12 February 1998) and Trinidad & Tobago (29 November 1994). In total, Grenada identified thirteen "agreements" in its List of Tax agreements: three bilateral agreements and the CARICOM Agreement.

[87] Revisions to the CARICOM Agreement require an agreement from its eleven treaty partners.

4	Dominica	Yes
5	Guyana*	No
6	Jamaica	Yes
7	Saint Kitts and Nevis	Yes
8	Saint Lucia	Yes
9	Saint Vincent and the Grenadines	Yes
10	South Africa	Yes
11	Switzerland	Yes
12	Trinidad and Tobago	Yes
13	United Kingdom	Yes

Guernsey

A. Progress in the implementation of the minimum standard

Guernsey has 14 tax agreements in force as reported in its response to the Peer Review questionnaire. Ten of those agreements comply with the minimum standard.

Guernsey signed the MLI in 2017 and deposited its instrument of ratification on 12 February 2019. The MLI entered into force for Guernsey on 1 June 2019. The agreements modified by the MLI come into compliance with the minimum standard once the provisions of the MLI take effect.

Guernsey has not listed its agreements with Jersey and Qatar under the MLI but indicated in its response to the Peer Review questionnaire that steps have been taken (other than under the MLI) to implement the minimum standard in these two agreements.

Guernsey is implementing the minimum standard through the inclusion of the preamble statement and the PPT.[88]

B. Conclusion

No jurisdiction has raised any concerns about their agreements with Guernsey.

Summary of the jurisdiction response - Guernsey

	1.Treaty partners	2. Compliance with the standard	3. Signature of a complying instrument	4. Minimum standard provision used
1	Cyprus*	Yes MLI		PPT
2	Estonia	Yes other		PPT
3	Hong Kong (China)	No	Yes MLI	PPT
4	Isle of Man	Yes other		PPT
5	Jersey	No	No	PPT
6	Liechtenstein	Yes MLI		PPT
7	Luxembourg	Yes MLI		PPT
8	Malta	Yes MLI		PPT
9	Mauritius	Yes MLI		PPT
10	Monaco	Yes MLI		PPT
11	Qatar	No	No	PPT
12	Seychelles	No	Yes MLI	PPT
13	Singapore	Yes MLI		PPT
14	United Kingdom	Yes other		PPT

[88] For its agreements listed under the MLI, Guernsey is implementing the preamble statement (Article 6 of the MLI) and the PPT (Article 7 of the MLI).

Haiti

A. Progress in the implementation of the minimum standard

Haiti has no tax agreements in force as reported in its response to the Peer Review questionnaire.

B. Conclusion

No jurisdiction has raised any concerns about Haiti.

Honduras

A. Progress in the implementation of the minimum standard

Honduras has no tax agreements in force as reported in its response to the Peer Review questionnaire.

B. Conclusion

No jurisdiction has raised any concerns about Honduras.

Hong Kong (China)

A. Progress in the implementation of the minimum standard

Hong Kong (China) has 42 tax agreements in force as reported in its response to the Peer Review questionnaire. Four of those agreements comply with the minimum standard.

Hong Kong (China) joined the MLI in 2017 and has listed its non-compliant agreements in its draft definitive list of agreements to be covered under the MLI. The agreements modified by the MLI come into compliance with the minimum standard once the provisions of the MLI take effect.

Hong Kong (China) is implementing the minimum standard through the inclusion of the preamble statement and the PPT.[89]

B. Conclusion

Recommendation

It is recommended that the steps to have the MLI take effect with respect to Hong Kong (China)'s listed agreements be completed, as those agreements will only be modified by the MLI (and come into compliance with the minimum standard) once the provisions of the MLI take effect.

Summary of the jurisdiction response – Hong Kong (China)

	1.Treaty partners	2. Compliance with the standard	3. Signature of a complying instrument	4. Minimum standard provision used
1	Austria	No	Yes MLI	PPT
2	Belarus	Yes other		PPT
3	Belgium	No	Yes MLI	PPT
4	Brunei Darussalam	No	No	PPT
5	Cambodia*	No	No	PPT
6	Canada	No	Yes MLI	PPT
7	Czech Republic	No	Yes MLI	PPT
8	Estonia	Yes other		PPT
9	Finland	Yes other		PPT
10	France	No	Yes MLI	PPT
11	Guernsey	No	Yes MLI	PPT
12	Hungary	No	Yes MLI	PPT
13	India	No	No	PPT
14	Indonesia	No	Yes MLI	PPT

[89] For its agreements listed under the MLI, Hong Kong (China) is implementing the preamble statement (Article 6 of the MLI) and the PPT (Article 7 of the MLI). Hong Kong (China) has made a reservation pursuant to Article 6(4) of the MLI not to apply Article 6(1) of the MLI with respect to agreements that already contain the relevant preamble language (covering one agreement). Hong Kong (China) has also made a reservation pursuant to Article 7(15)(b) of the MLI not to apply Article 7(1) of the MLI with respect to agreements that already contain a PPT (covering two agreements).

15	Ireland	No	Yes MLI	PPT
16	Italy	No	Yes MLI	PPT
17	Japan	No	Yes MLI	PPT
18	Jersey	No	Yes MLI	PPT
19	Korea	No	Yes MLI	PPT
20	Kuwait*	No	Yes MLI	PPT
21	Latvia	No	Yes MLI	PPT
22	Liechtenstein	No	Yes MLI	PPT
23	Luxembourg	No	Yes MLI	PPT
24	Malaysia	No	Yes MLI	PPT
25	Malta	No	Yes MLI	PPT
26	Mexico	No	Yes MLI	PPT
27	Netherlands	No	Yes MLI	PPT
28	New Zealand	No	Yes MLI	PPT
29	Pakistan	No	Yes MLI	PPT
30	Portugal	No	Yes MLI	PPT
31	Qatar	No	Yes MLI	PPT
32	Romania	No	Yes MLI	PPT
33	Russian Federation	No	Yes MLI	PPT
34	Saudi Arabia	No	No	PPT
35	Serbia	Yes other		PPT
36	South Africa	No	Yes MLI	PPT
37	Spain	No	Yes MLI	PPT
38	Switzerland	No	No	PPT
39	Thailand	No	No	PPT
40	United Arab Emirates	No	Yes MLI	PPT
41	United Kingdom	No	Yes MLI	PPT
42	Viet Nam	No	No	PPT

Hungary

A. Progress in the implementation of the minimum standard

Hungary has 82 tax agreements in force as reported in its response to the Peer Review questionnaire. None of those agreements comply with the minimum standard.

Hungary signed the MLI in 2017 and deposited its instrument of ratification on 25 March 2021. The MLI entered into force for Hungary on 1 July 2021. The agreements modified by the MLI come into compliance with the minimum standard once the provisions of the MLI take effect.

Hungary has not listed its agreements with Mongolia, Montenegro and Switzerland under the MLI but indicated in its response to the Peer Review questionnaire that steps have been taken (other than under the MLI) to implement the minimum standard in its agreement with Switzerland. Hungary also indicated in its response to the Peer Review questionnaire that the agreements with Mongolia and Montenegro do not give rise to material treaty-shopping concerns for Hungary.

Hungary is implementing the minimum standard through the inclusion of the preamble statement and the PPT.[90]

B. Conclusion

No jurisdiction has raised any concerns about their agreements with Hungary.

Summary of the jurisdiction response - Hungary

	1.Treaty partners	2. Compliance with the standard	3. Signature of a complying instrument	4. Minimum standard provision used
1	Albania	No	Yes MLI	PPT
2	Armenia	No	Yes MLI	PPT
3	Australia	No	Yes MLI	PPT
4	Austria	No	Yes MLI	PPT
5	Azerbaijan*	No	No	PPT
6	Bahrain	No	Yes MLI	PPT
7	Belarus	No	No	PPT
8	Belgium	No	Yes MLI	PPT
9	Bosnia-Herzegovina	No	Yes MLI	PPT
10	Brazil	No	No	PPT
11	Bulgaria	No	Yes MLI	PPT
12	Canada	No	Yes MLI	PPT
13	China (People's Republic of)	No	Yes MLI	PPT
14	Croatia	No	Yes MLI	PPT
15	Cyprus*	No	Yes MLI	PPT
16	Czech Republic	No	Yes MLI	PPT
17	Denmark	No	Yes MLI	PPT
18	Egypt	No	Yes MLI	PPT

[90] For its agreements listed under the MLI, Hungary is implementing the preamble statement (Article 6 of the MLI) and the PPT (Article 7 of the MLI).

19	Estonia	No	Yes MLI	PPT
20	Finland	No	Yes MLI	PPT
21	France	No	Yes MLI	PPT
22	Georgia	No	Yes MLI	PPT
23	Germany	No	Yes MLI	PPT
24	Greece	No	Yes MLI	PPT
25	Hong Kong (China)	No	Yes MLI	PPT
26	Iceland	No	Yes MLI	PPT
27	India	No	Yes MLI	PPT
28	Indonesia	No	Yes MLI	PPT
29	Ireland	No	Yes MLI	PPT
30	Israel	No	Yes MLI	PPT
31	Italy	No	Yes MLI	PPT
32	Japan	No	Yes MLI	PPT
33	Kazakhstan	No	Yes MLI	PPT
34	Korea	No	Yes MLI	PPT
35	Kuwait*	No	No	PPT
36	Latvia	No	Yes MLI	PPT
37	Liechtenstein	No	Yes MLI	PPT
38	Lithuania	No	Yes MLI	PPT
39	Luxembourg	No	Yes MLI	PPT
40	Malaysia	No	Yes MLI	PPT
41	Malta	No	Yes MLI	PPT
42	Mexico	No	Yes MLI	PPT
43	Morocco	No	Yes MLI	PPT
44	Netherlands	No	Yes MLI	PPT
45	North Macedonia	No	Yes MLI	PPT
46	Norway	No	No	PPT
47	Oman	No	Yes MLI	PPT
48	Pakistan	No	Yes MLI	PPT
49	Philippines*	No	No	PPT
50	Poland	No	Yes MLI	PPT
51	Portugal	No	Yes MLI	PPT
52	Qatar	No	Yes MLI	PPT
53	Romania	No	Yes MLI	PPT
54	Russian Federation	No	Yes MLI	PPT
55	San Marino	No	Yes MLI	PPT
56	Saudi Arabia	No	Yes MLI	PPT
57	Serbia	No	Yes MLI	PPT
58	Singapore	No	Yes MLI	PPT
59	Slovak republic	No	Yes MLI	PPT
60	Slovenia	No	Yes MLI	PPT
61	South Africa	No	Yes MLI	PPT
62	Spain	No	Yes MLI	PPT
63	Sweden	No	Yes MLI	PPT
64	Switzerland	No	No	PPT
65	Thailand	No	No	PPT
66	Tunisia	No	Yes MLI	PPT
67	Turkey	No	Yes MLI	PPT
68	Ukraine	No	Yes MLI	PPT
69	United Arab Emirates	No	Yes MLI	PPT
70	United Kingdom	No	Yes MLI	PPT
71	United States	No	No	PPT

72	Uruguay	No	Yes MLI	PPT
73	Viet Nam	No	No	PPT

Other agreements

	1.Treaty partners	2. Inclusive Framework member
1	Chinese Taipei*	No
2	Iran*	No
3	Iraq	No
4	Kosovo*	No
5	Kyrgyzstan*	No
6	Moldova*	No
7	Mongolia	Yes
8	Montenegro	Yes
9	Turkmenistan*	No
10	Uzbekistan*	No

Iceland

A. Progress in the implementation of the minimum standard

Iceland has 41 tax agreements in force as reported in its response to the Peer Review questionnaire, including the multilateral Nordic Convention concluded with Denmark, the Faroe Islands, Finland, Norway and Sweden (the Nordic Convention).[91] Twenty-five of those agreements, including the Nordic Convention, comply with the minimum standard.

Iceland signed the MLI in 2017 and deposited its instrument of ratification on 26 September 2019. The MLI entered into force for Iceland on 1 January 2020. On 14 December 2021, Iceland made an additional notification to expand its list of agreements to be covered under the MLI. The agreements modified by the MLI come into compliance with the minimum standard once the provisions of the MLI take effect.

Iceland has not listed its agreements with Germany and Greenland under the MLI but indicated in its response to the Peer Review questionnaire that steps have been taken (other than under the MLI) to implement the minimum standard in those agreements.

Iceland is implementing the minimum standard through the inclusion of the preamble statement and PPT.[92]

B. Conclusion

Iceland gave effect to its plan to implement the minimum standard in its agreement Austria by making a notification on 14 December 2021 to expand its list of agreements to be covered under the MLI to include that agreement.

Summary of the jurisdiction response - Iceland

	1.Treaty partners	2. Compliance with the standard	3. Signature of a complying instrument	4. Minimum standard provision used
1	Albania	Yes MLI		PPT
2	Barbados	No	Yes MLI	PPT
3	Belgium	Yes MLI		PPT
4	Canada	Yes MLI		PPT
5	China (People's Republic of)	No	Yes MLI	PPT
6	Croatia	No	Yes MLI	PPT
7	Cyprus*	Yes MLI		PPT
8	Czech Republic	Yes MLI		PPT
9	Denmark	Yes other		PPT
10	Estonia	No	Yes MLI	PPT
11	Faroe Islands	Yes other		PPT

[91] See the Multilateral convention concluded by Denmark, Finland, the Faroe Islands, Iceland, Norway and Sweden: for the avoidance of double taxation with respect to taxes on income and on capital (1996, 1997, 2008 and 2018). In total, Iceland identified 45 "agreements" in its List of Tax agreements: 40 bilateral agreements and the Nordic Convention concluded with five treaty partners.

[92] For its agreements listed under the MLI, Iceland is implementing the preamble statement (Article 6 of the MLI) and the PPT (Article 7 of the MLI). Under Article 7(7)(a) of the MLI, Iceland is also implementing the simplified LOB (Article 7(8 to 13) of the MLI) in agreements concluded with treaty partners that have adopted the simplified LOB.

12	Finland	Yes other		PPT
13	France	Yes MLI		PPT
14	Georgia	Yes MLI		PPT
15	Germany	No	No	
16	Greece	No	Yes MLI	PPT
17	Greenland	No	No	
18	Hungary	No	Yes MLI	PPT
19	India	Yes MLI		PPT+LOB
20	Ireland	Yes MLI		PPT
21	Italy	No	Yes MLI	PPT
22	Japan	Yes other		PPT+LOB
23	Korea	Yes MLI		PPT
24	Latvia	Yes MLI		PPT
25	Lichtenstein	Yes other		PPT
26	Lithuania	Yes MLI		PPT
27	Luxembourg	Yes MLI		PPT
28	Malta	Yes MLI		PPT
29	Mexico	No	Yes MLI	PPT
30	Netherlands	Yes MLI		PPT
31	Norway	Yes other		PPT
32	Poland	Yes MLI		PPT
33	Portugal	Yes MLI		PPT
34	Romania	No	Yes MLI	PPT
35	Russian Federation	Yes MLI		PPT
36	Slovak Republic	Yes MLI		PPT
37	Slovenia	Yes MLI		PPT
38	Spain	No	Yes MLI	PPT
39	Sweden	Yes other		PPT
40	Switzerland	No	Yes MLI	PPT
41	Ukraine	Yes MLI		PPT
42	United Kingdom	Yes MLI		PPT+LOB
43	United States	No	No	D-LOB
44	Viet Nam	No	No	PPT

Other agreements

	1.Treaty partners	2. Inclusive Framework member
1	Austria	Yes

India

A. Progress in the implementation of the minimum standard

India has 95 tax agreements in force as reported in its response to the Peer Review questionnaire. Forty-two of those agreements comply with the minimum standard.

India signed the MLI in 2017 and deposited its instrument of ratification on 25 June 2019, listing its non-compliant agreements. The MLI entered into force for India on 1 October 2019. The agreements modified by the MLI come into compliance with the minimum standard once the provisions of the MLI take effect.

India is implementing the minimum standard through the inclusion of the preamble statement and the PPT combined with the LOB.[93]

B. Conclusion

No jurisdiction has raised any concerns about their agreements with India.

Summary of the jurisdiction response - India

	1.Treaty partners	2. Compliance with the standard	3. Signature of a complying instrument	4. Minimum standard provision used
1	Albania	Yes MLI		PPT
2	Armenia	No	Yes MLI	PPT + LOB
3	Australia	Yes MLI		PPT
4	Austria	Yes MLI		PPT
5	Bangladesh*	No	No	
6	Belarus	No	No	
7	Belgium	Yes MLI		PPT
8	Bhutan*	No	No	
9	Botswana	No	No	
10	Brazil	No	No	
11	Bulgaria	No	Yes MLI	PPT+LOB
12	Canada	Yes MLI		PPT
13	China (People's Republic of)	Yes other		PPT
14	Colombia	No	Yes MLI	PPT+LOB
15	Croatia	No	Yes MLI	PPT
16	Cyprus*	Yes MLI		PPT
17	Czech Republic	Yes MLI		PPT
18	Denmark	Yes MLI		PPT + LOB
19	Egypt	Yes MLI		PPT
20	Estonia	No	Yes MLI	PPT
21	Ethiopia*	No	No	
22	Fiji*	No	Yes MLI	PPT

93 For its agreements listed under the MLI, India is implementing the preamble statement (Article 6 of the MLI), the PPT (Article 7 of the MLI) and the simplified LOB (Article 7(6) of the MLI). India expressed a statement, in accordance with Article 7(17)(a) of the MLI, that while it accepts the application of PPT alone as an interim measure, it intends where possible to adopt an LOB provision in addition to or in replacement of the PPT through bilateral negotiation.

23	Finland	Yes MLI		PPT
24	France	Yes MLI		PPT
25	Georgia	Yes MLI		PPT
26	Germany	No	No	
27	Greece	No	Yes MLI	PPT + LOB
28	Hong Kong (China)	No	No	
29	Hungary	No	Yes MLI	PPT
30	Iceland	Yes MLI		PPT + LOB
31	Indonesia	Yes MLI		PPT
32	Iran*	Yes other		PPT
33	Ireland	Yes MLI		PPT
34	Israel	Yes MLI		PPT
35	Italy	No	Yes MLI	PPT
36	Japan	Yes MLI		PPT
37	Jordan	Yes MLI		PPT
38	Kazakhstan	Yes MLI		PPT + LOB
39	Kenya	No	Yes MLI	PPT+LOB
40	Korea	Yes MLI		PPT
41	Kuwait*	No	Yes MLI	PPT
42	Kyrgyzstan*	No	No	
43	Latvia	Yes MLI		PPT
44	Libya*	No	No	
45	Lithuania	Yes MLI		PPT
46	Luxembourg	Yes MLI		PPT
47	Malaysia	No	Yes MLI	PPT
48	Malta	Yes MLI		PPT
49	Mauritius	No	No	
50	Mexico	No	Yes MLI	PPT
51	Mongolia	No		
52	Montenegro	No	No	
53	Morocco	No	Yes MLI	PPT
54	Mozambique*	No	No	
55	Myanmar*	No	No	
56	Namibia	No	No	
57	Nepal*	No	No	
58	Netherlands	Yes MLI		PPT
59	New Zealand	Yes MLI		PPT
60	North Macedonia	No	Yes MLI	PPT
61	Norway	Yes MLI		PPT + LOB
62	Oman	No	No	
63	Philippines*	No	No	
64	Poland	Yes MLI		PPT
65	Portugal	Yes MLI		PPT
66	Qatar	Yes MLI		PPT
67	Romania	No	Yes MLI	PPT
68	Russian Federation	Yes MLI		PPT + LOB
69	Saudi Arabia	Yes MLI		PPT
70	Serbia	Yes MLI		PPT
71	Singapore	Yes MLI		PPT
72	Slovak Republic	Yes MLI		PPT + LOB
73	Slovenia	Yes MLI		PPT
74	South Africa	No	Yes MLI	PPT
75	Spain	No	Yes MLI	PPT

76	Sri Lanka	No	No	
77	Sudan*	No	No	
78	Sweden	No	Yes MLI	PPT
79	Switzerland	No	No	
80	Syria*	No	No	
81	Tajikistan*	No	No	
82	Tanzania*	No	No	
83	Thailand	No	No	
84	Trinidad and Tobago	No	No	
85	Turkey	No	Yes MLI	PPT
86	Turkmenistan*	No	No	
87	United Arab Emirates	Yes MLI		PPT
88	Uganda*	No	No	
89	Ukraine	Yes MLI		PPT
90	United Kingdom	Yes MLI		PPT
91	United States	No	No	
92	Uruguay	Yes MLI		PPT+LOB
93	Uzbekistan*	No	No	
94	Viet Nam	No	No	
95	Zambia	No	No	

Indonesia

A. Progress in the implementation of the minimum standard

Indonesia has 70 tax agreements in force as reported in its response to the Peer Review questionnaire. Twenty-one of those agreements comply with the minimum standard.

Indonesia signed the MLI in 2017 and deposited its instrument of ratification on 28 April 2020. The MLI entered into force for Indonesia on 1 August 2020. The agreements modified by the MLI come into compliance with the minimum standard once the provisions of the MLI take effect.

Indonesia reserved the right to delay the entry into effect of the provisions of the MLI until Indonesia has completed its internal procedures for this purpose with respect to each of its listed agreements.[94] Indonesia notified that it completed its internal procedures for the entry into effect of the MLI with respect to its agreements with Australia, Belgium, Canada, Denmark, Finland, France, India, Japan, Korea, Luxembourg, Netherlands, New Zealand, Poland, Portugal, Qatar, the Russian Federation, Serbia, Singapore, the Slovak Republic, Sweden, the United Arab Emirates and the United Kingdom on 26 November 2020, and with respect to its agreements with Croatia, Egypt, Hungary, Malaysia and Pakistan on 21 October 2021.

Indonesia has not listed its agreements with, Austria, Belarus, Germany, Jordan, Mongolia, Morocco, Papua New Guinea, Sri Lanka, Tunisia and Ukraine under the MLI. These agreements will therefore not, at this stage, be modified by the MLI. Jordan, Morocco, Tunisia, Papua New Guinea and Ukraine have listed their agreements with Indonesia under the MLI. Indonesia indicated in its response to the Peer Review questionnaire that steps have been taken (other than under the MLI) to implement the minimum standard in its agreement with Austria and Germany. Indonesia indicated in its response to the Peer Review questionnaire that the agreements with Mongolia, Morocco, Papua New Guinea, Sri Lanka, Tunisia and Ukraine do not give rise to material treaty-shopping concerns for Indonesia.

Indonesia is implementing the minimum standard through the inclusion of the preamble statement and the PPT.[95]

B. Conclusion

Jordan, Morocco, Tunisia, Papua New Guinea and Ukraine have listed their agreements with Indonesia under the MLI, which amount to requests to implement the minimum standard.

Indonesia has developed a plan for the implementation of the minimum standard in its agreements with Belarus, Jordan, Mongolia, Morocco, Papua New Guinea, Sri Lanka, Tunisia and Ukraine. Indonesia indicated in its response to the Peer Review questionnaire that it intends to expand its list of agreements to be covered under the MLI to include those agreements.

---

94 The reservation was made under Article 35(7)(a) of the MLI.

95 For its agreements listed under the MLI, Indonesia is implementing the preamble statement (Article 6 of the MLI) and the PPT (Article 7 of the MLI).

Summary of the jurisdiction response - Indonesia

	1.Treaty partners	2. Compliance with the standard	3. Signature of a complying instrument	4. Minimum standard provision used
1	Armenia	No	Yes MLI	PPT
2	Australia	Yes MLI		PPT
3	Austria	No	No	
4	Belgium	Yes MLI		PPT
5	Brunei Darussalam	No	No	PPT
6	Bulgaria	No	Yes MLI	PPT
7	Canada	Yes MLI		
8	China (People's Republic of)	No	Yes MLI	PPT
9	Croatia	No	Yes MLI	PPT
10	Czech Republic	No	No	PPT
11	Denmark	Yes MLI		PPT
12	Egypt	No	Yes MLI	PPT
13	Finland	Yes MLI		PPT
14	France	Yes MLI		PPT
15	Hong Kong (China)	No	Yes MLI	PPT
16	Hungary	No	Yes MLI	PPT
17	Germany	No	No	
18	India	Yes MLI		PPT
19	Italy	No	Yes MLI	PPT
20	Japan	Yes MLI		PPT
21	Korea	Yes MLI		PPT
22	Lao People's Democratic Republic*	No	No	PPT
23	Luxembourg	Yes MLI		PPT
24	Malaysia	No	Yes MLI	PPT
25	Mexico	No	Yes MLI	PPT
26	Netherlands	Yes MLI		PPT
27	New Zealand	Yes MLI		PPT
28	Norway	No	No	PPT
29	Pakistan	No	Yes MLI	PPT
30	Philippines*	No	No	PPT
31	Poland	Yes MLI		PPT
32	Portugal	Yes MLI		PPT
33	Qatar	Yes MLI		PPT
34	Romania	No	Yes MLI	PPT
35	Russian Federation	Yes MLI		PPT
36	Serbia	Yes MLI		PPT
37	Seychelles	No	Yes MLI	PPT
38	Singapore	Yes MLI		PPT
39	Slovak Republic	Yes MLI		PPT
40	South Africa	No	Yes MLI	PPT
41	Spain	No	Yes MLI	PPT
42	Sweden	Yes MLI		PPT
43	Switzerland	No	No	PPT
44	Thailand	No	No	PPT
45	Turkey	No	Yes MLI	PPT
46	United Arab Emirates	Yes MLI		PPT
47	United Kingdom	Yes MLI		PPT
48	United States	No	No	PPT

49	Viet Nam	No	No	PPT

Other agreements

	1.Treaty partners	2. Inclusive Framework member
1	Algeria*	No
2	Bangladesh*	No
3	Belarus	Yes
4	Cambodia*	No
5	Chinese Taipei*	No
6	Democratic People's Republic of Korea*	No
7	Iran*	No
8	Jordan	Yes
9	Kuwait*	No
10	Mongolia	Yes
11	Morocco	Yes
12	Papua New Guinea	Yes
13	Sri Lanka	Yes
14	Sudan*	No
15	Suriname	No
16	Syrian Arab Republic*	No
17	Tajikistan*	No
18	Tunisia	Yes
19	Ukraine	Yes
20	Uzbekistan*	No
21	Venezuela*	No

Ireland

A. Progress in the implementation of the minimum standard

Ireland has 73 tax agreements in force as reported in its response to the Peer Review questionnaire. Forty of those agreements comply with the minimum standard.

Ireland signed the MLI in 2017 and deposited its instrument of ratification on 29 January 2019. The MLI entered into force for Ireland on 1 May 2019. The agreements modified by the MLI come into compliance with the minimum standard once the provisions of the MLI take effect.

Ireland has not listed its agreement with Germany under the MLI but has signed a bilateral complying instrument with respect to that agreement. The bilateral complying instruments with respect to the agreements with the Netherlands and Switzerland both started to take effect in January 2021.

Ireland is implementing the minimum standard through the inclusion of the preamble statement and the PPT.[96]

B. Conclusion

No jurisdiction has raised any concerns about their agreements with Ireland.

Summary of the jurisdiction response - Ireland

	1.Treaty partners	2. Compliance with the standard	3. Signature of a complying instrument	4. Minimum standard provision used
1	Albania	Yes MLI		PPT
2	Armenia	No	Yes MLI	PPT
3	Australia	Yes MLI		PPT
4	Austria	Yes MLI		PPT
5	Bahrain	No	Yes MLI	PPT
6	Belarus	No	No	PPT
7	Belgium	Yes MLI		PPT
8	Bosnia-Herzegovina	Yes MLI		PPT
9	Botswana	No	No	PPT
10	Bulgaria	No	Yes MLI	PPT
11	Canada	Yes MLI		PPT
12	Chile	No	Yes MLI	PPT
13	China (People's Republic of)	No	Yes MLI	PPT
14	Croatia	No	Yes MLI	PPT
15	Cyprus*	Yes MLI		PPT
16	Czech Republic	Yes MLI		PPT
17	Denmark	Yes MLI		PPT
18	Egypt	Yes MLI		PPT
19	Estonia	No	Yes MLI	PPT
20	Ethiopia	No	No	PPT

[96] For its agreements listed under the MLI, Ireland is implementing the preamble statement (Article 6 of the MLI) and the PPT (Article 7 of the MLI).

21	Finland	Yes MLI		PPT
22	France	Yes MLI		PPT
23	Georgia	Yes MLI		PPT
24	Germany	No	Yes other	PPT
25	Greece	No	Yes MLI	PPT
26	Hong Kong (China)	No	Yes MLI	PPT
27	Hungary	No	Yes MLI	PPT
28	Iceland	Yes MLI		PPT
29	India	Yes MLI		PPT
30	Israel	Yes MLI		PPT
31	Italy	No	Yes MLI	PPT
32	Japan	Yes MLI		PPT
33	Kazakhstan	Yes MLI		PPT
34	Korea	Yes MLI		PPT
35	Kuwait*	No	Yes MLI	PPT
36	Latvia	Yes MLI		PPT
37	Lithuania	Yes MLI		PPT
38	Luxembourg	Yes MLI		PPT
39	Malaysia	No	Yes MLI	PPT
40	Malta	Yes MLI		PPT
41	Mexico	No	Yes MLI	PPT
42	Moldova	No	No	PPT
43	Montenegro	No	No	PPT
44	Morocco	No	Yes MLI	PPT
45	Netherlands	Yes other		PPT
46	New Zealand	Yes MLI		PPT
47	North Macedonia	No	Yes MLI	PPT
48	Norway	Yes MLI		PPT
49	Pakistan	Yes MLI		PPT
50	Panama	No	Yes MLI	PPT
51	Poland	Yes MLI		PPT
52	Portugal	Yes MLI		PPT
53	Qatar	Yes MLI		PPT
54	Romania	No	Yes MLI	PPT
55	Russian Federation	Yes MLI		PPT
56	Saudi Arabia	Yes MLI		PPT
57	Serbia	Yes MLI		PPT
58	Singapore	Yes MLI		PPT
59	Slovak Republic	Yes MLI		PPT
60	Slovenia	Yes MLI		PPT
61	South Africa	No	Yes MLI	PPT
62	Spain	No	Yes MLI	PPT
63	Sweden	No	Yes MLI	PPT
64	Switzerland	Yes other		PPT
65	Thailand	No	No	PPT
66	Turkey	No	Yes MLI	PPT
67	Ukraine	Yes MLI		PPT
68	United Arab Emirates	Yes MLI		PPT
69	United Kingdom	Yes MLI		PPT
70	United States	No	No	LOB
71	Uzbekistan*	No	No	PPT
72	Viet Nam	No	No	PPT
73	Zambia	No	No	PPT

Isle of Man

A. Progress in the implementation of the minimum standard

The Isle of Man has ten tax agreements in force as reported in its response to the Peer Review questionnaire. Six of those agreements comply with the minimum standard.

The Isle of Man signed the MLI in 2017 and deposited its instrument of ratification on 25 October 2017. The MLI entered into force for the Isle of Man on 1 July 2018. The agreements modified by the MLI come into compliance with the minimum standard once the provisions of the MLI take effect.

The Isle of Man has not listed its agreement with Jersey under the MLI but indicated in its response to the Peer Review questionnaire that steps have been taken (other than under the MLI) to implement the minimum standard in that agreement.

The Isle of Man is implementing the minimum standard through the inclusion of the preamble statement and the PPT.[97]

B. Conclusion

No jurisdiction has raised any concerns about their agreements with the Isle of Man.

Summary of the jurisdiction response – Isle of Man

	1.Treaty partners	2. Compliance with the standard	3. Signature of a complying instrument	4. Minimum standard provision used
1	Bahrain	No	Yes MLI	PPT
2	Estonia	No	Yes MLI	PPT
3	Guernsey	Yes other		PPT
4	Jersey	No	No	PPT
5	Luxembourg	Yes MLI		PPT
6	Malta	Yes MLI		PPT
7	Qatar	Yes MLI		PPT
8	Seychelles	No	Yes MLI	PPT
9	Singapore	Yes MLI		PPT
10	United Kingdom	Yes other		PPT

[97] For its agreements listed under the MLI, the Isle of Man is implementing the preamble statement (Article 6 of the MLI) and the PPT (Article 7 of the MLI).

Israel

A. Progress in the implementation of the minimum standard

Israel has 58 tax agreements in force as reported in its response to the Peer Review questionnaire. Twenty-eight of those agreements comply with the minimum standard.

Israel signed the MLI in 2017 and deposited its instrument of ratification on 13 September 2018. The MLI entered into force for Israel on 1 January 2019. The agreements modified by the MLI come into compliance with the minimum standard once the provisions of the MLI take effect.

Israel has not listed its agreements with Germany and Switzerland under the MLI but indicated in its response to the Peer Review questionnaire that steps have been taken (other than under the MLI) to implement the minimum standard in those two agreements .

Israel is implementing the minimum standard through the inclusion of the preamble statement and the PPT.[98]

B. Conclusion

No jurisdiction has raised any concerns about their agreements with Israel.

Summary of the jurisdiction response - Israel

	1.Treaty partners	2. Compliance with the standard	3. Signature of a complying instrument	4. Minimum standard provision used
1	Armenia	No	No	PPT
2	Australia	Yes other		PPT
3	Austria	Yes MLI		PPT
4	Azerbaijan*	No	No	PPT
5	Belarus	No	No	PPT
6	Belgium	Yes MLI		PPT
7	Brazil	No	No	PPT
8	Bulgaria	No	Yes MLI	PPT
9	Canada	Yes MLI		PPT
10	China (People's Republic of)	No	Yes MLI	PPT
11	Chinese Taipei*	No	No	PPT
12	Croatia	No	Yes MLI	PPT
13	Czech Republic	Yes MLI		PPT
14	Denmark	Yes MLI		PPT
15	Estonia	No	Yes MLI	PPT
16	Ethiopia*	No	No	PPT
17	Finland	Yes MLI		PPT
18	France	Yes MLI		PPT
19	Georgia	Yes MLI		PPT
20	Germany	No	No	PPT

98 For its agreements listed under the MLI, Israel is implementing the preamble statement (Article 6 of the MLI) and the PPT (Article 7 of the MLI).

21	Greece	No	Yes MLI	PPT
22	Hungary	No	Yes MLI	PPT
23	India	Yes MLI		PPT
24	Ireland	Yes MLI		PPT
25	Italy	No	Yes MLI	PPT
26	Jamaica	No	Yes MLI	PPT
27	Japan	Yes MLI		PPT
28	Korea	Yes MLI		PPT
29	Latvia	Yes MLI		PPT
30	Lithuania	Yes MLI		PPT
31	Luxembourg	Yes MLI		PPT
32	Malta	Yes MLI		PPT
33	Mexico	No	Yes MLI	PPT
34	Moldova*	No	No	PPT
35	Netherlands	Yes MLI		PPT
36	North Macedonia	No	Yes MLI	PPT
37	Norway	No	No	PPT
38	Panama	Yes MLI		PPT
39	Philippines*	No	No	PPT
40	Poland	Yes MLI		PPT
41	Portugal	Yes MLI		PPT
42	Romania	No	Yes MLI	PPT
43	Russian Federation	Yes MLI		PPT
44	Serbia	Yes other		PPT
45	Singapore	Yes MLI		PPT
46	Slovak Republic	Yes MLI		PPT
47	Slovenia	Yes MLI		PPT
48	South Africa	No	Yes MLI	PPT
49	Spain	No	Yes MLI	PPT
50	Sweden	No	Yes MLI	PPT
51	Switzerland	No	No	PPT
52	Thailand	No	No	PPT
53	Turkey	No	Yes MLI	PPT
54	Ukraine	Yes MLI		PPT
55	United Kingdom	Yes other		PPT
56	United States	No	No	PPT
57	Uzbekistan*	No	No	PPT
58	Viet Nam	No	No	PPT

Italy

A. Progress in the implementation of the minimum standard

Italy has 100 tax agreements in force as reported in its response to the Peer Review questionnaire. Two of those agreements comply with the minimum standard.

Italy signed the MLI in 2017. The agreements modified by the MLI come into compliance with the minimum standard once the provisions of the MLI take effect. Italy has not listed its agreements with Albania, Belarus, Congo, Montenegro, North Macedonia, Oman, and Panama. These agreements will therefore not, at this stage, be modified by the MLI. Albania, North Macedonia, Oman and Panama have listed their agreements with Italy under the MLI.

Italy indicated in its response to the Peer Review questionnaire that steps have been taken (other than under the MLI) to implement the minimum standard in its agreements with Brazil, Norway and Uzbekistan*.

Italy indicated in its response to the Peer Review questionnaire that the agreements with Belarus, Congo, Ecuador*, Ethiopia*, Ghana*, Kyrgyzstan*, Montenegro, Mozambique*, Syria*, Tajikistan* and Venezuela* do not give rise to material treaty-shopping concerns for Italy as they contain specific features and as Italy's domestic anti-abuse legislation applies.

Italy is implementing the minimum standard through the inclusion of the preamble statement and the PPT.[99]

B. Conclusion

Albania, North Macedonia, Oman and Panama have listed their agreements with Italy under the MLI, which amount to requests to implement the minimum standard. Italy has developed a plan for the implementation of the minimum standard in its agreements with Albania, North Macedonia, Oman and Panama. Italy indicated in its response to the Peer Review questionnaire that it intends to expand its list of agreements to be covered under the MLI to include those agreements.

Recommendation

It is recommended that Italy completes the steps to have the MLI take effect with respect to its agreements listed under the MLI as those agreements will only be modified by the MLI (and come into compliance with the minimum standard) once the provisions of the MLI take effect.

Summary of the jurisdiction response - Italy

	1.Treaty partners	2. Compliance with the standard	3. Signature of a complying instrument	4. Minimum standard provision used

[99] For its agreements listed under the MLI, Italy is implementing the preamble statement (Article 6 of the MLI) and the PPT (Article 7 of the MLI). Italy has made a reservation pursuant to Article 7(15)(b) of the MLI not to apply Article 7(1) of the MLI with respect to agreements that already contain a PPT (covering thirteen agreements).

1	Argentina	No	Yes MLI	PPT
2	Armenia	No	Yes MLI	PPT
3	Australia	No	Yes MLI	PPT
4	Austria	No	Yes MLI	PPT
5	Azerbaijan*	No	No	PPT
6	Bangladesh*	No	No	PPT
7	Barbados	No	Yes MLI	PPT
8	Belgium	No	Yes MLI	PPT
9	Bosnia-Herzegovina	No	Yes MLI	PPT
10	Brazil	No	No	PPT
11	Bulgaria	No	Yes MLI	PPT
12	Canada	No	Yes MLI	PPT
13	Chile	Yes Other		PPT
14	China (People's Republic of)	No	Yes MLI	PPT
15	Côte d'Ivoire	No	Yes MLI	PPT
16	Croatia	No	Yes MLI	PPT
17	Cyprus*	No	Yes MLI	PPT
18	Czech Republic	No	Yes MLI	PPT
19	Denmark	No	Yes MLI	PPT
20	Egypt	No	Yes MLI	PPT
21	Estonia	No	Yes MLI	PPT
22	Finland	No	Yes MLI	PPT
23	France	No	Yes MLI	PPT
24	Georgia	No	Yes MLI	PPT
25	Germany	No	Yes MLI	PPT
26	Greece	No	Yes MLI	PPT
27	Hong Kong (China)	No	Yes MLI	PPT
28	Hungary	No	Yes MLI	PPT
29	Iceland	No	Yes MLI	PPT
30	India	No	Yes MLI	PPT
31	Indonesia	No	Yes MLI	PPT
32	Ireland	No	Yes MLI	PPT
33	Israel	No	Yes MLI	PPT
34	Japan	No	Yes MLI	PPT
35	Jordan	No	Yes MLI	PPT
36	Kazakhstan	No	Yes MLI	PPT
37	Korea	No	Yes MLI	PPT
38	Kuwait*	No	No	PPT
39	Latvia	No	Yes MLI	PPT
40	Lebanon*	No	No	PPT
41	Lithuania	No	Yes MLI	PPT
42	Luxembourg	No	Yes MLI	PPT
43	Malaysia	No	Yes MLI	PPT
44	Malta	No	Yes MLI	PPT
45	Mauritius	No	Yes MLI	PPT
46	Mexico	No	Yes MLI	PPT
47	Moldova*	No	No	PPT
48	Morocco	No	Yes MLI	PPT
49	Netherlands	No	Yes MLI	PPT
50	New Zealand	No	Yes MLI	PPT
51	Norway	No	No	PPT
52	Pakistan	No	Yes MLI	PPT
53	Philippines*	No	No	PPT

54	Poland	No	Yes MLI	PPT
55	Portugal	No	Yes MLI	PPT
56	Qatar	No	Yes MLI	PPT
57	Romania	No	Yes MLI	PPT
58	Russian Federation	No	Yes MLI	PPT
59	San Marino	No	Yes MLI	PPT
60	Saudi Arabia	No	Yes MLI	PPT
61	Senegal	No	Yes MLI	PPT
62	Serbia	No	Yes MLI	PPT
63	Singapore	No	Yes MLI	PPT
64	Slovak Republic	No	Yes MLI	PPT
65	Slovenia	No	Yes MLI	PPT
66	South Africa	No	Yes MLI	PPT
67	Spain	No	Yes MLI	PPT
68	Sri Lanka	No	No	PPT
69	Sweden	No	Yes MLI	PPT
70	Switzerland	No	Yes MLI	PPT
71	Tanzania*	No	No	PPT
72	Thailand	No	No	PPT
73	Trinidad and Tobago	No	No	D-LOB
74	Tunisia	No	Yes MLI	PPT
75	Turkey	No	Yes MLI	PPT
76	Uganda*	No	No	PPT
77	Ukraine	No	Yes MLI	PPT
78	United Arab Emirates	No	Yes MLI	PPT
79	United Kingdom	No	Yes MLI	PPT
80	United States	No	No	LOB
81	Uruguay	Yes Other		PPT
82	Uzbekistan*	No	No	PPT
83	Viet Nam	No	No	PPT
84	Zambia	No	No	PPT

Other agreements

	1.Treaty partners	2. Inclusive Framework member
1	Albania	Yes
2	Algeria*	No
3	Belarus	Yes
4	Congo	Yes
5	Ecuador*	No
6	Ethiopia*	No
7	Ghana*	No
8	Kyrgyzstan*	No
9	Montenegro	Yes
10	North Macedonia	Yes
11	Mozambique*	No
12	Oman	Yes
13	Panama	Yes
14	Syrian Arab Republic*	No
15	Tajikistan*	No
16	Venezuela*	No

Jamaica

A. Progress in the implementation of the minimum standard

Jamaica has 15 tax agreements in force, as reported in its response to the Peer Review questionnaire, including the multilateral agreement among the members of the CARICOM concluded with ten treaty partners (the CARICOM Agreement).[100] One of those agreements, the agreement with Japan, complies with the minimum standard.

Jamaica signed the MLI in 2018 and listed its non-compliant bilateral agreements. The agreements modified by the MLI come into compliance with the minimum standard once the provisions of the MLI take effect.

Jamaica is implementing the minimum standard through the inclusion of the preamble statement and PPT combined with the LOB.[101]

B. Conclusion

Jamaica acknowledges that the CARICOM Agreement does not at this stage comply with the minimum standard and that discussions to bring this agreement up to date would be contemplated.[102]

[100] Agreement Among the Governments of the Member States of the Caribbean Community for the Avoidance of Double Taxation and the Prevention of Fiscal Evasion with Respect to Taxes on Income, Profits or Gains and Capital Gains and for the Encouragement of Regional Trade and Investment, St. Michael Barbados, 6 July 1994; between: Antigua and Barbuda (18 February 1998), Barbados (7 July 1995), Belize (30 November 1994), Dominica (19 June 1996), Grenada (1 March 1996), Guyana* (26 November 1997), Jamaica (16 February 1995), St. Kitts/Nevis (8 May 1997), St. Lucia (22 May 1995) St. Vincent (12 February 1998) and Trinidad & Tobago (29 November 1994). In total, Jamaica identified 24 "agreements" in its List of Tax agreements: 14 bilateral agreements and the CARICOM Agreement concluded with ten of its treaty partners.

[101] For its agreements listed under the MLI, Jamaica is implementing the preamble statement (Article 6 of the MLI) and the PPT (Article 7 of the MLI). Under Article 7(7)(a) of the MLI, Jamaica is also implementing the simplified LOB (Article 7(8 to 13) of the MLI) in agreements concluded with treaty partners that adopted the simplified LOB..

[102] Revisions to the CARICOM Agreement require an agreement from its eleven treaty partners.

Recommendation

It is recommended that Jamaica completes the steps to have the MLI take effect with respect to its agreements listed under the MLI as those agreements will only be modified by the MLI (and come into compliance with the minimum standard) once the provisions of the MLI take effect.

Summary of the jurisdiction response - Jamaica

	1.Treaty partners	2. Compliance with the standard	3. Signature of a complying instrument	4. Minimum standard provision used
1	Antigua and Barbuda	No	No	PPT+LOB
2	Belize	No	No	PPT+LOB
3	Barbados	No	No	PPT+LOB
4	Canada	No	Yes MLI	PPT
5	China (People's Republic of)	No	Yes MLI	PPT
6	Denmark	No	Yes MLI	PPT
7	Dominica	No	No	PPT+LOB
8	France	No	Yes MLI	PPT
9	Germany	No	No	PPT+LOB
10	Grenada	No	No	PPT+LOB
11	Guyana*	No	No	PPT+LOB
12	Israel	No	Yes MLI	PPT
13	Japan	Yes other		PPT
14	Mexico	No	Yes MLI	PPT+LOB
15	Norway	No	No	PPT+LOB
16	Saint Kitts and Nevis	No	No	PPT+LOB
17	Saint Lucia	No	No	PPT+LOB
18	Saint Vincent and the Grenadines	No	No	PPT+LOB
19	Spain	No	Yes MLI	PPT
20	Sweden	No	Yes MLI	PPT
21	Switzerland	No	No	PPT+LOB
22	Trinidad and Tobago	No	No	PPT+LOB
23	United Kingdom	No	Yes MLI	PPT
24	United States	No	No	PPT+LOB

Japan

A. Progress in the implementation of the minimum standard

Japan has 75 tax agreements in force as reported in its response to the Peer Review questionnaire. Forty-four of those agreements comply with the minimum standard.

Japan signed the MLI in 2017 and deposited its instrument of acceptance on 26 September 2018. The MLI entered into force for Japan on 1 January 2019. Subsequently, Japan made additional notifications to expand its list of agreements to be covered under the MLI.[103] The agreements modified by the MLI come into compliance with the minimum standard once the provisions of the MLI take effect. Japan has not listed its agreements with Armenia, Belarus, Brazil, Brunei Darussalam, Georgia, Sri Lanka, Switzerland, Thailand, the United States, Viet Nam and Zambia, which have not joined the MLI or have joined the MLI but not listed the agreements with Japan. These agreements will therefore not, at this stage, be modified by the MLI. Japan indicated that it would list such agreements once the treaty partners join the MLI and list the agreements with Japan except for the cases where the agreement will be updated through bilateral negotiations to be compliant with the minimum standard.

Japan has signed a bilateral complying instrument with respect to its agreement with Georgia.

Japan indicated in its response to the Peer Review questionnaire that steps have been taken (other than under the MLI) to implement the minimum standard in its agreements with Azerbaijan* and Switzerland.[104]

Japan indicated in its response to the Peer Review questionnaire that the agreements with Armenia, Belarus, Brazil, Brunei Darussalam, Sri Lanka, Thailand, Viet Nam and Zambia do not give rise to material treaty-shopping concerns for Japan.

Japan is implementing the minimum standard through the inclusion of the preamble statement and the PPT for its compliant agreements with Canada, Chile, Czech Republic, Ecuador*, Egypt, Finland, India, Indonesia, Ireland, Israel, Jamaica, Kazakhstan, Korea, Luxembourg, Norway, Oman, Pakistan, Peru, Poland, Portugal, Qatar, Saudi Arabia, Singapore, the Slovak Republic, Slovenia, Ukraine and the United Arab Emirates. Japan is implementing the minimum standard through the inclusion of the preamble statement and the PPT combined with the LOB for its compliant agreements with Australia, Austria, Belgium, Croatia, Denmark, Estonia, France, Germany, Iceland, Latvia, Lithuania, Netherlands, New Zealand, Russian Federation, Spain, the United Kingdom and Uzbekistan*.[105]

B. Conclusion

No jurisdiction has raised any concerns about their agreements with Japan.

---

[103] Japan made additional notifications to expand its list of agreements to be covered under the MLI on 14 February 2020 and on 22 July 2020.

[104] Japan and Switzerland signed an amending protocol to the 1971 Japan-Switzerland income tax treaty, as amended by the 2010 protocol, on 16 July 2021.

[105] For its agreements listed under the MLI, Japan is implementing the preamble statement (Article 6 of the MLI) and the PPT (Article 7 of the MLI). Japan has made a reservation pursuant to Article 6(4) of the MLI not to apply Article 6(1) of the MLI with respect to agreements that already contain the relevant preamble language (covering one agreement).

Summary of the jurisdiction response - Japan

	1.Treaty partners	2. Compliance with the standard	3. Signature of a complying instrument	4. Minimum standard provision used
1	Australia	Yes MLI		PPT+LOB
2	Austria	Yes other		PPT+LOB
3	Azerbaijan*	No	No	
4	Belgium	Yes other		PPT+LOB
5	Bulgaria	No	Yes MLI	PPT
6	Canada	Yes MLI		PPT
7	Chile	Yes other		PPT
8	China (People's Republic of)	No	Yes MLI	PPT
9	Croatia	Yes other		PPT+LOB
10	Czech Republic	Yes MLI		PPT
11	Denmark	Yes other		PPT+LOB
12	Ecuador*	Yes other		PPT
13	Egypt	Yes MLI		PPT
14	Estonia	Yes other		PPT+LOB
15	Fiji*	No	Yes MLI	PPT
16	Finland	Yes MLI		PPT
17	France	Yes MLI		PPT+LOB
18	Georgia	No	Yes other	PPT+LOB
19	Germany	Yes other		PPT+LOB
20	Hong Kong (China)	No	Yes MLI	PPT
21	Hungary	No	Yes MLI	PPT
22	Iceland	Yes other		PPT+LOB
23	India	Yes MLI		PPT
24	Indonesia	Yes MLI		PPT
25	Ireland	Yes MLI		PPT
26	Israel	Yes MLI		PPT
27	Italy	No	Yes MLI	PPT
28	Jamaica	Yes other		PPT
29	Kazakhstan	Yes MLI		PPT
30	Korea	Yes MLI		PPT
31	Kuwait*	No	Yes MLI	PPT
32	Latvia	Yes other		PPT+LOB
33	Lithuania	Yes other		PPT+LOB
34	Luxembourg	Yes MLI		PPT
35	Malaysia	No	Yes MLI	PPT
36	Mexico	No	Yes MLI	PPT
37	Netherlands	Yes MLI		PPT+LOB
38	New Zealand	Yes MLI		PPT+LOB
39	Norway	Yes MLI		PPT
40	Oman	Yes MLI		PPT
41	Pakistan	Yes MLI		PPT
42	Peru	Yes other		PPT
43	Poland	Yes MLI		PPT
44	Portugal	Yes MLI		PPT
45	Qatar	Yes MLI		PPT
46	Romania	No	Yes MLI	PPT
47	Russian Federation	Yes other		PPT+LOB
48	Saudi Arabia	Yes MLI		PPT
49	Singapore	Yes MLI		PPT

50	Slovak Republic	Yes MLI		PPT
51	Slovenia	Yes other		PPT
52	South Africa	No	Yes MLI	PPT
53	Spain	Yes other		PPT+LOB
54	Sweden	No	Yes MLI	PPT+LOB
55	Switzerland	No	No	PPT+LOB
56	Turkey	No	Yes MLI	PPT
57	Ukraine	Yes MLI		PPT
58	United Arab Emirates	Yes MLI		PPT
59	United Kingdom	Yes MLI		PPT+LOB
60	United States	No	No	D-LOB
61	Uzbekistan*	Yes other		PPT+LOB

Other agreements

	1.Treaty partners	2. Inclusive Framework member
1	Armenia	Yes
2	Bangladesh*	No
3	Belarus	Yes
4	Brazil	Yes
5	Brunei Darussalam	Yes
6	Kyrgyzstan*	No
7	Moldova*	No
8	Philippines*	No
9	Sri Lanka	Yes
10	Tajikistan*	No
11	Thailand	Yes
12	Turkmenistan*	No
13	Viet Nam	Yes
14	Zambia	Yes

Jersey

A. Progress in the implementation of the minimum standard

Jersey has 15 tax agreements in force as reported in its response to the Peer Review questionnaire. Eight of those agreements comply with the minimum standard.

Jersey signed the MLI in 2017 and deposited its instrument of ratification on 15 December 2018. The MLI entered into force for Jersey on 1 July 2018. The agreements modified by the MLI come into compliance with the minimum standard once the provisions of the MLI take effect. Jersey has not listed its agreement with Mauritius. This agreement will therefore not, at this stage, be modified by the MLI. Mauritius has listed its agreement with Jersey under the MLI.

Jersey indicated in its response to the Peer Review questionnaire that steps have been taken (other than under the MLI) to implement the minimum standard in its agreements with Guernsey and the Isle of Man.

Jersey is implementing the minimum standard through the inclusion of the preamble statement and the PPT.[106]

B. Conclusion

Recommendation

It is recommended that Jersey formulates a plan for the implementation of the minimum standard in its agreement for which no steps have yet been taken and that were concluded with members of the BEPS Inclusive Framework (Mauritius).

Summary of the jurisdiction response – Jersey

	1.Treaty partners	2. Compliance with the standard	3. Signature of a complying instrument	4. Minimum standard provision used
1	Cyprus*	Yes MLI		PPT
2	Estonia	No	Yes MLI	PPT
3	Guernsey	No	No	PPT
4	Hong Kong (China)	No	Yes MLI	PPT
5	Isle of Man	No	No	PPT
6	Liechtenstein	Yes other		PPT
7	Luxembourg	Yes MLI		PPT
8	Malta	Yes MLI		PPT
9	Qatar	Yes MLI		PPT
10	Rwanda*	No	No	
11	Seychelles	No	Yes MLI	PPT
12	Singapore	Yes MLI		PPT

106 For its agreements listed under the MLI, Jersey is implementing the preamble statement (Article 6 of the MLI) and the PPT (Article 7 of the MLI).

13	United Arab Emirates	Yes MLI		PPT
14	United Kingdom	Yes other		PPT

Other agreements

	1.Treaty partners	2. Inclusive Framework member
1	Mauritius	Yes

Jordan

A. Progress in the implementation of the minimum standard

Jordan has 37 tax agreements in force as reported in its response to the Peer Review questionnaire. Fifteen of those agreements comply with the minimum standard.

Jordan signed the MLI in 2019 and deposited its instrument of ratification on 22 September 2020, listing its non-compliant agreements. The MLI entered into force for Jordan on 1 January 2021. The agreements modified by the MLI come into compliance with the minimum standard once the provisions of the MLI take effect.

Jordan is implementing the minimum standard through the inclusion of the preamble statement and the PPT.[107]

B. Conclusion

No jurisdiction has raised any concerns about their agreements with Jordan.

Summary of the jurisdiction response - Jordan

	1.Treaty partners	2. Compliance with the standard	3. Signature of a complying instrument	4. Minimum standard provision used
1	Algeria*	No	No	
2	Azerbaijan*	No	No	
3	Bahrain	no	Yes MLI	PPT
4	Bosnia-Herzegovina	Yes MLI		PPT
5	Bulgaria	No	Yes MLI	PPT
6	Canada	Yes MLI		PPT
7	Croatia	No	Yes MLI	PPT
8	Czech Republic	No	No	
9	Egypt	Yes MLI		PPT
10	France	Yes MLI		PPT
11	India	Yes MLI		PPT
12	Indonesia	No	No	
13	Iran*	No	No	
14	Italy	No	Yes MLI	PPT
15	Korea	Yes MLI		PPT
16	Kuwait*	No	No	
17	Lebanon*	No	No	
18	Malaysia	No	Yes MLI	PPT
19	Malta	Yes MLI		PPT
20	Morocco	No	Yes MLI	PPT
21	Netherlands	Yes MLI		PPT
22	Palestine*	No	No	
23	Pakistan	Yes MLI		PPT

107 For its agreements listed under the MLI, Jordan is implementing the preamble statement (Article 6 of the MLI) and the PPT (Article 7 of the MLI).

24	Poland	Yes MLI		PPT
25	Qatar	Yes MLI		PPT
26	Romania	No	Yes MLI	PPT
27	Saudi Arabia	Yes MLI		PPT
28	Sudan*	No	No	
29	Syria*	No	No	
30	Tajikistan*	No	No	
31	Tunisia	No	Yes MLI	PPT
32	Turkey	No	Yes MLI	PPT
33	Ukraine	Yes MLI		PPT
34	United Arab Emirates	Yes MLI		PPT
35	United Kingdom	Yes MLI		PPT
36	Uzbekistan*	No	No	
37	Yemen*	No	No	

Kazakhstan

A. Progress in the implementation of the minimum standard

Kazakhstan has 55 tax agreements in force as reported in its response to the Peer Review questionnaire. Twenty-three of those agreements comply with the minimum standard.

Kazakhstan signed the MLI in 2018 and deposited its instrument of ratification on 24 June 2020, listing its non-compliant agreements. The MLI entered into force for Kazakhstan on 1 October 2020. The agreements modified by the MLI come into compliance with the minimum standard once the provisions of the MLI take effect.

Kazakhstan is implementing the minimum standard through the inclusion of the preamble statement and the PPT combined with the LOB.[108]

B. Conclusion

No jurisdiction has raised any concerns about their agreements with Kazakhstan.

Summary of the jurisdiction response - Kazakhstan

	1.Treaty partners	2. Compliance with the standard	3. Signature of a complying instrument	4. Minimum standard provision used
1	Armenia	No	Yes MLI	PPT+LOB
2	Austria	No	No	
3	Azerbaijan*	No	No	
4	Belarus	No	No	
5	Belgium	Yes MLI		PPT
6	Bulgaria	No	Yes MLI	PPT
7	Canada	Yes MLI		PPT
8	China (People's Republic of)	No	Yes MLI	PPT
9	Croatia	No	Yes MLI	PPT
10	Czech Republic	No	No	
11	Estonia	No	Yes MLI	PPT
12	Finland	Yes MLI		PPT
13	France	Yes MLI		PPT
14	Georgia	No	No	
15	Germany	No	No	
16	Hungary	No	Yes MLI	PPT
17	India	Yes MLI		PPT+LOB
18	Iran*	No	No	
19	Ireland	Yes MLI		PPT
20	Italy	No	Yes MLI	PPT
21	Japan	Yes MLI		PPT
22	Korea	Yes MLI		PPT
23	Kyrgyzstan*	No	No	

108 For its agreements listed under the MLI, Kazakhstan is implementing the preamble statement (Article 6 of the MLI) and the PPT (Article 7 of the MLI). Kazakhstan has also adopted the simplified LOB pursuant to Article 7(6) of the MLI.

24	Latvia	Yes MLI		PPT
25	Lithuania	Yes MLI		PPT
26	Luxembourg	Yes MLI		PPT
27	Malaysia	No	Yes MLI	PPT
28	Moldova*	No	No	
29	Mongolia	No	No	
30	Netherlands	Yes MLI		PPT
31	North Macedonia	No	Yes MLI	
32	Norway	No	No	
33	Pakistan	Yes MLI		PPT+LOB
34	Poland	Yes MLI		PPT
35	Qatar	No	No	PPT+LOB
36	Romania	No	Yes MLI	PPT
37	Russian Federation	Yes MLI		PPT+LOB
38	Saudi Arabia	Yes MLI		PPT
39	Serbia	Yes MLI		PPT
40	Singapore	Yes MLI		PPT
41	Slovak Republic	Yes MLI		PPT+LOB
42	Slovenia	Yes MLI		PPT
43	Spain	No	Yes MLI	PPT
44	Sweden	No	Yes MLI	PPT
45	Switzerland	No	No	
46	Tajikistan*	No	No	
47	Turkey	No	Yes MLI	PPT
48	Turkmenistan*	No	No	
49	Ukraine	Yes MLI		PPT
50	United Arab Emirates	Yes MLI		PPT
51	United Kingdom	Yes MLI		PPT
52	United States	No	No	
53	Uzbekistan*	No	No	
54	Viet Nam	No	No	

Other agreements

	1.Treaty partners	2. Inclusive Framework member
1	Cyprus*	No

Kenya

A. Progress in the implementation of the minimum standard

Kenya has 15 tax agreements in force as reported in its response to the Peer Review questionnaire. None of those agreements comply with the minimum standard.

Kenya signed the MLI in 2019. The agreements modified by the MLI come into compliance with the minimum standard once the provisions of the MLI take effect.

Kenya indicated has not listed its agreements with Germany, Korea and Zambia under the MLI, but indicated in its response to the Peer Review questionnaire that steps have been taken (other than under the MLI) to implement the minimum standard in its agreement with Germany and Korea. Korea has listed its agreement with Kenya under the MLI.

Kenya is implementing the minimum standard through the inclusion of the preamble statement and the PPT combined with the LOB.[109]

B. Conclusion

Korea has listed its agreement with Kenya under the MLI, which amounts to a request to implement the minimum standard.

Kenya has developed a plan for the implementation of the minimum standard in its agreements with Zambia. Kenya indicated in its response to the Peer Review questionnaire that it intends to expand its list of agreements to be covered under the MLI to include that agreement.

Recommendation

It is recommended that Kenya completes the steps to have the MLI take effect with respect to its agreements listed under the MLI as those agreements will only be modified by the MLI (and come into compliance with the minimum standard) once the provisions of the MLI take effect.

Summary of the jurisdiction response - Kenya

	1.Treaty partners	2. Compliance with the standard	3. Signature of a complying instrument	4. Minimum standard provision used
1	Canada	No	Yes MLI	PPT
2	Denmark	No	Yes MLI	PPT+LOB
3	France	No	Yes MLI	
4	Germany	No	No	
5	India	No	Yes MLI	PPT+LOB
6	Norway	No	No	
7	Korea	No	No	

109 For its agreements listed under the MLI, Kenya is implementing the preamble statement (Article 6 of the MLI) and the PPT combined with the LOB (Article 7 of the MLI).

8	Qatar	No	Yes MLI	PPT
9	Seychelles	No	Yes MLI	PPT
10	South Africa	No	Yes MLI	PPT
11	Sweden	No	Yes MLI	PPT
12	United Arab Emirates	No	Yes MLI	PPT
13	United Kingdom	No	Yes MLI	PPT

Other agreements

	1.Treaty partners	2. Inclusive Framework member
1	Iran*	No
2	Zambia	Yes

Korea

A. Progress in the implementation of the minimum standard

Korea has 94 tax agreements in force as reported in its response to the Peer Review questionnaire. Forty-one of those agreements comply with the minimum standard.

Korea signed the MLI in 2017 and deposited its instrument of ratification on 13 May 2020. The MLI entered into force for Korea on 1 September 2020. The agreements modified by the MLI come into compliance with the minimum standard once the provisions of the MLI take effect.

Korea has not listed its agreements with Albania, Austria, Belarus, Brazil, Germany, and Turkey, but indicated in its response to the Peer Review questionnaire that steps have been taken (other than under the MLI) to implement the minimum standard in the agreements with Albania, Austria, Belarus, Brazil, Ecuador*, Ethiopia*, Germany, Iran*, Kyrgyzstan*, Lao People's Democratic Republic*, Myanmar*, Nepal*, Tajikistan*, Turkey and Venezuela*. Albania and Turkey have listed their agreements with Korea under the MLI.

Korea is implementing the minimum standard through the inclusion of the preamble statement and the PPT.[110]

B. Conclusion

No jurisdiction has raised any concerns about their agreements with Korea.

Albania and Turkey have listed their agreements with Korea under the MLI, which amount to requests to implement the minimum standard.

Summary of the jurisdiction response - Korea

	1.Treaty partners	2. Compliance with the standard	3. Signature of a complying instrument	4. Minimum standard provision used
1	Albania	No	No	PPT
2	Algeria*	No	No	PPT
3	Australia	Yes MLI		PPT
4	Austria	No	No	PPT
5	Azerbaijan*	No	No	PPT
6	Bahrain	No	Yes MLI	PPT
7	Bangladesh*	No	No	PPT
8	Belarus	No	No	PPT
9	Belgium	Yes MLI		PPT
10	Brazil	No	No	PPT
11	Brunei Darussalam	No	No	PPT
12	Bulgaria	No	Yes MLI	PPT
13	Cambodia*	Yes other		PPT
14	Canada	Yes MLI		PPT

110 For its agreements listed under the MLI, Korea is implementing the preamble statement (Article 6 of the MLI) and the PPT (Article 7 of the MLI).

15	Chile	No	Yes MLI	PPT
16	China (People's Republic of)	No	Yes MLI	PPT
17	Colombia	No	Yes MLI	PPT
18	Croatia	No	Yes MLI	PPT
19	Czech Republic	Yes other		PPT
20	Denmark	Yes MLI		PPT
21	Ecuador*	No	No	PPT
22	Egypt	Yes MLI		PPT
23	Estonia	No	Yes MLI	PPT
24	Ethiopia*	No	No	PPT
25	Fiji*	No	Yes MLI	PPT
26	Finland	Yes MLI		PPT
27	France	Yes MLI		PPT
28	Gabon	No	No	PPT
29	Georgia	Yes MLI		PPT
30	Germany	No	No	PPT
31	Greece	No	Yes MLI	PPT
32	Hong Kong (China)	No	Yes MLI	PPT
33	Hungary	No	Yes MLI	PPT
34	Iceland	Yes MLI		PPT
35	India	Yes MLI		PPT
36	Indonesia	Yes MLI		PPT
37	Iran*	No	No	PPT
38	Ireland	Yes MLI		PPT
39	Israel	Yes MLI		PPT
40	Italy	No	Yes MLI	PPT
41	Japan	Yes MLI		PPT
42	Jordan	Yes MLI		PPT
43	Kazakhstan	Yes MLI		PPT
44	Kenya	No	No	PPT
45	Kuwait*	No	Yes MLI	PPT
46	Kyrgyzstan*	No	No	PPT
47	Lao People's Democratic Republic*	No	No	PPT
48	Latvia	Yes MLI		PPT
49	Lithuania	Yes MLI		PPT
50	Luxembourg	Yes MLI		PPT
51	Malaysia	No	Yes MLI	PPT
52	Malta	Yes MLI		PPT
53	Mexico	No	Yes MLI	PPT
54	Mongolia	No	No	PPT
55	Morocco	No	Yes MLI	PPT
56	Myanmar*	No	No	PPT
57	Nepal*	No	No	PPT
58	Netherlands	Yes MLI		PPT
59	New Zealand	Yes MLI		PPT
60	Norway	No	No	PPT
61	Oman	Yes MLI		PPT
62	Pakistan	No	Yes MLI	PPT
63	Panama	No	Yes MLI	PPT
64	Papua New Guinea	No	Yes MLI	PPT

65	Peru	No	Yes MLI	PPT
66	Philippines*	No	No	PPT
67	Poland	Yes MLI		PPT
68	Portugal	Yes MLI		PPT
69	Qatar	Yes MLI		PPT
70	Romania	No	Yes MLI	PPT
71	Russian Federation	Yes MLI		PPT
72	Saudi Arabia	Yes MLI		PPT
73	Serbia	Yes MLI		PPT
74	Singapore	Yes other		PPT
75	Slovak Republic	Yes MLI		PPT
76	Slovenia	Yes MLI		PPT
77	South Africa	No	Yes MLI	PPT
78	Spain	No	Yes MLI	PPT
79	Sri Lanka	No	No	PPT
80	Sweden	No	Yes MLI	PPT
81	Switzerland	Yes other		PPT
82	Tajikistan*	No	No	PPT
83	Thailand	No	No	PPT
84	Tunisia	No	Yes MLI	PPT
85	Turkey	No	No	PPT
86	Turkmenistan*	Yes other		PPT
87	Ukraine	Yes MLI		PPT
88	United Arab Emirates	Yes MLI		PPT
89	United Kingdom	Yes MLI		PPT
90	United States	No	No	PPT
91	Uruguay	Yes MLI		PPT
92	Uzbekistan*	Yes other		PPT
93	Venezuela*	No	No	PPT
94	Viet Nam	No	No	PPT

Latvia

A. Progress in the implementation of the minimum standard

Latvia has 62 tax agreements in force as reported in its response to the Peer Review questionnaire. Thirty-four of those agreements comply with the minimum standard.

Latvia signed the MLI in 2017 and deposited its instrument of ratification on 29 October 2019. The MLI entered into force for Latvia on 1 February 2020. On 20 April 2020, Latvia made an additional notification to expand its list of agreements to be covered under the MLI. The agreements modified by the MLI come into compliance with the minimum standard once the provisions of the MLI take effect.

Latvia has not listed its agreement with Germany under the MLI but indicated in its response to the Peer Review questionnaire that steps have been taken (other than under the MLI) to implement the minimum standard in this agreement.

Latvia is implementing the minimum standard through the inclusion of the preamble statement and the PPT.[111]

B. Conclusion

No jurisdiction has raised any concerns about their agreements with Latvia.

Summary of the jurisdiction response - Latvia

	1.Treaty partners	2. Compliance with the standard	3. Signature of a complying instrument	4. Minimum standard provision used
1	Albania*	Yes MLI		PPT
2	Armenia	No	Yes MLI	PPT
3	Austria	Yes MLI		PPT
4	Azerbaijan*	No	No	PPT
5	Belarus	No	No	PPT
6	Belgium	Yes MLI		PPT
7	Bulgaria	No	Yes MLI	PPT
8	Canada	Yes MLI		PPT
9	China (People's Republic of)	No	Yes MLI	PPT
10	Croatia	No	Yes MLI	PPT
11	Cyprus*	Yes MLI		PPT
12	Czech Republic	Yes MLI		PPT
13	Denmark	Yes MLI		PPT
14	Estonia	No	Yes MLI	PPT
15	Finland	Yes MLI		PPT
16	France	Yes MLI		PPT
17	Georgia	Yes MLI		PPT
18	Germany	No	No	PPT
19	Greece	No	Yes MLI	PPT

[111] For its agreements listed under the MLI, Latvia is implementing the preamble statement (Article 6 of the MLI) and the PPT (Article 7 of the MLI).

20	Hong Kong (China)	No	Yes MLI	PPT
21	Hungary	No	Yes MLI	PPT
22	Iceland	Yes MLI		PPT
23	India	Yes MLI		PPT
24	Ireland	Yes MLI		PPT
25	Israel	Yes MLI		PPT
26	Italy	No	Yes MLI	PPT
27	Japan	Yes other		PPT+LOB
28	Kazakhstan	Yes MLI		PPT
29	Korea	Yes MLI		PPT
30	Kuwait*	No	No	PPT
31	Kyrgyzstan*	No	No	PPT
32	Lithuania	Yes MLI		PPT
33	Luxembourg	Yes MLI		PPT
34	Malta	Yes MLI		PPT
35	Mexico	No	Yes MLI	PPT
36	Moldova*	No	No	PPT
37	Montenegro*	No	No	PPT
38	Morocco	No	Yes MLI	PPT
39	Netherlands	Yes MLI		PPT
40	North Macedonia	No	Yes MLI	PPT
41	Norway	Yes MLI		PPT
42	Poland	Yes MLI		PPT
43	Portugal	Yes MLI		PPT
44	Qatar	Yes MLI		PPT
45	Romania	No	Yes MLI	PPT
46	Russian Federation	Yes MLI		PPT
47	Serbia	Yes MLI		PPT
48	Singapore	Yes MLI		PPT
49	Slovak Republic	Yes MLI		PPT
50	Slovenia	Yes MLI		PPT
51	Spain	No	Yes MLI	PPT
52	Sweden	No	Yes MLI	PPT
53	Switzerland	Yes Other		PPT
54	Tajikistan*	No	No	PPT
55	Turkey	No	Yes MLI	PPT
56	Turkmenistan*	No	No	PPT
57	Ukraine	Yes MLI		PPT
58	United Arab Emirates	Yes MLI		PPT
59	United Kingdom	Yes MLI		PPT
60	United States	No	No	PPT
61	Uzbekistan*	No	No	PPT
62	Viet Nam	No	No	PPT

Liberia

A. Progress in the implementation of the minimum standard

Liberia has one tax agreement in force, the agreement with Germany, as reported in its response to the Peer Review questionnaire. This agreement does not comply with the minimum standard.

Liberia has not signed the MLI.

Liberia indicated in its response to the Peer Review questionnaire that steps have been taken (other than under the MLI) to implement the minimum standard in its agreement with Germany.

Liberia is implementing the minimum standard through the inclusion of the preamble statement and the PPT.

B. Conclusion

No jurisdiction has raised any concerns about Liberia.

Summary of the jurisdiction response - Liberia

	1.Treaty partners	2. Compliance with the standard	3. Signature of a complying instrument	4. Minimum standard provision used
1	Germany	No	No	

Liechtenstein

A. Progress in the implementation of the minimum standard

Liechtenstein has 21 tax agreements in force as reported in its response to the Peer Review questionnaire. Sixteen of those agreements comply with the minimum standard.

Liechtenstein signed the MLI in 2017 and deposited its instrument of ratification on 19 December 2019. The MLI entered into force for Liechtenstein on 1 April 2020. The agreements modified by the MLI come into compliance with the minimum standard once the provisions of the MLI take effect.

Liechtenstein has not listed its agreement with Switzerland under the MLI but has signed a bilateral complying instrument with respect to its agreements with Germany and Switzerland.

Liechtenstein is implementing the minimum standard through the inclusion of the preamble statement and the PPT.[112]

B. Conclusion

No jurisdiction has raised any concerns about their agreements with Liechtenstein.

Summary of the jurisdiction response – Liechtenstein

	1.Treaty partners	2. Compliance with the standard	3. Signature of a complying instrument	4. Minimum standard provision used
1	Andorra	No	Yes MLI	PPT
2	Austria	Yes other		PPT
3	Czech Republic	Yes MLI		PPT
4	Georgia	Yes MLI		PPT
5	Germany	No	Yes other	PPT
6	Guernsey	Yes MLI		PPT
7	Hong Kong (China)	No	Yes MLI	PPT
8	Hungary	No	Yes MLI	PPT
9	Iceland	Yes other		PPT
10	Jersey	Yes other		PPT
11	Lithuania	Yes other		PPT
12	Luxembourg	Yes MLI		PPT
13	Malta	Yes MLI		PPT
14	Monaco	Yes other		PPT
15	Netherlands	Yes other		PPT
16	San Marino	Yes MLI		PPT
17	Singapore	Yes MLI		PPT
18	Switzerland	No	Yes other	PPT
19	United Arab Emirates	Yes MLI		PPT
20	United Kingdom	Yes MLI		PPT
21	Uruguay	Yes MLI		PPT

112 For its agreements listed under the MLI, Liechtenstein is implementing the preamble statement (Article 6 of the MLI) and the PPT (Article 7 of the MLI).

Lithuania

A. Progress in the implementation of the minimum standard

Lithuania has 56 tax agreements in force as reported in its response to the Peer Review questionnaire. Thirty-three of those agreements comply with the minimum standard.

Lithuania signed the MLI in 2017 and deposited its instrument of ratification on 11 September 2018. The MLI entered into force for the Lithuania on 1 January 2019. The agreements modified by the MLI come into compliance with the minimum standard once the provisions of the MLI take effect.

Lithuania indicated in its response to the Peer Review questionnaire that steps have been taken (other than under the MLI) to implement the minimum standard in its agreement with Germany. Lithuania is implementing the minimum standard through the inclusion of the preamble statement and the PPT.[113]

B. Conclusion

No jurisdiction has raised any concerns about their agreements with Lithuania.

Summary of the jurisdiction response - Lithuania

	1.Treaty partners	2. Compliance with the standard	3. Signature of a complying instrument	4. Minimum standard provision used
1	Armenia	No	Yes MLI	PPT
2	Austria	Yes MLI		PPT
3	Azerbaijan*	No	No	PPT
4	Belarus	No	No	PPT
5	Belgium	Yes MLI		PPT
6	Bulgaria	No	Yes MLI	PPT
7	Canada	Yes MLI		PPT
8	China (People's Republic of)	No	Yes MLI	PPT
9	Croatia	No	Yes MLI	PPT
10	Cyprus*	Yes MLI		PPT
11	Czech Republic	Yes MLI		PPT
12	Denmark	Yes MLI		PPT
13	Estonia	No	Yes MLI	PPT
14	Finland	Yes MLI		PPT
15	France	Yes MLI		PPT
16	Georgia	Yes MLI		PPT
17	Germany	No	No	PPT
18	Greece	No	Yes MLI	PPT
19	Hungary	No	Yes MLI	PPT
20	Iceland	Yes MLI		PPT
21	India	Yes MLI		PPT
22	Ireland	Yes MLI		PPT
23	Israel	Yes MLI		PPT

113 For its agreements listed under the MLI, Lithuania is implementing the preamble statement (Article 6 of the MLI) and the PPT (Article 7 of the MLI).

24	Italy	No	Yes MLI	PPT
25	Japan	Yes other		PPT+LOB
26	Kazakhstan	Yes MLI		PPT
27	Korea	Yes MLI		PPT
28	Kuwait*	No	Yes MLI	PPT
29	Kyrgyzstan*	No	No	PPT
30	Latvia	Yes MLI		PPT
31	Liechtenstein	Yes other		PPT
32	Luxembourg	Yes MLI		PPT
33	Malta	Yes MLI		PPT
34	Mexico	No	Yes MLI	PPT
35	Moldova*	No	No	PPT
36	Netherlands	Yes MLI		PPT
37	North Macedonia	No	Yes MLI	PPT
38	Norway	Yes MLI		PPT
39	Poland	Yes MLI		PPT
40	Portugal	Yes MLI		PPT
41	Romania	No	Yes MLI	PPT
42	Russian Federation	Yes MLI		PPT
43	Serbia	Yes MLI		PPT
44	Singapore	Yes MLI		PPT
45	Slovak Republic	Yes MLI		PPT
46	Slovenia	Yes MLI		PPT
47	Spain	No	Yes MLI	PPT
48	Sweden	No	Yes MLI	PPT
49	Switzerland	Yes MLI		PPT
50	Turkey	No	Yes MLI	PPT
51	Turkmenistan*	No	No	PPT
52	Ukraine	Yes MLI		PPT
53	United Arab Emirates	Yes MLI		PPT
54	United Kingdom	Yes MLI		PPT
55	United States	No	No	PPT
56	Uzbekistan*	No	No	PPT

Luxembourg

A. Progress in the implementation of the minimum standard

Luxembourg has 83 tax agreements in force as reported in its response to the Peer Review questionnaire. Forty-six of those agreements comply with the minimum standard.

Luxembourg signed the MLI in 2017 and deposited its instrument of ratification on 9 April 2019, listing its non-compliant agreements. The MLI entered into force for Luxembourg on 1 August 2019. The agreements modified by the MLI come into compliance with the minimum standard once the provisions of the MLI take effect.

Luxembourg is implementing the minimum standard through the inclusion of the preamble statement and the PPT.[114]

B. Conclusion

No jurisdiction has raised any concerns about their agreements with Luxembourg.

Summary of the jurisdiction response - Luxembourg

	1.Treaty partners	2. Compliance with the standard	3. Signature of a complying instrument	4. Minimum standard provision used
1	Andorra	No	Yes MLI	PPT
2	Armenia	No	Yes MLI	PPT
3	Austria	Yes MLI		PPT
4	Azerbaijan*	No	No	PPT
5	Bahrain	No	Yes MLI	PPT
6	Barbados	No	Yes MLI	PPT
7	Belgium	Yes MLI		PPT
8	Brazil	No	No	PPT
9	Brunei Darussalam	No	No	PPT
10	Bulgaria	No	Yes MLI	PPT
11	Canada	Yes MLI		PPT
12	China (People's Republic of)	No	Yes MLI	PPT
13	Chinese Taipei*	No	No	PPT
14	Croatia	No	Yes MLI	PPT
15	Cyprus*	Yes other		PPT
16	Czech Republic	Yes MLI		PPT
17	Denmark	Yes MLI		PPT
18	Estonia	No	Yes MLI	PPT
19	Finland	Yes MLI		PPT
20	France	Yes other		PPT

114 For its agreements listed under the MLI, Luxembourg is implementing the preamble statement (Article 6 of the MLI) and the PPT (Article 7 of the MLI). Luxembourg has made a reservation pursuant to Article 6(4) MLI not to apply Article 6(1) of the MLI with respect to agreements that already contain the relevant preamble language (covering one agreement). Luxembourg has also made a reservation pursuant to Article 7(15)(b) MLI not to apply Article 7(1) of the MLI with respect to agreements that already contain a PPT (covering one agreement).

21	Georgia	Yes MLI		PPT
22	Germany	No	Yes MLI	PPT
23	Greece	No	Yes MLI	PPT
24	Guernsey	Yes MLI		PPT
25	Hong Kong (China)	No	Yes MLI	PPT
26	Hungary	No	Yes MLI	PPT
27	Iceland	Yes MLI		PPT
28	India	Yes MLI		PPT
29	Indonesia	Yes MLI		PPT
30	Ireland	Yes MLI		PPT
31	Isle of Man	Yes MLI		PPT
32	Israel	Yes MLI		PPT
33	Italy	No	Yes MLI	PPT
34	Japan	Yes MLI		PPT
35	Jersey	Yes MLI		PPT
36	Kazakhstan	Yes MLI		PPT
37	Korea	Yes MLI		PPT
38	Kosovo*	Yes other		PPT
39	Lao People's Democratic Republic*	No	No	PPT
40	Latvia	Yes MLI		PPT
41	Liechtenstein	Yes MLI		PPT
42	Lithuania	Yes MLI		PPT
43	Malaysia	No	Yes MLI	PPT
44	Malta	Yes MLI		PPT
45	Mauritius	Yes MLI		PPT
46	Mexico	No	Yes MLI	PPT
47	Moldova*	No	No	PPT
48	Monaco	Yes MLI		PPT
49	Morocco	No	Yes MLI	PPT
50	Netherlands	Yes MLI		PPT
51	North Macedonia	No	Yes MLI	PPT
52	Norway	Yes MLI		PPT
53	Panama	No	Yes MLI	PPT
54	Poland	Yes MLI		PPT
55	Portugal	Yes MLI		PPT
56	Qatar	Yes MLI		PPT
57	Romania	No	Yes MLI	PPT
58	Russian Federation	Yes MLI		PPT
59	San Marino	Yes MLI		PPT
60	Saudi Arabia	Yes MLI		PPT
61	Senegal	Yes other		PPT
62	Serbia	Yes MLI		PPT
63	Seychelles	No	Yes MLI	PPT
64	Singapore	Yes MLI		PPT
65	Slovak Republic	Yes MLI		PPT
66	Slovenia	Yes MLI		PPT
67	South Africa	No	Yes MLI	PPT
68	Spain	No	Yes MLI	PPT
69	Sri Lanka	No	No	PPT
70	Sweden	No	Yes MLI	PPT
71	Switzerland	Yes MLI		PPT
72	Tajikistan*	No	No	PPT
73	Thailand	No	No	PPT

74	Trinidad and Tobago	No	No	PPT
75	Tunisia	No	Yes MLI	PPT
76	Turkey	No	Yes MLI	PPT
77	Ukraine	Yes MLI		PPT
78	United Arab Emirates	Yes MLI		PPT
79	United Kingdom	Yes MLI		PPT
80	United States	No	No	D-LOB
81	Uruguay	Yes MLI		PPT
82	Uzbekistan*	Yes other		PPT
83	Viet Nam	No	No	PPT

Macau (China)

A. Progress in the implementation of the minimum standard

Macau (China) has four tax agreements in force, as reported in its response to the Peer Review questionnaire. None of those agreements comply with the minimum standard.

Macau (China) has not joined the MLI.

Macau (China) indicated in its response to the Peer Review questionnaire that steps have been taken (other than under the MLI) to implement the minimum standard in its agreements with Cabo Verde, Mozambique*, Portugal and Viet Nam.

B. Conclusion

No jurisdiction has raised any concerns about their agreements with Macau (China).

Summary of the jurisdiction response – Macau, China

	1.Treaty partners	2. Compliance with the standard	3. Signature of a complying instrument	6. Other comments
1	Cabo Verde	No	No	Macao has already sent proposal for amending Protocol
2	Mozambique*	No	No	Macao already held the first round of negotiations for amending Protocol
3	Portugal	No	No	Macao sent an invitation to start conversations as to amend the existing DTA through an amending Protocol
4	Viet Nam	No	No	Macao sent an invitation to start conversations as to amend the existing DTA through an amending Protocol

Malaysia

A. Progress in the implementation of the minimum standard

Malaysia has 73 tax agreements in force as reported in its response to the Peer Review questionnaire. One of those, the agreement with Cambodia*, complies with the minimum standard.

Malaysia signed the MLI in 2018 and deposited its instrument of ratification on 18 February 2021, listing its non-compliant agreements. The MLI entered into force for Malaysia on 1 June 2021. The agreements modified by the MLI come into compliance with the minimum standard once the provisions of the MLI take effect.

Malaysia is implementing the minimum standard through the inclusion of the preamble statement and the PPT.[115]

B. Conclusion

No jurisdiction has raised any concerns about their agreements with Malaysia.

Summary of the jurisdiction response - Malaysia

	1.Treaty partners	2. Compliance with the standard	3. Signature of a complying instrument	4. Minimum standard provision used
1	Albania	No	Yes MLI	PPT
2	Australia	No	Yes MLI	PPT
3	Austria	No	No	PPT
4	Bahrain	No	Yes MLI	PPT
5	Bangladesh*	No	No	PPT
6	Belgium	No	Yes MLI	PPT
7	Bosnia-Herzegovina	No	Yes MLI	PPT
8	Brunei Darussalam	No	No	PPT
9	Cambodia*	Yes other		PPT
10	Canada	No	Yes MLI	PPT
11	Chile	No	Yes MLI	PPT
12	China (People's Republic of)	No	Yes MLI	PPT
13	Croatia	No	Yes MLI	PPT
14	Czech Republic	No	No	PPT
15	Denmark	No	Yes MLI	PPT
16	Egypt	No	Yes MLI	PPT
17	Fiji*	No	Yes MLI	PPT
18	Finland	No	Yes MLI	PPT
19	France	No	Yes MLI	PPT
20	Germany	No	No	PPT
21	Hong Kong (China)	No	Yes MLI	PPT
22	Hungary	No	Yes MLI	PPT
23	India	No	Yes MLI	PPT

[115] For its agreements listed under the MLI, Malaysia is implementing the preamble statement (Article 6 of the MLI) and the PPT (Article 7 of the MLI).

24	Indonesia	No	Yes MLI	PPT
25	Iran*	No	No	PPT
26	Ireland	No	Yes MLI	PPT
27	Italy	No	Yes MLI	PPT
28	Japan	No	Yes MLI	PPT
29	Jordan	No	Yes MLI	PPT
30	Kazakhstan	No	Yes MLI	PPT
31	Korea	No	Yes MLI	PPT
32	Kuwait*	No	Yes MLI	PPT
33	Kyrgyzstan*	No	No	PPT
34	Lao People's Democratic Republic*	No	No	PPT
35	Lebanon*	No	No	PPT
36	Luxembourg	No	Yes MLI	PPT
37	Malta	No	Yes MLI	PPT
38	Mauritius	No	Yes MLI	PPT
39	Mongolia	No	No	PPT
40	Morocco	No	Yes MLI	PPT
41	Myanmar*	No	No	PPT
42	Namibia	No	No	PPT
43	Netherlands	No	Yes MLI	PPT
44	New Zealand	No	Yes MLI	PPT
45	Norway	No	No	PPT
46	Pakistan	No	Yes MLI	PPT
47	Papua New Guinea	No	Yes MLI	PPT
48	Philippines*	No	No	PPT
49	Poland	No	Yes MLI	PPT
50	Qatar	No	Yes MLI	PPT
51	Romania	No	Yes MLI	PPT
52	Russian Federation	No	Yes MLI	PPT
53	San Marino	No	Yes MLI	PPT
54	Saudi Arabia	No	Yes MLI	PPT
55	Seychelles	No	Yes MLI	PPT
56	Singapore	No	Yes MLI	PPT
57	Slovak Republic	No	Yes MLI	PPT
58	South Africa	No	Yes MLI	PPT
59	Spain	No	Yes MLI	PPT
60	Sri Lanka	No	No	PPT
61	Sudan*	No	No	PPT
62	Sweden	No	Yes MLI	PPT
63	Switzerland	No	No	PPT
64	Syrian Arab Republic*	No	No	PPT
65	Thailand	No	No	PPT
66	Turkey	No	Yes MLI	PPT
67	Turkmenistan*	No	No	PPT
68	United Arab Emirates	No	Yes MLI	PPT
69	United Kingdom	No	Yes MLI	PPT
70	Uzbekistan*	No	No	PPT
71	Venezuela*	No	No	PPT
72	Viet Nam	No	No	PPT
73	Zimbabwe*	No	No	PPT

Maldives

A. Progress in the implementation of the minimum standard

The Maldives has one tax agreement in force, the agreement with the United Arab Emirates, as reported in its response to the Peer Review questionnaire. This agreement does not comply with the minimum standard.

The Maldives has not signed the MLI.

B. Conclusion

The Maldives is currently developing a plan, in consultation with the Secretariat, for the implementation of the minimum standard in its agreement with the United Arab Emirates.

Other agreements

This Table shows the agreements that are not compliant, not subject to a complying instrument, not covered by a general statement on the implementation of the detailed LOB and for which no steps have been taken to implement the minimum standard.

	1.Treaty partners	2. Inclusive Framework member
1	United Arab Emirates	Yes

Malta

A. Progress in the implementation of the minimum standard

Malta has 77 tax agreements in force, as reported in its response to the Peer Review questionnaire. Forty-three of those agreements comply with the minimum standard.

Malta signed the MLI in 2017 and deposited its instrument of ratification on 18 December 2018. The MLI entered into force for Malta on 1 April 2019. The agreements modified by the MLI come into compliance with the minimum standard once the provisions of the MLI take effect.[116] Malta has not listed its agreements with Botswana, Bulgaria, Monaco and Switzerland under the MLI. These agreements will therefore not, at this stage, be modified under the MLI.

Malta has signed a bilateral complying instrument with respect to its agreement with Switzerland. Malta has also indicated in its response to the Peer Review questionnaire that steps have been taken (other than under the MLI) to implement the minimum standard in the agreements with Botswana, Bulgaria, Georgia, Moldova*, Monaco, Montenegro and the United States.

Malta is implementing the minimum standard through the inclusion of the preamble statement and the PPT.[117]

B. Conclusion

No jurisdiction has raised any concerns about their agreements with Malta.

Summary of the jurisdiction response - Malta

	1.Treaty partners	2. Compliance with the standard	3. Signature of a complying instrument	4. Minimum standard provision used
1	Albania	Yes MLI		PPT
2	Andorra	No	Yes MLI	PPT
3	Australia	Yes MLI		PPT
4	Austria	Yes MLI		PPT
5	Azerbaijan*	No	No	
6	Bahrain	No	Yes MLI	PPT
7	Barbados	No	Yes MLI	PPT
8	Belgium	Yes MLI		PPT
9	Botswana	No	No	
10	Bulgaria	No	No	
11	Canada	Yes MLI		PPT
12	China (People's Republic of)	No	Yes MLI	PPT
13	Croatia	No	Yes MLI	PPT

[116] Malta chose to replace, under Article 35(3) of the MLI, the reference to "taxable periods beginning on or after the expiration of a period" with a reference to "taxable periods beginning on or after 1 January of the next calendar year beginning on or after the expiration of a period" for the purposes of its own application of Article 35(1)(b) and (5)(b) (Entry into effect) of the MLI.

[117] For its agreements listed under the MLI, Malta is implementing the preamble statement (Article 6 of the MLI) and the PPT (Article 7 of the MLI).

14	Czech Republic	Yes MLI		PPT
15	Cyprus*	Yes MLI		PPT
16	Denmark	Yes MLI		PPT
17	Egypt	Yes MLI		PPT
18	Estonia	No	Yes MLI	PPT
19	Finland	Yes MLI		PPT
20	France	Yes MLI		PPT
21	Georgia	No	No	PPT
22	Germany	No	Yes MLI	PPT
23	Greece	No	Yes MLI	PPT
24	Guernsey	Yes MLI		PPT
25	Hong Kong (China)	No	Yes MLI	PPT
26	Hungary	No	Yes MLI	PPT
27	Iceland	Yes MLI		PPT
28	India	Yes MLI		PPT
29	Ireland	Yes MLI		PPT
30	Isle of Man	Yes MLI		PPT
31	Israel	Yes MLI		PPT
32	Italy	No	Yes MLI	PPT
33	Jersey	Yes MLI		PPT
34	Jordan	Yes MLI		PPT
35	Korea	Yes MLI		PPT
36	Kosovo*	Yes other		PPT
37	Kuwait*	No	Yes MLI	PPT
38	Latvia	Yes MLI		PPT
39	Lebanon*	No	No	
40	Libya*	No	No	
41	Liechtenstein	Yes MLI		PPT
42	Lithuania	Yes MLI		PPT
43	Luxembourg	Yes MLI		PPT
44	Malaysia	No	Yes MLI	PPT
45	Mauritius	Yes MLI		PPT
46	Mexico	No	Yes MLI	PPT
47	Moldova*	No	No	
48	Monaco	No	No	
49	Montenegro	No	No	
50	Morocco	No	Yes MLI	PPT
51	Netherlands	Yes MLI		PPT
52	Norway	Yes MLI		PPT
53	Pakistan	Yes MLI		PPT
54	Poland	Yes MLI		PPT
55	Portugal	Yes MLI		PPT
56	Qatar	Yes MLI		PPT
57	Romania	No	Yes MLI	PPT
58	Russian Federation	Yes MLI		PPT
59	San Marino	Yes MLI		PPT
60	Saudi Arabia	Yes MLI		PPT
61	Serbia	Yes MLI		PPT
62	Singapore	Yes MLI		PPT
63	Slovak Republic	Yes MLI		PPT
64	Slovenia	Yes MLI		PPT
65	South Africa	No	Yes MLI	PPT
66	Spain	No	Yes MLI	PPT

67	Sweden	No	Yes MLI	PPT
68	Switzerland	No	Yes other	PPT
69	Syria*	No	No	
70	Tunisia	No	Yes MLI	PPT
71	Turkey	No	Yes MLI	PPT
72	Ukraine	Yes MLI		PPT
73	United Arab Emirates	Yes MLI		PPT
74	United Kingdom	Yes MLI		PPT
75	United States	No	No	PPT
76	Uruguay	Yes MLI		PPT
77	Viet Nam	No	No	PPT

Mauritius

A. Progress in the implementation of the minimum standard

Mauritius has 44 tax agreements in force[118], as reported in its response to the Peer Review questionnaire. Twelve of those agreements comply with the minimum standard.

Mauritius signed the MLI in 2017 and deposited its instrument of ratification on 18 October 2019. The MLI entered into force for Mauritius on 1 February 2020. The agreements that will be modified by the MLI will come into compliance with the minimum standard once the provisions of the MLI take effect

Mauritius has not listed its agreement with India under the MLI indicated in its response to the Peer Review questionnaire that steps have been taken (other than under the MLI) to implement the minimum standard in that agreement. India has listed its agreement with Mauritius under the MLI.

Mauritius is implementing the minimum standard in its tax agreements through the inclusion of the preamble statement and the PPT.[119]

B. Conclusion

No jurisdiction has raised any concerns about their agreements with Mauritius.

India has listed its agreement with Mauritius under the MLI, which amounts to a request to implement the minimum standard.

Summary of the jurisdiction response - Mauritius

	1.Treaty partners	2. Compliance with the standard	3. Signature of a complying instrument	4. Minimum standard provision used
1	Bangladesh*	No	No	PPT
2	Barbados	No	Yes MLI	PPT
3	Belgium	Yes MLI		PPT
4	Botswana	No	No	PPT
5	Cabo Verde	No	No	PPT
6	China (People's Republic of)	No	Yes MLI	PPT
7	Congo	No	No	PPT
8	Croatia	No	Yes MLI	PPT
9	Cyprus*	Yes MLI		PPT
10	Egypt	No	Yes MLI	PPT
11	France	Yes MLI		PPT
12	Germany	No	No	PPT
13	Ghana*	No	No	PPT
14	Guernsey	Yes MLI		PPT

118 Mauritius also concluded a new agreement with Lesotho* in 2021. This agreement was not in force on 31 May 2021 and has therefore not been assessed for the purposes of the 2021 Action 6 peer review.

119 For its agreements listed under the MLI, Mauritius is implementing the preamble statement (Article 6 of the MLI) and the PPT (Article 7 of the MLI). Mauritius has stated that while it accepts the application of the PPT under the MLI, it intends where possible to adopt an LOB provision through bilateral negotiation.

15	India	No	No	PPT
16	Italy	No	Yes MLI	PPT
17	Jersey	No	No	PPT
18	Kuwait*	No	Yes MLI	PPT
19	Lesotho*	No	No	PPT
20	Luxembourg	Yes MLI		PPT
21	Madagascar*	No	No	PPT
22	Malaysia	No	Yes MLI	PPT
23	Malta	Yes MLI		PPT
24	Monaco	Yes MLI		PPT
25	Mozambique*	No	No	PPT
26	Namibia	No	No	PPT
27	Nepal*	No	No	PPT
28	Oman	Yes MLI		PPT
29	Pakistan	No	Yes MLI	PPT
30	Qatar	Yes MLI		PPT
31	Rwanda*	No	No	PPT
32	Seychelles	No	Yes MLI	PPT
33	Singapore	Yes MLI		PPT
34	South Africa	No	Yes MLI	PPT
35	Sri Lanka	No	No	PPT
36	Eswatini	No	No	PPT
37	Sweden	No	Yes MLI	PPT
38	Thailand	No	No	PPT
39	Tunisia	No	No	PPT
40	Uganda*	No	No	PPT
41	United Arab Emirates	Yes MLI		PPT
42	United Kingdom	Yes MLI		PPT
43	Zambia	No	No	PPT
44	Zimbabwe*	No	No	PPT

Mexico

A. Progress in the implementation of the minimum standard

Mexico has 60 tax agreements in force, as reported in its response to the Peer Review questionnaire. Three of those agreements comply with the minimum standard.

Mexico signed the MLI in 2017 and listed its non-compliant agreements. The agreements that will be modified by the MLI will come into compliance with the minimum standard once the provisions of the MLI take effect.

Mexico indicated in its response to the Peer Review questionnaire that steps have been taken (other than under the MLI) to implement the minimum standard in its agreement with Germany.

Mexico is implementing the minimum standard through the inclusion of the preamble statement and the PPT combined with the LOB.[120]

B. Conclusion

Recommendation

It is recommended that Mexico completes the steps to have the MLI take effect with respect to its agreements listed under the MLI as those agreements will only be modified by the MLI (and come into compliance with the minimum standard) once the provisions of the MLI take effect.

Summary of the jurisdiction response - Mexico

	1.Treaty partners	2. Compliance with the standard	3. Signature of a complying instrument	4. Minimum standard provision used
1	Argentina	Yes other		PPT+LOB
2	Australia	No	Yes MLI	PPT
3	Austria	No	Yes MLI	PPT
4	Bahrain	No	Yes MLI	PPT
5	Barbados	No	Yes MLI	PPT
6	Belgium	No	Yes MLI	PPT
7	Brazil	No	No	
8	Canada	No	Yes MLI	PPT
9	Chile	No	Yes MLI	PPT+LOB
10	China (People's Republic of)	No	Yes MLI	PPT

120 For its agreements listed under the MLI, Mexico is implementing the preamble statement (Article 6 of the MLI) and the PPT (Article 7 of the MLI). Mexico has also adopted the simplified LOB under Article 7(6) of the MLI. Mexico has made a reservation pursuant to Article 6(4) of the MLI not to apply Article 6(1) of the MLI with respect to agreements which already contain the relevant preamble language (covering four agreements). Mexico has also made a reservation pursuant to Article 7(15)(b) of the MLI not to apply Article 7(1) of the MLI with respect to agreements which already contain a PPT (covering three agreements)..

11	Colombia	No	Yes MLI	PPT
12	Costa Rica	No	Yes MLI	PPT
13	Czech Republic	No	Yes MLI	PPT
14	Denmark	No	Yes MLI	PPT+LOB
15	Ecuador*	No	No	PPT
16	Estonia	No	Yes MLI	PPT
17	Finland	No	Yes MLI	PPT
18	France	No	Yes MLI	PPT
19	Germany	No	No	PPT
20	Greece	No	Yes MLI	PPT
21	Hong Kong (China)	No	Yes MLI	PPT
22	Hungary	No	Yes MLI	PPT
23	Iceland	No	Yes MLI	PPT
24	India	No	Yes MLI	PPT
25	Indonesia	No	Yes MLI	PPT
26	Ireland	No	Yes MLI	PPT
27	Israel	No	Yes MLI	PPT
28	Italy	No	Yes MLI	PPT
29	Jamaica	No	Yes MLI	PPT
30	Japan	No	Yes MLI	PPT
31	Korea	No	Yes MLI	PPT
32	Kuwait*	No	Yes MLI	PPT
33	Latvia	No	Yes MLI	PPT
34	Lithuania	No	Yes MLI	PPT
35	Luxembourg	No	Yes MLI	PPT
36	Malta	No	Yes MLI	PPT
37	Netherlands	No	Yes MLI	PPT
38	New Zealand	No	Yes MLI	PPT
39	Norway	No	Yes MLI	PPT+LOB
40	Panama	No	Yes MLI	PPT
41	Peru	No	Yes MLI	PPT
42	Philippines*	Yes other		PPT
43	Poland	No	Yes MLI	PPT
44	Portugal	No	Yes MLI	PPT
45	Qatar	No	Yes MLI	PPT
46	Romania	No	Yes MLI	PPT
47	Russian Federation	No	Yes MLI	PPT+LOB
48	Saudi Arabia	No	Yes MLI	PPT
49	Singapore	No	Yes MLI	PPT
50	Slovak Republic	No	Yes MLI	PPT+LOB
51	South Africa	No	Yes MLI	PPT
52	Spain	Yes other		PPT
53	Sweden	No	Yes MLI	PPT
54	Switzerland	No	Yes MLI	PPT
55	Turkey	No	Yes MLI	PPT
56	Ukraine	No	Yes MLI	PPT
57	United Arab Emirates	No	Yes MLI	PPT
58	United Kingdom	No	Yes MLI	PPT
59	United States	No	No	
60	Uruguay	No	Yes MLI	PPT

Monaco

A. Progress in the implementation of the minimum standard

Monaco has ten tax agreements in force, as reported in its response to the Peer Review questionnaire. Six of those agreements comply with the minimum standard.

Monaco signed the MLI in 2017 and deposited its instrument of ratification on 10 January 2019. The MLI entered into force for Monaco on 1 May 2019. The agreements modified by the MLI come into compliance with the minimum standard once the provisions of the MLI take effect.

Monaco has not listed its agreement with Malta under the MLI but indicated in its response to the Peer Review questionnaire that steps have been taken (other than under the MLI) to implement the minimum standard in its agreements with Malta and Mali*.

Monaco is implementing the minimum standard through the inclusion of the preamble statement and the PPT.[121]

B. Conclusion

No jurisdiction has raised any concerns about their agreements with Monaco.

Summary of the jurisdiction response - Monaco

	1.Treaty partners	2. Compliance with the standard	3. Signature of a complying instrument	4. Minimum standard provision used
1	France	Yes MLI		PPT
2	Guernsey	Yes MLI		PPT
3	Liechtenstein	Yes other		PPT
4	Luxembourg	Yes MLI		PPT
5	Mali*	No	No	
6	Malta	No	No	
7	Mauritius	Yes MLI		PPT
8	Qatar	Yes MLI		PPT
9	Saint Kitts and Nevis	No	No	
10	Seychelles	No	Yes MLI	PPT

[121] For its agreements listed under the MLI, Monaco is implementing the preamble statement (Article 6 of the MLI) and the PPT (Article 7 of the MLI).

Mongolia

A. Progress in the implementation of the minimum standard

Mongolia has 25 tax agreements in force, as reported in its response to the Peer Review questionnaire. None of those agreements comply with the minimum standard.

Mongolia has not signed the MLI.

Mongolia indicated in its response to the Peer Review questionnaire that it intends to join the MLI in early 2022.

In their responses to the Peer Review questionnaire, Hungary and Indonesia indicated that their agreements with Mongolia did not give rise to material treaty shopping concerns, for their respective jurisdictions.

B. Conclusion

Mongolia has developed a plan for the implementation of the minimum standard in its agreements with Austria, Belarus, Belgium, Bulgaria, Canada, China (People's Republic of), Czech Republic, France, Germany, Hungary, India, Indonesia, Kazakhstan, Korea, Malaysia, Poland, Russian Federation, Singapore, Switzerland, Turkey, Ukraine, United Kingdom and Viet Nam. Mongolia indicated in its response to the Peer Review questionnaire that it intends to sign the MLI in early 2022 and list those agreements to be covered.

Other agreements

This Table shows the agreements that are not compliant, not subject to a complying instrument, not covered by a general statement on the implementation of the detailed LOB and for which no steps have been taken to implement the minimum standard.

	1.Treaty partners	2. Inclusive Framework member
1	Austria	Yes
2	Belarus	Yes
3	Belgium	Yes
4	Bulgaria	Yes
5	Canada	Yes
6	China (People's Republic of)	Yes
7	Czech Republic	Yes
8	Democratic People's Republic of Korea*	No
9	France	Yes
10	Germany	Yes
11	Hungary	Yes
12	India	Yes
13	Indonesia	Yes
14	Kazakhstan	Yes
15	Korea	Yes
16	Kyrgyzstan*	No
17	Malaysia	Yes
18	Poland	Yes

19	Russian Federation	Yes
20	Singapore	Yes
21	Switzerland	Yes
22	Turkey	Yes
23	Ukraine	Yes
24	United Kingdom	Yes
25	Viet Nam	Yes

Montenegro

A. Progress in the implementation of the minimum standard

Montenegro has 44 tax agreements in force, as reported in its response to the Peer Review questionnaire. None of those agreements comply with the minimum standard.

Montenegro has not signed the MLI.

Montenegro indicated in its response to the Peer Review questionnaire that steps have been taken (other than under the MLI) to implement the minimum standard in its agreements with the Czech Republic, Poland, the Slovak Republic and Slovenia.

Montenegro indicated in its response to the Peer Review questionnaire that it intends to join the MLI.

In their responses to the Peer Review questionnaire, Hungary, Italy and Sweden indicated that their agreements with Montenegro did not give rise to material shopping concerns for their respective jurisdictions.

B. Conclusion

Montenegro has developed a plan for the implementation of the minimum standard in its agreements with Albania, Austria, Belarus, Belgium, Bosnia-Herzegovina, Bulgaria, China, Croatia, Denmark, Egypt, Finland, France, Germany, Hungary, India, Ireland, Italy, Latvia, Malaysia, Malta, Netherlands, North Macedonia, Norway, Portugal, Romania, the Russian Federation, Serbia, Sri Lanka, Sweden, Switzerland, Turkey, Ukraine, the United Emirates and the United Kingdom. Montenegro indicated in its response to the Peer Review questionnaire that it intends to sign the MLI and list those agreements to be covered.

Summary of the jurisdiction response - Montenegro

	1.Treaty partners	2. Compliance with the standard	3. Signature of a complying instrument	4. Minimum standard provision used
1	Czech Republic	No	No	
2	Poland	No	No	
3	Slovak Republic	No	No	
4	Slovenia	No	No	

Other agreements

	1.Treaty partners	2. Inclusive Framework member
1	Albania	Yes
2	Austria	Yes
3	Azerbaijan*	No
4	Belarus	Yes
5	Belgium	Yes
6	Bosnia-Herzegovina	Yes
7	Bulgaria	Yes
8	China	Yes

9	Croatia	Yes
10	Cyprus*	No
11	Denmark	Yes
12	Democratic People's Republic of Korea*	No
13	Egypt	Yes
14	Finland	Yes
15	France	Yes
16	Germany	Yes
17	Hungary	Yes
18	India	Yes
19	Iran*	No
20	Ireland	Yes
21	Italy	Yes
22	Kuwait*	No
23	Latvia	Yes
24	Malaysia	Yes
25	Malta	Yes
26	Moldova*	No
27	Netherlands	Yes
28	North Macedonia	Yes
29	Norway	Yes
30	Portugal	Yes
31	Romania	Yes
32	Russian Federation	Yes
33	Serbia	Yes
34	Sri Lanka	Yes
35	Sweden	Yes
36	Switzerland	Yes
37	Turkey	Yes
38	Ukraine	Yes
39	United Emirates	Yes
40	United Kingdom	Yes

Montserrat

A. Progress in the implementation of the minimum standard

Montserrat has two tax agreements in force, as reported in its response to the Peer Review questionnaire. Neither of those agreements comply with the minimum standard.

Montserrat has not joined the MLI.

Montserrat indicated in its response to the Peer Review questionnaire that steps have been taken (other than under the MLI) to implement the minimum standard in its arrangement with the United Kingdom.

In its response to the Peer Review questionnaire, Switzerland indicated that its agreement with Montserrat did not give rise to material treaty shopping concerns for Switzerland.

B. Conclusion

No jurisdiction has raised any concerns about their agreements with Montserrat.

Summary of the jurisdiction response - Montserrat

	1.Treaty partners	2. Compliance with the standard	3. Signature of a complying instrument	4. Minimum standard provision used
1	United Kingdom	No	No	PPT

Other agreements

	1.Treaty partners	2. Inclusive Framework member
1	Switzerland	Yes

Morocco

A. Progress in the implementation of the minimum standard

Morocco has 57 tax agreements in force, as reported in its response to the Peer Review questionnaire, including the Arab Maghreb Union Income Agreement concluded with four treaty partners (the UMA Agreement).[122] None of those agreements comply with the minimum standard.

Morocco signed the MLI in 2019 and listed its non-compliant tax agreements. The agreements that will be modified by the MLI will come into compliance with the minimum standard once the provisions of the MLI take effect.

Morocco is implementing the minimum standard through the inclusion of the preamble statement and the PPT.[123]

B. Conclusion

Recommendation

It is recommended that Morocco completes the steps to have the MLI take effect with respect to its agreements listed under the MLI as those agreements will only be modified by the MLI (and come into compliance with the minimum standard) once the provisions of the MLI take effect.

Summary of the jurisdiction response - Morocco

	1.Treaty partners	2. Compliance with the standard	3. Signature of a complying instrument	4. Minimum standard provision used
1	Algeria*	No	No	PPT
2	Austria	No	No	PPT
3	Bahrain	No	Yes MLI	PPT
4	Belgium	No	Yes MLI	PPT
5	Bulgaria	No	Yes MLI	PPT
6	Cameroon	No	Yes MLI	PPT
7	Canada	No	Yes MLI	PPT
8	Chine (People's Republic of)	No	Yes MLI	PPT
9	Côte d'Ivoire	No	Yes MLI	PPT
10	Croatia	No	Yes MLI	PPT
11	Czech Republic	No	No	PPT
12	Denmark	No	Yes MLI	PPT
13	Egypt	No	Yes MLI	PPT

122 In total, Morocco identified 60 "agreements" in its List of Tax agreements: 56 bilateral agreements and the UMA Agreement concluded with four of its treaty partners.

123 For its agreements listed under the MLI, Morocco is implementing the preamble statement (Article 6 of the MLI) and the PPT (Article 7 of the MLI).

14	Ethiopia*	No	No	PPT
15	Finland	No	Yes MLI	PPT
16	France	No	Yes MLI	PPT
17	Gabon	No	Yes MLI	PPT
18	Germany	No	No	PPT
19	Greece	No	Yes MLI	PPT
20	Guinea*	No	No	PPT
21	Hungary	No	Yes MLI	PPT
22	India	No	Yes MLI	PPT
23	Indonesia	No	No	PPT
24	Ireland	No	Yes MLI	PPT
25	Italy	No	Yes MLI	PPT
26	Jordan	No	Yes MLI	PPT
27	Korea	No	Yes MLI	PPT
28	Kuwait*	No	Yes MLI	PPT
29	Latvia	No	Yes MLI	PPT
30	Lebanon*	No	No	PPT
31	Libya*	No	No	PPT
32	Luxembourg	No	Yes MLI	PPT
33	Malaysia	No	Yes MLI	PPT
34	Mali*	No	No	PPT
35	Malta	No	Yes MLI	PPT
36	Mauritania*	No	No	PPT
37	Netherlands	No	Yes MLI	PPT
38	North Macedonia	No	Yes MLI	PPT
39	Norway	No	No	PPT
40	Oman	No	Yes MLI	PPT
41	Pakistan	No	Yes MLI	PPT
42	Poland	No	Yes MLI	PPT
43	Portugal	No	Yes MLI	PPT
44	Qatar	No	Yes MLI	PPT
45	Romania	No	Yes MLI	PPT
46	Russian Federation	No	Yes MLI	PPT
47	Rwanda*	No	No	PPT
48	Senegal	No	Yes MLI	PPT
49	Singapore	No	Yes MLI	PPT
50	Spain	No	Yes MLI	PPT
51	Switzerland	No	No	PPT
52	Syria*	No	No	PPT
53	Tunisia	No	Yes MLI	PPT
54	Turkey	No	Yes MLI	PPT
55	Ukraine	No	Yes MLI	PPT
56	United Arab Emirates	No	Yes MLI	PPT
57	United Kingdom	No	Yes MLI	PPT
58	United States	No	No	PPT
59	Viet Nam	No	No	PPT
60	Zambia	No	No	PPT

Namibia

A. Progress in the implementation of the minimum standard

Namibia has eleven tax agreements in force, as reported in its response to the Peer Review questionnaire. None of those agreements comply with the minimum standard.

Namibia signed the MLI in September 2021 and listed its non-compliant agreements. The agreements modified by the MLI come into compliance with the minimum standard once the provisions of the MLI take effect.

Namibia is implementing the minimum standard through the inclusion of the preamble statement and the PPT combined with the LOB.[124]

B. Conclusion

Acknowledging that Namibia signed the MLI in September 2021, no recommendation is made that Namibia ratifies the MLI in 2021. However, it is expected that Namibia will swiftly start the process to complete the steps to have the MLI take effect with respect to its agreements listed under the MLI, as those agreement will only be modified by the MLI (and come into compliance with the minimum standard) once the provisions of the MLI take effect.

Summary of the jurisdiction response - Namibia

	1.Treaty partners	2. Compliance with the standard	3. Signature of a complying instrument	4. Minimum standard provision used
1	Botswana	No	No	PPT + LOB
2	France	No	Yes MLI	PPT + LOB
3	Germany	No	No	PPT + LOB
4	India	No	Yes MLI	PPT + LOB
5	Malaysia	No	Yes MLI	PPT + LOB
6	Mauritius	No	Yes MLI	PPT + LOB
7	Romania	No	Yes MLI	PPT + LOB
8	Russian Federation	No	No	PPT + LOB
9	South Africa	No	Yes MLI	PPT + LOB
10	Sweden	No	Yes MLI	PPT + LOB
11	United Kingdom	No	Yes MLI	PPT + LOB

124 For its agreements listed under the MLI, Namibia is implementing the preamble statement (Article 6 of the MLI) and the PPT (Article 7 of the MLI) and the simplified LOB (Article 7(6) of the MLI). Namibia expressed a statement, in accordance with Article 7(17)(a) of the MLI, that while it accepts the application of PPT alone as an interim measure, it intends where possible to adopt an LOB provision in addition to or in replacement of the PPT through bilateral negotiation.

Netherlands

A. Progress in the implementation of the minimum standard

The Netherlands has 94 tax agreements in force, as reported in its response to the Peer Review questionnaire. Forty-five of the Netherlands' agreements comply with the minimum standard.

The Netherlands signed the MLI in 2017 and deposited its instrument of acceptance in 2019. The MLI entered into force for the Netherlands on 1 July 2019. On 25 November 2021, the Netherlands made an additional notification to expand its list of agreements to be covered under the MLI. The agreements modified by the MLI come into compliance with the minimum standard once the provisions of the MLI take effect. The Netherlands has not listed its agreements with Brazil, Bulgaria, Poland, Spain and Ukraine. These agreements will therefore not, at this stage, be modified by the MLI. Poland and Ukraine have listed their agreements with the Netherlands under the MLI.

The Netherlands has signed a bilateral complying instrument with respect to its agreements with Bulgaria, Germany, Poland and Ukraine.

The Netherlands indicated in its response to the Peer Review questionnaire that steps have been taken (other than under the MLI) to implement the minimum standard in its agreements with Aruba, Belgium, Brazil, Curaçao, Sint Maarten*, Spain and the United States.

The Netherlands' arrangements with Aruba, Curaçao and Sint Maarten* are arrangements governed by the domestic law of the Kingdom of the Netherlands.

The Netherlands is implementing the minimum standard through the inclusion of the preamble statement and the PPT.[125]

B. Conclusion

No jurisdiction has raised any concerns about their agreements with the Netherlands.

Summary of the jurisdiction response - Netherlands

	1.Treaty partners	2. Compliance with the standard	3. Signature of a complying instrument	4. Minimum standard provision used
1	Albania	Yes MLI		PPT
2	Algeria*	Yes other		PPT
3	Argentina	No	Yes MLI	PPT
4	Armenia	No	Yes MLI	PPT
5	Aruba	No	No	
6	Australia	Yes MLI		PPT
7	Austria	Yes MLI		PPT
8	Azerbaijan*	No	No	PPT
9	Bahrain	No	Yes MLI	PPT
10	Bangladesh*	No	No	PPT

[125] For its agreements listed under the MLI, Netherlands is implementing the preamble statement (Article 6 of the MLI) and the PPT (Article 7 of the MLI). Netherlands' agreements with Aruba, Curaçao and Sint Maarten* are not listed under the MLI as they are arrangements governed by the domestic law of the Kingdom of Netherlands.

11	Barbados	Yes MLI		PPT
12	Belarus	No	No	PPT
13	Belgium	No	No	
14	Bosnia-Herzegovina	Yes MLI		PPT
15	Brazil	No	No	
16	Bulgaria	No	Yes other	PPT
17	Canada	Yes MLI		PPT
18	China (People's Republic of)	No	Yes MLI	PPT
19	Croatia	No	Yes M:LI	PPT
20	Curaçao	No	No	
21	Czech Republic	Yes MLI		PPT
22	Denmark	Yes other		PPT
23	Egypt	Yes MLI		PPT
24	Estonia	No	Yes MLI	PPT
25	Ethiopia*	No	No	PPT
26	Finland	Yes MLI		PPT
27	France	Yes MLI		PPT
28	Georgia	Yes MLI		PPT
29	Germany	No	Yes other	PPT
30	Ghana*	Yes other		PPT
31	Greece	No	Yes MLI	PPT
32	Hong Kong (China)	No	Yes MLI	PPT
33	Hungary	No	Yes MLI	PPT
34	Iceland	Yes MLI		PPT
35	India	Yes MLI		PPT
36	Indonesia	Yes MLI		PPT
37	Ireland	Yes other		PPT
38	Israel	Yes MLI		PPT
39	Italy	No	Yes MLI	PPT
40	Japan	Yes MLI		PPT+LOB
41	Jordan	Yes MLI		PPT
42	Kazakhstan	Yes MLI		PPT
43	Korea	Yes MLI		PPT
44	Kuwait*	No	No	PPT
45	Latvia	Yes MLI		PPT
46	Liechtenstein	Yes other		PPT
47	Lithuania	Yes MLI		PPT
48	Luxembourg	Yes MLI		PPT
49	Malaysia	No	Yes MLI	PPT
50	Malta	Yes MLI		PPT
51	Mexico	No	Yes MLI	PPT
52	Moldova*	No	No	PPT
53	Montenegro	No	No	PPT
54	Morocco	No	Yes MLI	PPT
55	New Zealand	Yes MLI		PPT
56	Nigeria	No	Yes MLI	PPT
57	North Macedonia	No	Yes MLI	PPT
58	Norway	Yes MLI		PPT
59	Oman	Yes MLI		PPT
60	Pakistan	Yes MLI		PPT
61	Panama	Yes MLI		PPT
62	Philippines*	No	No	PPT
63	Poland	No	Yes other	PPT

64	Portugal	Yes MLI		PPT
65	Qatar	Yes MLI		PPT
66	Romania	No	Yes MLI	PPT
67	Russian Federation	Yes MLI		PPT
68	Saudi Arabia	Yes MLI		PPT
69	Serbia	Yes MLI		PPT
70	Singapore	Yes MLI		PPT
71	Sint Maarten*	No	No	
72	Slovak Republic	Yes MLI		PPT
73	Slovenia	Yes MLI		PPT
74	South Africa	No	Yes MLI	PPT
75	Spain	No	No	
76	Sri Lanka	No	No	PPT
77	Suriname*	No	No	PPT
78	Sweden	No	Yes MLI	PPT
79	Switzerland	Yes other		PPT
80	Tajikistan*	No	No	PPT
81	Thailand	No	No	PPT
82	Tunisia	No	Yes MLI	PPT
83	Turkey	No	Yes MLI	PPT
84	Uganda*	No		PPT
85	Ukraine		Yes other	PPT
86	United Arab Emirates	Yes MLI		PPT
87	United Kingdom	Yes MLI		PPT
88	United States	No	No	PPT
89	Uzbekistan*	Yes other		PPT
90	Venezuela*	No	No	PPT
91	Viet Nam	No	No	PPT
92	Zambia	No	No	PPT
93	Zimbabwe*	No	No	PPT

Other agreements

	1.Treaty partners	2. Inclusive Framework member
1	Chinese Taipei*	No

New Zealand

A. Progress in the implementation of the minimum standard

New Zealand has 40 tax agreements in force, as reported in its response to the Peer Review questionnaire. Twenty-one of those agreements comply with the minimum standard.

New Zealand signed the MLI in 2017 and deposited its instrument of ratification on the 27 June 2018, listing its non-compliant agreements. The MLI entered into force for New Zealand on 1 October 2018. The agreements modified by the MLI come into compliance with the minimum standard once the provisions of the MLI take effect.

New Zealand has signed a bilateral complying instrument with respect to its agreement with Switzerland.

New Zealand indicated in its response to the Peer Review questionnaire that steps have been taken (other than under the MLI) to implement the minimum standard in its agreements with Austria, Germany and Norway.

New Zealand is implementing the minimum standard through the inclusion of the preamble statement and the PPT.[126]

B. Conclusion

No jurisdiction has raised any concerns about their agreements with New Zealand.

Summary of the jurisdiction response – New Zealand

	1.Treaty partners	2. Compliance with the standard	3. Signature of a complying instrument	4. Minimum standard provision used
1	Australia	Yes MLI		PPT
2	Austria	No	No	PPT
3	Belgium	Yes MLI		PPT
4	Canada	Yes MLI		PPT
5	Chile	No	Yes MLI	PPT
6	China (People's Republic of)	Yes other		PPT
7	Czech Republic	Yes MLI		PPT
8	Denmark	Yes MLI		PPT
9	Fiji*	No	Yes MLI	PPT
10	Finland	Yes MLI		PPT
11	France	Yes MLI		PPT
12	Germany	No	No	PPT
13	Hong Kong (China)	No	Yes MLI	PPT
14	India	Yes MLI		PPT
15	Indonesia	Yes MLI		PPT
16	Ireland	Yes MLI		PPT
17	Italy	No	Yes MLI	PPT

[126] For its agreements listed under the MLI, New Zealand is implementing the preamble statement (Article 6 of the MLI) and the PPT (Article 7 of the MLI).

18	Japan	Yes MLI		PPT + LOB
19	Korea	Yes MLI		PPT
20	Malaysia	No	Yes MLI	PPT
21	Mexico	No	Yes MLI	PPT
22	Netherlands	Yes MLI		PPT
23	Norway	No	No	PPT
24	Papua New Guinea	No	Yes MLI	PPT
25	Philippines*	No	No	PPT
26	Poland	Yes MLI		PPT
27	Russian Federation	Yes MLI		PPT
28	Samoa	Yes other		PPT
29	Singapore	Yes MLI		PPT
30	South Africa	No	Yes MLI	PPT
31	Spain	No	Yes MLI	PPT
32	Sweden	No	Yes MLI	PPT
33	Switzerland	Yes other		PPT
34	Thailand	No	No	PPT
35	Turkey	No	Yes MLI	PPT
36	United Arab Emirates	Yes MLI		PPT
37	United Kingdom	Yes MLI		PPT
38	United States	No	No	D-LOB
39	Viet Nam	No	No	PPT

Other agreements

	1.Treaty partners	2. Inclusive Framework member
1	Chinese Taipei*	No

Nigeria

A. Progress in the implementation of the minimum standard

Nigeria has 15 tax agreements in force, as reported in its response to the Peer Review questionnaire. None of those agreements comply with the minimum standard.

Nigeria signed the MLI in 2017 and listed its non-compliant agreements. The agreements that will be modified by the MLI will come into compliance with the minimum standard once the provisions of the MLI take effect.

Nigeria is implementing the minimum standard through the inclusion of the preamble statement and the PPT.[127]

B. Conclusion

Recommendation

It is recommended that Nigeria completes the steps to have the MLI take effect with respect to its agreements listed under the MLI as those agreements will only be modified by the MLI (and come into compliance with the minimum standard) once the provisions of the MLI take effect.

Summary of the jurisdiction response - Nigeria

	1.Treaty partners	2. Compliance with the standard	3. Signature of a complying instrument	4. Minimum standard provision used
1	Belgium	No	Yes MLI	PPT
2	Canada	No	Yes MLI	PPT
3	China (People's Republic of)	No	Yes MLI	PPT
4	Czech Republic	No	Yes MLI	PPT
5	France	No	Yes MLI	PPT
6	Netherlands	No	Yes MLI	PPT
7	Pakistan	No	Yes MLI	PPT
8	Philippines*	No	No	PPT
9	Romania	No	Yes MLI	PPT
10	Singapore	No	Yes MLI	PPT
11	Slovak Republic	No	Yes MLI	PPT
12	South Africa	No	Yes MLI	PPT
13	Spain	No	Yes MLI	PPT
14	Sweden	No	Yes MLI	PPT
15	United Kingdom	No	Yes MLI	PPT

[127] For its agreements listed under the MLI, Nigeria is implementing the preamble statement (Article 6 of the MLI) and the PPT (Article 7 of the MLI).

North Macedonia

A. Progress in the implementation of the minimum standard

The Republic of North Macedonia has 48 tax agreements in force, as reported in its response to the Peer Review questionnaire. None of those agreements comply with the minimum standard.

The Republic of North Macedonia signed the MLI in 2020. The agreements that will be modified by the MLI will come into compliance with the minimum standard once the provisions of the MLI take effect.

The Republic of North Macedonia has not listed its agreement with Switzerland under the MLI but has signed a bilateral complying instrument with respect to that agreement.

The Republic of North Macedonia is implementing the minimum standard through the inclusion of the preamble statement and the PPT.[128]

B. Conclusion

Recommendation

It is recommended that the Republic of North Macedonia completes the steps to have the MLI take effect with respect to its agreements listed under the MLI as those agreements will only be modified by the MLI (and come into compliance with the minimum standard) once the provisions of the MLI take effect.

Summary of the jurisdiction response – North Macedonia

	1.Treaty partners	2. Compliance with the standard	3. Signature of a complying instrument	4. Minimum standard provision used
1	Albania	No	Yes MLI	PPT
2	Austria	No	No	PPT
3	Azerbaijan*	No	No	PPT
4	Belarus	No	No	PPT
5	Belgium	No	Yes MLI	PPT
6	Bosnia-Herzegovina	No	Yes MLI	PPT
7	Bulgaria	No	Yes MLI	PPT
8	China (People's Republic of)	No	Yes MLI	PPT
9	Chinese Taipei*	No	No	PPT
10	Croatia	No	Yes MLI	PPT
11	Czech Republic	No	No	PPT
12	Denmark	No	Yes MLI	PPT
13	Estonia	No	Yes MLI	PPT
14	Finland	No	Yes MLI	PPT

[128] For its agreements listed under the MLI, the Republic of North Macedonia is implementing the preamble statement (Article 6 of the MLI) and the PPT (Article 7 of the MLI).

15	France	No	Yes MLI	PPT
16	Germany	No	No	PPT
17	Hungary	No	Yes MLI	PPT
18	India	No	Yes MLI	PPT
19	Iran*	No	No	PPT
20	Ireland	No	Yes MLI	PPT
21	Israel	No	Yes MLI	PPT
22	Italy	No	No	PPT
23	Kazakhstan	No	Yes MLI	PPT
24	Kosovo*	No	No	PPT
25	Kuwait*	No	No	PPT
26	Latvia	No	Yes MLI	PPT
27	Lithuania	No	Yes MLI	PPT
28	Luxembourg	No	Yes MLI	PPT
29	Moldova*	No	No	PPT
30	Montenegro	No	No	PPT
31	Morocco	No	Yes MLI	PPT
32	Netherlands	No	Yes MLI	PPT
33	Norway	No	No	PPT
34	Poland	No	Yes MLI	PPT
35	Qatar	No	Yes MLI	PPT
36	Romania	No	Yes MLI	PPT
37	Russian Federation	No	No	PPT
38	Saudi Arabia	No	Yes MLI	PPT
39	Serbia	No	Yes MLI	PPT
40	Slovak Republic	No	Yes MLI	PPT
41	Slovenia	No	Yes MLI	PPT
42	Spain	No	Yes MLI	PPT
43	Sweden	No	Yes MLI	PPT
44	Switzerland	No	Yes other	PPT
45	Turkey	No	Yes MLI	PPT
46	Ukraine	No	Yes MLI	PPT
47	United Arab Emirates	No	Yes MLI	PPT
48	United Kingdom	No	Yes MLI	PPT

Norway

A. Progress in the implementation of the minimum standard

Norway has 85 tax agreements in force, as reported in its response to the Peer Review questionnaire, including the multilateral Nordic Convention concluded with Denmark, the Faroe Islands, Finland, Iceland and Sweden (the "Nordic Convention").[129] Twenty-one of those agreements, including the Nordic Convention, comply with the minimum standard.

Norway signed the MLI in 2017 and deposited its instrument of ratification on the 17 July 2019, listing 28 of its agreements in force. The MLI entered into force for Norway on 1 November 2019. The agreements modified by the MLI come into compliance with the minimum standard once the provisions of the MLI take effect.

Norway has not listed its agreements with Albania, Austria, Barbados, Belgium, Benin, Bosnia-Herzegovina, Brazil, Canada, Côte d'Ivoire, Croatia, Curaçao, Egypt, France, Germany, Greenland, Hungary, Indonesia, Israel, Italy, Jamaica, Kazakhstan, Kenya, Korea, Malaysia, Montenegro, Morocco, New Zealand, North Macedonia, Pakistan, Qatar, Senegal, Sierra Leone, Singapore, the Slovak Republic, Spain, Sri Lanka, Switzerland, Thailand, Tunisia, Ukraine, Viet Nam and Zambia to be covered under the MLI. These agreements will therefore not, at this stage, be modified by the MLI. Albania, Barbados, Bosnia-Herzegovina, Canada, Côte d'Ivoire, Croatia, Curaçao, Egypt, France, Hungary, Indonesia, Israel, Italy, Jamaica, Kazakhstan, Kenya, Korea, Malaysia, Morocco, New Zealand, North Macedonia, Pakistan, Senegal, Singapore, the Slovak Republic, Tunisia and Ukraine have listed their agreements with Norway under the MLI.

Norway has signed a bilateral complying instrument with respect to its agreement with Ghana*.

Norway indicated in its response to the Peer Review questionnaire that steps have been taken (other than under the MLI) to implement the minimum standard in its agreements with Austria, Belgium[130], Brazil, Canada, France, Germany, Israel, Italy, Korea, Malaysia, New Zealand, and Pakistan.

Norway indicated in its response to the Peer Review questionnaire that the agreements with Azerbaijan*, Bangladesh*, Gambia*, Malawi*, Nepal*, Uganda*, Venezuela*, and Zimbabwe* do not give rise to material treaty-shopping concerns for Norway.

Norway is implementing the minimum standard through the inclusion of the preamble statement and the PPT.[131]

---

[129] See the Multilateral convention concluded by Denmark, Finland, the Faroe Islands, Iceland, Norway and Sweden: for the avoidance of double taxation with respect to taxes on income and on capital (1996, 1997, 2008 and 2018). In total, Norway identified 89 "agreements" in its List of Tax agreements: 84 bilateral agreements and the Nordic Convention concluded with five of its treaty partners.

[130] A complying instrument was signed with respect to the agreement with Belgium on 8 September 2021.

[131] For its agreements listed under the MLI, Norway is implementing the preamble statement (Article 6 of the MLI) and the PPT (Article 7 of the MLI). Under Article 7(7)(a) of the MLI, Norway is also implementing the simplified LOB (Article 7(8 to 13) of the MLI) in agreements concluded with treaty partners that adopted the simplified LOB. Norway expressed a statement, in accordance with Article 7(17)(a) of the MLI, that while it accepts the application of PPT alone as an interim measure, it intends where possible to adopt an LOB provision in addition to or in replacement of the PPT through bilateral negotiation.

B. Conclusion

Albania, Barbados, Bosnia-Herzegovina, Canada, Côte d'Ivoire, Croatia, Curaçao, Egypt, France, Hungary, Indonesia, Israel, Italy, Jamaica, Kazakhstan, Kenya, Korea, Malaysia, Morocco, New Zealand, North Macedonia, Pakistan, Senegal, Singapore, the Slovak Republic, Tunisia and Ukraine have listed their agreements with Norway under the MLI, which amount to requests to implement the minimum standard.

Norway has developed a plan for the implementation of the minimum standard in its agreements with Albania, Barbados, Benin, Bosnia-Herzegovina, Côte d'Ivoire, Croatia, Curaçao, Egypt, Greenland, Hungary, Indonesia, Jamaica, Kazakhstan, Kenya, Montenegro, Morocco, the Republic of North Macedonia, Qatar, Senegal, Sierra Leone, Sri Lanka, Tunisia, Ukraine, Viet Nam and Zambia. Norway indicated in its response to the Peer Review questionnaire that bilateral discussions would be pursued with respect to those agreements.

Summary of the jurisdiction response - Norway

	1.Treaty partners	2. Compliance with the standard	3. Signature of a complying instrument	4. Minimum standard provision used
1	Argentina	No	Yes MLI	PPT-LOB
2	Australia	Yes MLI		PPT
3	Austria	No	No	
4	Belgium	No	No	PPT
5	Brazil	No	No	PPT+LOB
6	Bulgaria	No	Yes MLI	PPT
7	Canada	No	No	
8	Chile	No	Yes MLI	PPT+LOB
9	China (People's Republic of)	No	Yes MLI	
10	Cyprus*	Yes MLI		PPT
11	Czech Republic	Yes MLI		PPT
12	Denmark	Yes other		PPT
13	Estonia	No	Yes MLI	PPT
14	Faroe Islands	Yes other		PPT
15	Finland	Yes other		PPT
16	France	No	No	
17	Georgia	Yes MLI		PPT
18	Germany	No	No	
19	Ghana	No	Yes other	PPT+LOB
20	Greece	No	Yes MLI	PPT
21	Iceland	Yes other		PPT
22	India	Yes MLI		PPT+LOB
23	Ireland	Yes MLI		PPT
24	Israel	No	No	
25	Italy	No	No	
26	Japan	Yes MLI		PPT
27	Korea	No	No	
28	Latvia	Yes MLI		PPT
29	Lithuania	Yes MLI		PPT
30	Luxembourg	Yes MLI		PPT
31	Malaysia	No	No	
32	Malta	Yes MLI		PPT
33	Mexico	No	Yes MLI	PPT+LOB

34	Netherlands	Yes MLI		PPT
35	New Zealand	No	No	
36	Pakistan	No	No	
37	Poland	Yes MLI		PPT
38	Portugal	Yes MLI		PPT
39	Romania	No	Yes MLI	PPT
40	Russian Federation	Yes MLI		PPT
41	Serbia	Yes MLI		PPT
42	Singapore	No	No	
43	Slovak Republic	No	No	
44	Slovenia	Yes MLI		PPT
45	South Africa	No	Yes MLI	PPT
46	Spain	No	No	
47	Sweden	Yes other		PPT
48	Switzerland	Yes other		PPT
49	Thailand	No	No	
50	Trinidad and Tobago	No	No	D-LOB
51	Turkey	No	Yes MLI	PPT
52	United Kingdom	Yes MLI		PPT
53	United States	No	No	

Other agreements

	1.Treaty partners	2. Inclusive Framework member
1	Albania	Yes
2	Azerbaijan*	No
3	Bangladesh*	No
4	Barbados	Yes
5	Benin	Yes
6	Bosnia-Herzegovina	Yes
7	Côte d'Ivoire	Yes
8	Croatia	Yes
9	Curaçao	Yes
10	Egypt	Yes
11	Gambia*	No
12	Greenland	Yes
13	Hungary	Yes
14	Indonesia	Yes
15	Jamaica	Yes
16	Kazakhstan	Yes
17	Kenya	Yes
18	Malawi*	No
19	Montenegro	Yes
20	Morocco	Yes
21	Nepal*	No
22	North Macedonia	Yes
23	Philippines*	No
24	Qatar	Yes
25	Senegal	Yes
26	Sierra Leone	Yes
27	Sint Maarten*	No
28	Sri Lanka	Yes

29	Tanzania*	No
30	Tunisia	Yes
31	Uganda*	No
32	Ukraine	Yes
33	Venezuela*	No
34	Viet Nam	Yes
35	Zambia	Yes
36	Zimbabwe*	No

Oman

A. Progress in the implementation of the minimum standard

Oman has 35 tax agreements in force, as reported in its response to the Peer Review questionnaire. Nine of those agreements comply with the minimum standard.

Oman signed the MLI in 2019 and deposited its instrument of ratification on the 7 July 2020. The MLI entered into force for Oman on 1 November 2020. The agreements that will be modified by the MLI will come into compliance with the minimum standard once the provisions of the MLI take effect.

Oman has not listed its agreement with India under the MLI but indicated that steps have been taken (other than under the MLI) to implement the minimum standard in that agreement. India has listed its agreement with Oman under the MLI.

Oman is implementing the minimum standard through the inclusion of the preamble statement and the PPT.[132]

B. Conclusion

No jurisdiction has raised any concerns about their agreements with Oman.

India has listed its agreement with Oman under the MLI, which amounts to a request to implement the minimum standard.

Summary of the jurisdiction response - Oman

	1.Treaty partners	2. Compliance with the standard	3. Signature of a complying instrument	4. Minimum standard provision used
1	Algeria*	No	No	PPT
2	Belarus	No	No	PPT
3	Brunei Darussalam	No	No	PPT
4	Canada	Yes MLI		PPT
5	China (People's Republic of)	No	Yes MLI	
6	Croatia	No	Yes MLI	PPT
7	France	Yes MLI		
8	Hungary	No	Yes MLI	
9	India	No	No	
10	Iran*	No	No	
11	Italy	No	No	
12	Japan	Yes MLI		PPT
13	Korea	Yes MLI		PPT
14	Lebanon*	No	No	PPT
15	Mauritius	Yes MLI		
16	Moldova*	No	No	PPT
17	Morocco	No	Yes MLI	

[132] For its agreements listed under the MLI, Oman is implementing the preamble statement (Article 6 of the MLI) and the PPT (Article 7 of the MLI).

18	Netherlands	Yes MLI		
19	Pakistan	No	Yes MLI	
20	Portugal	Yes MLI		PPT
21	Seychelles	No	Yes MLI	PPT
22	Singapore	Yes MLI		PPT
23	Sri Lanka	No	No	PPT
24	South Africa	No	Yes MLI	PPT
25	Spain	No	Yes MLI	PPT
26	Sudan*	No	No	
27	Switzerland	No	No	
28	Syrian Arab Republic*	No	No	
29	Thailand	No	No	PPT
30	Tunisia	No	Yes MLI	
31	Turkey	No	Yes MLI	
32	United Kingdom	Yes MLI		PPT
33	Uzbekistan*	No	No	PPT
34	Viet Nam	No	No	PPT
35	Yemen*	No	No	PPT

Pakistan

A. Progress in the implementation of the minimum standard

Pakistan has 67 tax agreements in force, as reported in its response to the Peer Review questionnaire. Twenty-nine of those agreements comply with the minimum standard.

Pakistan signed the MLI in 2017 and deposited its instrument of ratification on 18 December 2020, listing its non-compliant agreements. The MLI entered into force for Pakistan on 1 April 2021. The agreements modified by the MLI come into compliance with the minimum standard once the provisions of the MLI take effect.

Pakistan is implementing the minimum standard through the inclusion of the preamble statement and the PPT.[133]

B. Conclusion

No jurisdiction has raised any concerns about their agreements with Pakistan.

Summary of the jurisdiction response - Pakistan

	1.Treaty partners	2. Compliance with the standard	3. Signature of a complying instrument	4. Minimum standard provision used
1	Austria	Yes MLI		PPT
2	Azerbaijan*	No	No	
3	Bahrain	No	Yes MLI	PPT
4	Bangladesh*	No	No	
5	Belarus	No	No	
6	Belgium	Yes MLI		PPT
7	Bosnia-Herzegovina	Yes MLI		PPT
8	Brunei Darussalam	No	No	
9	Bulgaria	Yes other		PPT
10	Canada	Yes MLI		PPT
11	China (People's Republic of)	No	Yes MLI	PPT
12	Czech Republic	Yes MLI		PPT
13	Denmark	Yes MLI		PPT+LOB
14	Egypt	Yes MLI		PPT
15	Finland	Yes MLI		PPT
16	France	Yes MLI		PPT
17	Germany	No	No	
18	Hong Kong (China)	No	Yes MLI	PPT
19	Hungary	No	Yes MLI	PPT
20	Indonesia	No	Yes MLI	PPT
21	Iran*	No	No	
22	Ireland	Yes MLI		PPT
23	Italy	No	Yes MLI	PPT

133 For its agreements listed under the MLI, Pakistan is implementing the preamble statement (Article 6 of the MLI) and the PPT (Article 7 of the MLI).

24	Japan	Yes MLI		PPT
25	Jordan	Yes MLI		PPT
26	Kazakhstan	Yes MLI		PPT + LOB
27	Kuwait*	No	Yes MLI	PPT
28	Kyrgyzstan*	No	No	
29	Lebanon*	No	No	
30	Libya*	No	No	
31	Malaysia	Yes MLI		PPT
32	Malta	Yes MLI		PPT
33	Mauritius	Yes MLI		PPT
34	Morocco	No	Yes MLI	PPT
35	Nepal*	No	No	
36	Netherlands	Yes MLI		PPT
37	Nigeria	No	Yes MLI	PPT
38	Norway	No	No	PPT + LOB
39	Oman	Yes MLI		PPT
40	Philippines*	No	No	
41	Poland	Yes MLI		PPT
42	Portuguese Republic	Yes MLI		PPT
43	Qatar	Yes MLI		PPT
44	Korea	Yes MLI		PPT
45	Romania	No	Yes MLI	PPT
46	Saudi Arabia	Yes MLI		PPT
47	Serbia	Yes MLI		PPT
48	Singapore	Yes MLI		PPT
49	South Africa	No	Yes MLI	PPT
50	Spain	No	Yes MLI	PPT
51	Sri-Lanka	No	No	
52	Sweden	No	Yes MLI	PPT
53	Switzerland	No	No	
54	Syria*	No	No	
55	Tajikistan*	No	No	
56	Thailand	No	No	
57	Tunisia	No	Yes MLI	PPT
58	Turkey	No	Yes MLI	PPT
59	Turkmenistan*	No	No	
60	United Arab Emirates	Yes MLI		PPT
61	United Kingdom	Yes MLI		PPT
62	Ukraine	Yes MLI		PPT
63	United States	No	No	D-LOB
64	Uzbekistan*	No	No	
65	Viet Nam	No	No	
66	Yemen*	No	No	

Panama

A. Progress in the implementation of the minimum standard

Panama has 17 tax agreements in force, as reported in its response to the Peer Review questionnaire. One of those agreements, the agreement with Israel, complies with the minimum standard.

Panama signed the MLI in 2018 and deposited its instrument of ratification on 5 November 2020, listing its non-compliant agreements. The MLI entered into force for Panama on 1 March 2021. The agreements modified by the MLI come into compliance with the minimum standard once the provisions of the MLI take effect.

Panama is implementing the minimum standard through the inclusion of the preamble statement and the PPT.[134]

B. Conclusion

No jurisdiction has raised any concerns about their agreements with Panama.

Summary of the jurisdiction response - Panama

	1.Treaty partners	2. Compliance with the standard	3. Signature of a complying instrument	4. Minimum standard provision used
1	Barbados	No	Yes MLI	PPT
2	Czech Republic	No	No	PPT
3	France	No	Yes MLI	PPT
4	Ireland	No	Yes MLI	PPT
5	Israel	Yes MLI		PPT
6	Italy	No	No	PPT
7	Korea	No	Yes MLI	PPT
8	Luxembourg	No	Yes MLI	PPT
9	Mexico	No	Yes MLI	
10	Netherlands	No	Yes MLI	PPT
11	Portugal	No	Yes MLI	PPT
12	Qatar	No	Yes MLI	PPT
13	Singapore	No	Yes MLI	PPT
14	Spain	No	Yes MLI	
15	United Arab Emirates	No	Yes MLI	PPT
16	United Kingdom	No	Yes MLI	PPT
17	Viet Nam	No	No	

[134] For its agreements listed under the MLI, Panama is implementing the preamble statement (Article 6 of the MLI) and the PPT (Article 7 of the MLI).

Papua New Guinea

A. Progress in the implementation of the minimum standard

Papua New Guinea has ten tax agreements in force, as reported in its response to the Peer Review questionnaire. None of those agreements comply with the minimum standard.

Papua New Guinea signed the MLI in 2019 and listed its non-compliant agreements. The agreements modified by the MLI come into compliance with the minimum standard once the provisions of the MLI take effect.

Papua New Guinea is implementing the minimum standard through the inclusion of the preamble statement and the PPT.[135]

B. Conclusion

Recommendation

It is recommended that Papua New Guinea completes the steps to have the MLI take effect with respect to its agreements listed under the MLI as those agreements will only be modified by the MLI (and come into compliance with the minimum standard) once the provisions of the MLI take effect.

Summary of the jurisdiction response - Papua New Guinea

	1.Treaty partners	2. Compliance with the standard	3. Signature of a complying instrument	4. Minimum standard provision used
1	Australia	No	Yes MLI	PPT
2	Canada	No	Yes MLI	PPT
3	China (People's Republic of)	No	Yes MLI	PPT
4	Fiji*	No	Yes MLI	PPT
5	Indonesia	No	No	PPT
6	Korea	No	Yes MLI	PPT
7	Malaysia	No	Yes MLI	PPT
8	New Zealand	No	Yes MLI	PPT
9	Singapore	No	Yes MLI	PPT
10	United Kingdom	No	Yes MLI	PPT

[135] For its agreements listed under the MLI, Papua New Guinea is implementing the preamble statement (Article 6 of the MLI) and the PPT (Article 7 of the MLI).

Paraguay

A. Progress in the implementation of the minimum standard

Paraguay has five tax agreements in force, as reported in its response to the Peer Review questionnaire. One of those agreements, the agreement with Uruguay, complies with the minimum standard.

Paraguay has not signed the MLI.

Paraguay indicated in its response to the Peer Review questionnaire that steps have been taken (other than under the MLI) to implement the minimum standard in its agreement with Chile.

Paraguay is implementing the minimum standard through the inclusion of the preamble statement and the PPT combined with the LOB.

B. Conclusion

Paraguay is currently developing a plan, in consultation with the Secretariat, for the implementation of the minimum standard in its agreements with Qatar and the United Arab Emirates.

Summary of the jurisdiction response - Paraguay

	1.Treaty partners	2. Compliance with the standard	3. Signature of a complying instrument	4. Minimum standard provision used
1	Chile	No	No	PPT + LOB
2	Uruguay	Yes other		PPT + LOB

Other agreements

	1.Treaty partners	2. Inclusive Framework member
1	Chinese Taipei*	No
2	Qatar	Yes
3	United Arab Emirates	Yes

Peru

A. Progress in the implementation of the minimum standard

Peru has nine tax agreements in force, as reported in its response to the Peer Review questionnaire, including the Decision 578 of the Andean Community Commission (Decision 578) for the members of the Andean Community (the Andean Community Agreement).[136] One of those agreements, the agreement with Japan, complies with the minimum standard.

Peru signed the MLI in 2018 and listed its non-compliant bilateral agreements. The agreements modified by the MLI come into compliance with the minimum standard once the provisions of the MLI take effect.

Peru indicated in its response to the Peer Review questionnaire that it is currently renegotiating the Andean Community Agreement to implement the minimum standard. Peru further indicated that steps had been taken (other than under the MLI) to implement the minimum standard in its agreements with Brazil and Switzerland.

Peru is implementing the minimum standard through the inclusion of the preamble statement and the PPT.[137]

B. Conclusion

Recommendation

It is recommended that Peru completes the steps to have the MLI take effect with respect to its agreements listed under the MLI as those agreements will only be modified by the MLI (and come into compliance with the minimum standard) once the provisions of the MLI take effect.

Summary of the jurisdiction response – Peru

	1.Treaty partners	2. Compliance with the standard	3. Signature of a complying instrument	4. Minimum standard provision used
1	Bolivia*	No	No	
2	Brazil	No	No	
3	Canada	No	Yes MLI	PPT
4	Chile	No	Yes MLI	PPT
5	Colombia	No	No	

136 The Decision of the Commission of the Andean Community 578 on the regime for the avoidance of double taxation and the prevention of fiscal evasion, adopted on 4 May 2004. The current members of the Andean Community are Bolivia*, Colombia, Ecuador* and Peru. In total, Peru identified eleven "agreements" in its List of Tax agreements: eight bilateral agreements and the Andean Community Agreement.

137 For its agreements listed under the MLI, Peru is implementing the preamble statement (Article 6 of the MLI) and the PPT (Article 7 of the MLI). Peru expressed a statement, in accordance with Article 7(17)(a) of the MLI, that while it accepts the application of the PPT under the MLI, it intends where possible to adopt an LOB provision through bilateral negotiation.

6	Ecuador*	No	No	
7	Japan	Yes other		PPT
8	Korea	No	Yes MLI	PPT
9	Mexico	No	Yes MLI	PPT
10	Portugal	No	Yes MLI	PPT
11	Switzerland	No	No	

Poland

A. Progress in the implementation of the minimum standard

Poland has 82 tax agreements in force, as reported in its response to the Peer Review questionnaire. Thirty-eight of those agreements comply with the minimum standard.

Poland signed the MLI in 2017 and deposited its instrument of ratification of the MLI on 23 January 2018. The MLI entered into force for Poland on 1 July 2018. The agreements modified by the MLI come into compliance with the minimum standard once the provisions of the MLI take effect.

Poland has signed a bilateral complying instrument with respect to its agreement with Netherlands.

Poland has not listed its agreements with Georgia, Germany, Montenegro, Switzerland and the United States under the MLI, but indicated in its response to the Peer Review questionnaire that steps had been taken (other than under the MLI) to implement the minimum standard in each of these agreements.

Poland is implementing the minimum standard through the inclusion of the preamble statement and the PPT.[138]

B. Conclusion

No jurisdiction has raised any concerns about their agreements with Poland.

Summary of the jurisdiction response - Poland

	1. Treaty partners	2. Compliance with the standard	3. Signature of a complying instrument	4. Minimum standard provision used
1	Albania	Yes MLI		PPT
2	Armenia	No	Yes MLI	PPT
3	Australia	Yes MLI		PPT
4	Austria	Yes MLI		PPT
5	Azerbaijan*	No	No	PPT
6	Bangladesh*	No	No	PPT
7	Belarus	No	No	PPT
8	Belgium	Yes MLI		PPT
9	Bosnia-Herzegovina	Yes MLI		PPT
10	Bulgaria	No	Yes MLI	PPT
11	Canada	Yes MLI		PPT
12	Chile	No	Yes MLI	PPT
13	China (People's Republic of)	No	Yes MLI	PPT
14	Croatia	No	Yes MLI	PPT
15	Cyprus*	Yes MLI		PPT
16	Czech Republic	Yes MLI		PPT
17	Denmark	Yes MLI		PPT
18	Egypt	Yes MLI		PPT

138 For its agreements listed under the MLI, Poland is implementing the preamble statement (Article 6 of the MLI) and the PPT (Article 7 of the MLI). Poland expressed a statement that while it accepts the application of the PPT under the MLI, it intends where possible to adopt an LOB provision through bilateral negotiation.

19	Estonia	No	Yes MLI	PPT
20	Ethiopia*	No	No	PPT
21	Finland	Yes MLI		PPT
22	France	Yes MLI		PPT
23	Georgia	No	No	
24	Germany	No	No	
25	Greece	No	Yes MLI	PPT
26	Hungary	No	Yes MLI	PPT
27	Iceland	Yes MLI		PPT
28	India	Yes MLI		PPT
29	Indonesia	Yes MLI		PPT
30	Iran*	No	No	PPT
31	Ireland	Yes MLI		PPT
32	Israel	Yes MLI		PPT
33	Italy	No	Yes MLI	PPT
34	Japan	Yes MLI		PPT
35	Jordan	Yes MLI		PPT
36	Kazakhstan	Yes MLI		PPT
37	Korea	Yes MLI		PPT
38	Kuwait*	No	No	PPT
39	Kyrgyzstan*	No	No	PPT
40	Latvia	Yes MLI		PPT
41	Lebanon*	No	No	PPT
42	Lithuania	Yes MLI		PPT
43	Luxembourg	Yes MLI		PPT
44	Malaysia	No	Yes MLI	PPT
45	Malta	Yes MLI		PPT
46	Mexico	No	Yes MLI	PPT
47	Moldova*	No	No	PPT
48	Mongolia	No	No	PPT
49	Montenegro	No	No	
50	Morocco	No	Yes MLI	PPT
51	Netherlands	No	Yes other	PPT
52	New Zealand	Yes MLI		PPT
53	North Macedonia	No	Yes MLI	PPT
54	Norway	Yes MLI		PPT
55	Pakistan	No	Yes MLI	PPT
56	Philippines*	No	No	PPT
57	Portugal	Yes MLI		PPT
58	Qatar	Yes MLI		PPT
59	Romania	No	Yes MLI	PPT
60	Russian Federation	Yes MLI		PPT
61	Saudi Arabia	Yes MLI		PPT
62	Serbia	Yes MLI		PPT
63	Singapore	Yes MLI		PPT
64	Slovak Republic	Yes MLI		PPT
65	Slovenia	Yes MLI		PPT
66	South Africa	No	Yes MLI	PPT
67	Spain	No	Yes MLI	PPT
68	Sri Lanka	No	No	PPT
69	Sweden	No	Yes MLI	PPT
70	Switzerland	No	No	
71	Syrian Arab Republic*	No	No	PPT

72	Tajikistan*	No	No	PPT
73	Thailand	No	No	PPT
74	Tunisia	No	Yes MLI	PPT
75	Turkey	No	Yes MLI	PPT
76	Ukraine	Yes MLI		PPT
77	United Arab Emirates	Yes MLI		PPT
78	United Kingdom	Yes MLI		PPT
79	United States	No	No	
80	Uzbekistan*	No	No	PPT
81	Viet Nam	No	No	PPT
82	Zimbabwe*	No	No	PPT

Portugal

A. Progress in the implementation of the minimum standard

Portugal has 78 tax agreements in force, as reported in its response to the Peer Review questionnaire. Thirty-five of those agreements comply with the minimum standard.

Portugal signed the MLI in 2017 and deposited its instrument of ratification on 28 February 2020, listing its non-compliant agreements. The MLI entered into force for Portugal on 1 June 2020. The agreements modified by the MLI come into compliance with the minimum standard once the provisions of the MLI take effect.

Portugal has signed a bilateral complying instrument with respect to its agreement with Sweden.

Portugal indicated in its response to the Peer Review questionnaire that steps have been taken (other than under the MLI) to implement the minimum standard in its agreements with Brazil, Cabo Verde, Germany, and Mozambique*.

Portugal is implementing the minimum standard through the inclusion of the preamble statement and the PPT.[139]

B. Conclusion

No jurisdiction has raised any concerns about their agreements with Portugal.

Summary of the jurisdiction response - Portugal

	1.Treaty partners	2. Compliance with the standard	3. Signature of a complying instrument	4. Minimum standard provision used
1	Algeria*	No	No	
2	Andorra	No	Yes MLI	PPT
3	Angola	Yes other		PPT
4	Austria	Yes MLI		PPT
5	Bahrain	No	Yes MLI	PPT
6	Barbados	No	Yes MLI	PPT
7	Belgium	Yes MLI		PPT
8	Brazil	No	No	
9	Bulgaria	No	Yes MLI	PPT
10	Cabo Verde	No	No	
11	Canada	Yes MLI		PPT
12	Chile	No	Yes MLI	PPT
13	China (People's Republic of)	No	Yes MLI	PPT
14	Colombia	No	Yes MLI	PPT
15	Côte d'Ivoire	No	Yes MLI	PPT
16	Croatia	No	Yes MLI	PPT
17	Cuba*	No	No	
18	Cyprus*	Yes MLI		PPT

[139] For its agreements listed under the MLI, Portugal is implementing the preamble statement (Article 6 of the MLI) and the PPT (Article 7 of the MLI).

19	Czech Republic	Yes MLI		PPT
20	Denmark	Yes MLI		PPT
21	Estonia	No	Yes MLI	PPT
22	Ethiopia*	No	No	
23	France	Yes MLI		PPT
24	Georgia	Yes MLI		PPT
25	Germany	No	No	
26	Greece	No	Yes MLI	PPT
27	Guinea-Bissau*	No	No	
28	Hong Kong (China)	No	Yes MLI	PPT
29	Hungary	No	Yes MLI	PPT
30	Iceland	Yes MLI		PPT
31	India	Yes MLI		PPT
32	Indonesia	Yes MLI		PPT
33	Ireland	Yes MLI		PPT
34	Israel	Yes MLI		PPT
35	Italy	No	Yes MLI	PPT
36	Japan	Yes MLI		PPT
37	Korea	Yes MLI		PPT
38	Kuwait*	No	Yes MLI	PPT
39	Latvia	Yes MLI		PPT
40	Lithuania	Yes MLI		PPT
41	Luxembourg	Yes MLI		PPT
42	Macau (China)	No	No	
43	Malta	Yes MLI		PPT
44	Mexico	No	Yes MLI	PPT
45	Moldova*	No	No	
46	Montenegro	No	No	
47	Morocco	No	Yes MLI	PPT
48	Mozambique*	No	No	
49	Netherlands	Yes MLI		PPT
50	Norway	Yes MLI		PPT
51	Oman	Yes MLI		PPT
52	Pakistan	No	Yes MLI	PPT
53	Panama	No	Yes MLI	PPT
54	Peru	No	Yes MLI	PPT
55	Poland	Yes MLI		PPT
56	Qatar	Yes MLI		PPT
57	Romania	No	Yes MLI	PPT
58	Russian Federation	Yes MLI		PPT
59	San Marino	Yes MLI		PPT
60	Sao Tome and Principe*	No	No	
61	Saudi Arabia	Yes MLI		PPT
62	Senegal	No	Yes MLI	PPT
63	Singapore	Yes MLI		PPT
64	Slovak Republic	Yes MLI		PPT
65	Slovenia	Yes MLI		PPT
66	South Africa	No	Yes MLI	PPT
67	Spain	No	Yes MLI	PPT
68	Sweden	No	Yes other	PPT
69	Switzerland	No	Yes MLI	PPT
70	Tunisia	No	Yes MLI	PPT
71	Turkey	No	Yes MLI	PPT

72	Ukraine	Yes MLI		PPT
73	United Arab Emirates	Yes MLI		PPT
74	United Kingdom	Yes MLI		PPT
75	United States	No	No	
76	Uruguay	Yes MLI		PPT
77	Venezuela*	No	No	
78	Viet Nam	No	No	

Qatar

A. Progress in the implementation of the minimum standard

Qatar has 78 tax agreements in force, as reported in its response to the Peer Review questionnaire. Twenty-nine of those agreements comply with the minimum standard.

Qatar signed the MLI in 2018 and deposited its instrument of ratification on 23 December 2019. The MLI entered into force for Qatar on April 1 2020. On 25 November 2021, Qatar made an additional notification to expand its list of agreements to be covered under the MLI. Qatar has not listed its agreements with Argentina, Austria, Guernsey, Norway, Switzerland and Ukraine. These agreements will therefore not, at this stage, be modified by the MLI. The agreements modified by the MLI come into compliance with the minimum standard once the provisions of the MLI take effect.

Qatar has signed a bilateral complying instrument with Bermuda.

Qatar indicated in its response to the Peer Review questionnaire that steps had been taken (other than under the MLI) to implement the minimum standard in the agreements with Austria, Guernsey, Kazakhstan, Switzerland and Ukraine.

Qatar is implementing the minimum standard through the inclusion of the preamble statement and the PPT.[140]

B. Conclusion

Qatar gave effect to its plan to implement the minimum standard in its agreements with Tunisia by making a notification on 25 November 2021 to expand its list of agreements to be covered under the MLI to include that agreement.

Qatar has developed a plan for the implementation of the minimum standard in its agreements with Argentina and Norway. Qatar indicated in its response to the Peer Review questionnaire that it intends to contact these jurisdictions to suggest a draft protocol to implement the minimum standard.

Summary of the jurisdiction response - Qatar

	1.Treaty partners	2. Compliance with the standard	3. Signature of a complying instrument	4. Minimum standard provision used
1	Albania	Yes MLI		PPT
2	Algeria*	No	No	PPT
3	Armenia	No	Yes MLI	PPT
4	Austria	No	No	PPT
5	Azerbaijan*	No	No	PPT
6	Barbados	Yes MLI		PPT
7	Belarus	No	No	PPT
8	Bermuda	Yes other		PPT
9	Bosnia-Herzegovina	Yes MLI		PPT
10	Bulgaria	No	Yes MLI	PPT

140 For its agreements listed under the MLI, Qatar is implementing the preamble statement (Article 6 of the MLI) and the PPT (Article 7 of the MLI).

11	Brunei Darussalam	No	No	PPT
12	Chad*	No	No	PPT
13	China (People's Republic of)	No	Yes MLI	PPT
14	Croatia	No	Yes MLI	PPT
15	Cuba*	No	No	PPT
16	Cyprus*	Yes MLI		PPT
17	Ecuador*	No	No	PPT
18	Fiji*	No	Yes MLI	PPT
19	France	Yes MLI		PPT
20	Georgia	No	No	PPT
21	Greece	No	Yes MLI	PPT
22	Guernsey	No	No	PPT
23	Hong Kong (China)	No	Yes MLI	PPT
24	Hungary	No	Yes MLI	PPT
25	India	Yes MLI		PPT
26	Indonesia	Yes MLI		PPT
27	Iran*	No	No	PPT
28	Ireland	Yes MLI		PPT
29	Isle of Man	Yes MLI		PPT
30	Italy	No	Yes MLI	PPT
31	Japan	Yes MLI		PPT
32	Jersey	Yes MLI		PTT
33	Jordan	Yes MLI		PPT
34	Kazakhstan	No	No	PPT
35	Kenya	No	Yes MLI	PPT
36	Korea	Yes MLI		PPT
37	Kyrgyzstan*	No	No	PPT
38	Latvia	Yes MLI		PPT
39	Lebanon*	No	No	PPT
40	Luxembourg	Yes MLI		PPT
41	Malaysia	Yes MLI		PPT
42	Malta	Yes MLI		PPT
43	Mauritius	Yes MLI		PPT
44	Mexico	No	Yes MLI	PPT
45	Monaco	Yes MLI		PPT
46	Morocco	No	Yes MLI	PPT
47	Nepal*	No	No	PPT
48	Netherlands	Yes MLI		PPT
49	Nigeria	No	Yes MLI	PPT
50	North Macedonia	No	Yes MLI	PPT
51	Pakistan	Yes MLI		PPT
52	Panama	No	Yes MLI	PPT
53	Philippines*	No	No	PPT
54	Poland	Yes MLI		PPT
55	Portugal	Yes MLI		PPT
56	Romania	No	Yes MLI	PPT
57	Russian Federation	Yes MLI		PPT
58	San Marino	Yes MLI		PPT
59	Senegal	No	Yes MLI	PPT
60	Serbia	Yes MLI		PPT
61	Seychelles	No	Yes MLI	PPT
62	Singapore	Yes MLI		PPT
63	Slovenia	Yes MLI		PPT

64	South Africa	No	Yes MLI	PPT
65	Spain	No	Yes MLI	PPT
66	Sri Lanka	No	No	PPT
67	Sudan*	No	No	PPT
68	Switzerland	No	No	PPT
69	Syrian Arab Republic*	No	No	PPT
70	Turkey	No	Yes MLI	PPT
71	Ukraine	No	No	PPT
72	United Kingdom	Yes MLI		PPT
73	Venezuela*	No	No	PPT
74	Viet Nam	No	No	PPT
75	Yemen*	No	No	PPT

Other agreements

	1.Treaty partners	2. Inclusive Framework member
1	Argentina	Yes
2	Norway	Yes
3	Tunisia	Yes

Romania

A. Progress in the implementation of the minimum standard

Romania has 88 tax agreements in force, as reported in its response to the Peer Review questionnaire. One of those agreements, the agreement with Spain, complies with the minimum standard.

Romania signed the MLI in 2017, and listed its non-compliant agreements. The agreements modified by the MLI come into compliance with the minimum standard once the provisions of the MLI take effect.

Romania is implementing the minimum standard through the inclusion of the preamble statement and the PPT.[141]

B. Conclusion

Recommendation

It is recommended that Romania completes the steps to have the MLI take effect with respect to its agreements listed under the MLI as those agreements will only be modified by the MLI (and come into compliance with the minimum standard) once the provisions of the MLI take effect.

Summary of the jurisdiction response - Romania

	1.Treaty partners	2. Compliance with the standard	3. Signature of a complying instrument	4. Minimum standard provision used
1	Albania	No	Yes MLI	PPT
2	Algeria*	No	No	PPT
3	Armenia	No	Yes MLI	PPT
4	Australia	No	Yes MLI	PPT
5	Austria	No	Yes MLI	PPT
6	Azerbaijan*	No	No	PPT
7	Bangladesh*	No	No	PPT
8	Belarus	No	No	PPT
9	Belgium	No	Yes MLI	PPT
10	Bosnia-Herzegovina	No	Yes MLI	PPT
11	Bulgaria	No	Yes MLI	PPT
12	Canada	No	Yes MLI	PPT
13	China (People's Republic of)	No	Yes MLI	PPT
14	Croatia	No	Yes MLI	PPT
15	Cyprus*	No	Yes MLI	PPT
16	Czech Republic	No	Yes MLI	PPT
17	Democratic People's Republic of Korea*	No	No	PPT

141 For its agreements listed under the MLI, Romania is implementing the preamble statement (Article 6 of the MLI) and the PPT (Article 7 of the MLI).

18	Denmark	No	Yes MLI	PPT
19	Ecuador*	No	No	PPT
20	Egypt	No	Yes MLI	PPT
21	Estonia	No	Yes MLI	PPT
22	Ethiopia*	No	No	PPT
23	Finland	No	Yes MLI	PPT
24	France	No	Yes MLI	PPT
25	Georgia	No	Yes MLI	PPT
26	Germany	No	Yes MLI	
27	Greece	No	Yes MLI	PPT
28	Hong Kong (China)	No	Yes MLI	PPT
29	Hungary	No	Yes MLI	PPT
30	Iceland	No	Yes MLI	PPT
31	India	No	Yes MLI	PPT
32	Indonesia	No	Yes MLI	PPT
33	Iran*	No	No	PPT
34	Ireland	No	Yes MLI	PPT
35	Israel	No	Yes MLI	PPT
36	Italy	No	Yes MLI	PPT
37	Japan	No	Yes MLI	PPT
38	Jordan	No	Yes MLI	PPT
39	Kazakhstan	No	Yes MLI	PPT
40	Korea	No	Yes MLI	PPT
41	Kuwait*	No	Yes MLI	PPT
42	Latvia	No	Yes MLI	PPT
43	Lebanon*	No	No	PPT
44	Lithuania	No	Yes MLI	PPT
45	Luxembourg	No	Yes MLI	PPT
46	Malaysia	No	Yes MLI	PPT
47	Malta	No	Yes MLI	PPT
48	Mexico	No	Yes MLI	PPT
49	Moldova*	No	No	PPT
50	Montenegro	No	No	PPT
51	Morocco	No	Yes MLI	PPT
52	Namibia	No	No	PPT
53	Netherlands	No	Yes MLI	PPT
54	Nigeria	No	Yes MLI	PPT
55	North Macedonia	No	Yes MLI	PPT
56	Norway	No	Yes MLI	PPT
57	Pakistan	No	Yes MLI	PPT
58	Philippines*	No	No	PPT
59	Poland	No	Yes MLI	PPT
60	Portugal	No	Yes MLI	PPT
61	Qatar	No	Yes MLI	PPT
62	Russian Federation	No	Yes MLI	PPT
63	San Marino	No	Yes MLI	PPT
64	Saudi Arabia	No	Yes MLI	PPT
65	Serbia	No	Yes MLI	PPT
66	Singapore	No	Yes MLI	PPT
67	Slovak Republic	No	Yes MLI	PPT
68	Slovenia	No	Yes MLI	PPT
69	South Africa	No	Yes MLI	PPT
70	Spain	Yes Other		PPT

71	Sri Lanka	No	No	PPT
72	Sudan*	No	No	PPT
73	Sweden	No	Yes MLI	PPT
74	Switzerland	No	No	
75	Syrian Arab Republic*	No	No	PPT
76	Tajikistan*	No	No	PPT
77	Thailand	No	No	PPT
78	Tunisia	No	Yes MLI	PPT
79	Turkey	No	Yes MLI	PPT
80	Turkmenistan*	No	No	PPT
81	Ukraine	No	Yes MLI	PPT
82	United Arab Emirates	No	Yes MLI	PPT
83	United Kingdom	No	Yes MLI	PPT
84	United States	No	No	PPT
85	Uruguay	No	Yes MLI	PPT
86	Uzbekistan*	No	No	PPT
87	Viet Nam	No	Yes MLI	PPT
88	Zambia	No	No	PPT

Russian Federation

A. Progress in the implementation of the minimum standard

The Russian Federation has 85 tax agreements in force, as reported in its response to the Peer Review questionnaire. Thirty-six of those agreements comply with the minimum standard.

The Russian Federation signed the MLI in 2017 and deposited its instrument of ratification on 18 June 2019. The MLI entered into force for Russian Federation on 1 October 2019. The agreements modified by the MLI come into compliance with the minimum standard once the provisions of the MLI take effect.

The Russian Federation has not listed its agreements with Brazil, Germany, Namibia, North Macedonia and Switzerland under the MLI. These agreements will therefore not, at this stage, be modified by the MLI. North Macedonia has listed the agreement with the Russian Federation under the MLI. North Macedonia has listed its agreement with Russian Federation under the MLI.

The agreements modified by the MLI come into compliance with the minimum standard once the provisions of the MLI take effect. The Russian Federation reserved the right to delay the entry into effect of the provisions of the MLI until the Russian Federation has completed its internal procedures for this purpose with respect to each of its listed agreements.[142] The Russian Federation notified that it completed its internal procedures for the entry into effect of the MLI with respect to its agreements with Australia, Austria, Belgium (old), Canada, Denmark, Finland, France, Iceland, India, Ireland, Israel, Latvia, Lithuania, Luxembourg, Malta, Netherlands, New Zealand, Norway, Poland, Qatar, Serbia, Singapore, the Slovak Republic, Slovenia, Ukraine, the United Arab Emirates and the United Kingdom on 30 April 2020, and with respect to its agreements with Cyprus*, the Czech Republic, Indonesia, Kazakhstan, Korea, Portugal and Saudi Arabia on 26 November 2020.

The Russian Federation indicated in its response to the Peer Review questionnaire that steps had been taken (other than under the MLI) to implement the minimum standard it the agreements with Brazil, Germany and Switzerland.

The Russian Federation further indicated in its response to the Peer Review questionnaire that the agreements with Namibia and North Macedonia do not give rise to material treaty-shopping concerns for the Russian Federation.

The Russian Federation is implementing the minimum standard through the inclusion of the preamble statement and the PPT combined with the LOB.[143]

B. Conclusion

The Russian Federation is encouraged to complete (and notify that it has completed) its internal procedures for the entry into effect of the MLI with respect to its agreements that are covered tax agreements under the MLI and for which no such notification has yet been made.

---

[142] The reservation was made under Article 35(7)(a) of the MLI.

[143] For its agreements listed under the MLI, the Russian Federation is implementing the preamble statement (Article 6 of the MLI) and the PPT (Article 7 of the MLI). The Russian Federation has also adopted for the simplified LOB under Article 7(6) of the MLI.

North Macedonia as listed its agreement with Russian Federation under the MLI, which amounts to a request to implement the minimum standard.

Recommendation

It is recommended that the Russian Federation formulates a plan for the implementation of the minimum standard in its agreement for which no steps have yet been taken and that was concluded with a member of the BEPS Inclusive Framework (North Macedonia).

Summary of the jurisdiction response – Russian Federation

	1.Treaty partners	2. Compliance with the standard	3. Signature of a complying instrument	4. Minimum standard provision used
1	Albania	No	Yes MLI	PPT
2	Algeria*	No	No	
3	Argentina	No	Yes MLI	PPT+LOB
4	Armenia	No	Yes MLI	PPT+LOB
5	Australia	Yes MLI		PPT
6	Austria	Yes MLI		PPT
7	Azerbaijan*	No	No	
8	Belarus	No	No	
9	Belgium	Yes MLI		PPT
10	Botswana	No	No	
11	Brazil	No	No	PPT
12	Bulgaria	No	Yes MLI	PPT+LOB
13	Canada	Yes MLI		PPT
14	Chile	No	Yes MLI	PPT+LOB
15	China (People's Republic of)	No	Yes MLI	PPT
16	Croatia	No	Yes MLI	PPT
17	Cuba*	No	No	
18	Cyprus*	Yes MLI		PPT
19	Czech Republic	Yes MLI		PPT
20	Denmark	Yes MLI		PPT+LOB
21	Ecuador*	No	No	
22	Egypt	No	Yes MLI	PPT
23	Finland	Yes MLI		PPT
24	France	Yes MLI		PPT
25	Germany	No	No	PPT
26	Greece	No	Yes MLI	PPT+LOB
27	Hong Kong (China)	No	Yes MLI	PPT+LOB
28	Hungary	No	Yes MLI	PPT
29	Iceland	Yes MLI		PPT+LOB
30	India	Yes MLI		PPT+LOB
31	Indonesia	Yes MLI		PPT
32	Ireland	Yes MLI		PPT
33	Israel	Yes MLI		PPT
34	Italy	No	Yes MLI	PPT
35	Japan	Yes other		PPT+LOB
36	Kazakhstan	Yes MLI		PPT+LOB

37	Korea	Yes MLI		PPT
38	Kuwait*	No	Yes MLI	PPT
39	Latvia	Yes MLI		PPT
40	Lebanon*	No	No	
41	Lithuania	Yes MLI		PPT
42	Luxembourg	Yes MLI		PPT
43	Malaysia	No	Yes MLI	PPT
44	Malta	Yes MLI		PPT
45	Mexico	No	Yes MLI	PPT+LOB
46	Moldova*	No	No	
47	Mongolia	No	No	
48	Montenegro	No	No	
49	Morocco	No	Yes MLI	PPT
50	Netherlands	Yes MLI		PPT
51	New Zealand	Yes MLI		PPT
52	Norway	Yes MLI		PPT+LOB
53	Philippines*	No	No	
54	Poland	Yes MLI		PPT
55	Portugal	Yes MLI		PPT
56	Qatar	Yes MLI		PPT
57	Romania	No	Yes MLI	PPT
58	Saudi Arabia	Yes MLI		PPT
59	Serbia	Yes MLI		PPT
60	Singapore	Yes MLI		PPT
61	Slovak Republic	Yes MLI		PPT+LOB
62	Slovenia	Yes MLI		PPT
63	South Africa	No	Yes MLI	PPT
64	Spain	No	Yes MLI	PPT
65	Sri Lanka	No	No	
66	Sweden	Yes other		PPT
67	Switzerland	No	No	PPT
68	Thailand	No	No	
69	Turkey	No	Yes MLI	PPT
70	Ukraine	Yes MLI		PPT
71	United Arab Emirates	Yes MLI		PPT
72	United Kingdom	Yes MLI		PPT
73	United States	No	No	
74	Venezuela*	No	No	
75	Viet Nam	No	No	PPT

Other agreements

	1.Treaty partners	2. Inclusive Framework member
1	Democratic People's Republic of Korea*	No
2	Iran*	No
3	Kyrgyzstan*	No
4	North Macedonia	Yes
5	Mali*	No
6	Namibia	Yes
7	Syrian Arab Republic*	No
8	Tajikistan*	No
9	Turkmenistan*	No
10	Uzbekistan*	No

Saint Kitts and Nevis

A. Progress in the implementation of the minimum standard

Saint Kitts and Nevis has nine tax agreements in force, as reported in its response to the Peer Review questionnaire, including the multilateral agreement among the members of the CARICOM concluded with ten treaty partners (the CARICOM Agreement).[144] None of those agreements comply with the minimum standard.

Saint Kitts and Nevis has not signed the MLI.

Saint Kitts and Nevis indicated that the agreement with Switzerland does not give rise to material treaty-shopping concerns for Saint Kitts and Nevis. In its response to the Peer Review questionnaire, Switzerland also indicated that its agreement with Saint Kitts and Nevis did not give rise to material treaty shopping concerns for Switzerland.

B. Conclusion

Saint Kitts and Nevis is currently developing a plan, in consultation with the Secretariat, for the implementation of the minimum standard in its agreements with Denmark, Monaco, New Zealand, Norway, San Marino, Sweden and the United Kingdom.

Saint Kitts and Nevis acknowledges that the CARICOM Agreement does not at this stage comply with the minimum standard and that discussions to bring this agreement up to date would be contemplated.[145]

Other agreements

This Table shows the agreements that are not compliant, not subject to a complying instrument, not covered by a general statement on the implementation of the detailed LOB and for which no steps have been taken to implement the minimum standard.

	1.Treaty partners	2. Inclusive Framework member
1	Antigua and Barbuda	Yes
2	Barbados	Yes
3	Belize	Yes
4	Denmark	Yes

[144] Agreement Among the Governments of the Member States of the Caribbean Community for the Avoidance of Double Taxation and the Prevention of Fiscal Evasion with Respect to Taxes on Income, Profits or Gains and Capital Gains and for the Encouragement of Regional Trade and Investment, St. Michael Barbados, 6 July 1994; between: Antigua and Barbuda (18 February 1998), Barbados (7 July 1995), Belize (30 November 1994), Dominica (19 June 1996), Grenada (1 March 1996), Guyana* (26 November 1997), Jamaica (16 February 1995), St. Kitts/Nevis (8 May 1997), St. Lucia (22 May 1995) St. Vincent (12 February 1998) and Trinidad & Tobago (29 November 1994). In total, Saint Kitts and Nevis identified 14 "agreements" in its List of Tax agreements: four bilateral agreements and the CARICOM Agreement concluded with ten of its treaty partners.

[145] Revisions to the CARICOM Agreement require an agreement from its eleven treaty partners.

5	Dominica	Yes
6	Grenada	Yes
7	Guyana*	No
8	Jamaica	Yes
9	Monaco	Yes
10	New Zealand	Yes
11	Norway	Yes
12	Saint Lucia	Yes
13	Saint Vincent and the Grenadines	Yes
14	San Marino	Yes
15	Sweden	Yes
16	Switzerland	Yes
17	Trinidad and Tobago	Yes
18	United Kingdom	Yes

Saint Lucia

A. Progress in the implementation of the minimum standard

Saint Lucia has two tax agreements, as reported in its response to the Peer Review questionnaire, including the multilateral agreement among the members of the CARICOM concluded with ten treaty partners (the CARICOM Agreement).[146] Neither of those agreements comply with the minimum standard.

Saint Lucia has not signed the MLI.

Saint Lucia indicated in its response to the Peer Review questionnaire that the agreement with Switzerland did not at this stage give rise to material treaty shopping concerns for Saint Lucia. In its response to the Peer Review questionnaire, Switzerland also indicated that its agreement with Saint Lucia did not give rise to material treaty shopping concerns for Switzerland.

B. Conclusion

Saint Lucia acknowledges that the CARICOM Agreement does not at this stage comply with the minimum standard and that discussions to bring this agreement up to date would be contemplated.[147]

Other agreements

This Table shows the agreements that are not compliant, not subject to a complying instrument, not covered by a general statement on the implementation of the detailed LOB and for which no steps have been taken to implement the minimum standard.

	1.Treaty partners	2. Inclusive Framework member
1	Antigua and Barbuda	Yes
2	Barbados	Yes
3	Belize	Yes
4	Dominica	Yes
5	Grenada	Yes
6	Guyana*	No
7	Jamaica	Yes
8	Saint Kitts and Nevis	Yes
9	Saint Vincent and the Grenadines	Yes
10	Switzerland	Yes
11	Trinidad and Tobago	Yes

[146] Agreement Among the Governments of the Member States of the Caribbean Community for the Avoidance of Double Taxation and the Prevention of Fiscal Evasion with Respect to Taxes on Income, Profits or Gains and Capital Gains and for the Encouragement of Regional Trade and Investment, St. Michael Barbados, 6 July 1994; between: Antigua and Barbuda (18 February 1998), Barbados (7 July 1995), Belize (30 November 1994), Dominica (19 June 1996), Grenada (1 March 1996), Guyana* (26 November 1997), Jamaica (16 February 1995), St. Kitts/Nevis (8 May 1997), St. Lucia (22 May 1995) St. Vincent (12 February 1998) and Trinidad & Tobago (29 November 1994). In total, Saint Lucia identified 11 "agreements" in its List of Tax agreements: one bilateral agreement and the CARICOM Agreement concluded with ten of its treaty partners.

[147] Revisions to the CARICOM Agreement require an agreement from its eleven treaty partners.

Saint Vincent and the Grenadines

A. Progress in the implementation of the minimum standard

Saint Vincent and the Grenadines has three tax agreements, as reported in its response to the Peer Review questionnaire, including the multilateral agreement among the members of the CARICOM concluded with ten treaty partners (the CARICOM Agreement).[148] None of those agreements comply with the minimum standard.

Saint Vincent and the Grenadines has not signed the MLI.

Saint Vincent and the Grenadines indicated in its response to the Peer Review questionnaire that steps have been contemplated to implement the minimum standard in its agreement with the United Arab Emirates.

Saint Vincent and the Grenadines also indicated that the agreement with Switzerland does not give rise to material treaty-shopping concerns for Saint Vincent and the Grenadines. In its response to the Peer Review questionnaire, Switzerland also indicated that its agreement with Saint Vincent and the Grenadines did not give rise to material treaty shopping concerns for Switzerland.

B. Conclusion

Saint Vincent and the Grenadines acknowledges that the CARICOM Agreement does not at this stage comply with the minimum standard and that discussions to bring this agreement up to date would be contemplated.[149]

Summary of the jurisdiction response – Saint Vincent and the Grenadines

	1.Treaty partners	2. Compliance with the standard	3. Signature of a complying instrument	4. Minimum standard provision used
1	United Arab Emirates	No	No	

Other agreements

	1.Treaty partners	2. Inclusive Framework member

[148] Agreement Among the Governments of the Member States of the Caribbean Community for the Avoidance of Double Taxation and the Prevention of Fiscal Evasion with Respect to Taxes on Income, Profits or Gains and Capital Gains and for the Encouragement of Regional Trade and Investment, St. Michael Barbados, 6 July 1994; between: Antigua and Barbuda (18 February 1998), Barbados (7 July 1995), Belize (30 November 1994), Dominica (19 June 1996), Grenada (1 March 1996), Guyana* (26 November 1997), Jamaica (16 February 1995), St. Kitts/Nevis (8 May 1997), St. Lucia (22 May 1995) St. Vincent (12 February 1998) and Trinidad & Tobago (29 November 1994). In total, Saint Vincent and the Grenadines identified twelve "agreements" in its List of Tax agreements: two bilateral agreements and the CARICOM Agreement concluded with ten of its treaty partners.

[149] Revisions to the CARICOM Agreement require an agreement from its eleven treaty partners.

1	Antigua and Barbuda	Yes
2	Barbados	Yes
3	Belize	Yes
4	Dominica	Yes
5	Grenada	Yes
6	Guyana*	No
7	Jamaica	Yes
8	Saint Kitts and Nevis	Yes
9	Saint Lucia	Yes
10	Switzerland	Yes
11	Trinidad and Tobago	Yes

Samoa

A. Progress in the implementation of the minimum standard

Samoa has one tax agreement in force, the agreement with New Zealand, as reported in its response to the Peer Review questionnaire. This agreement complies with the minimum standard.

B. Conclusion

No jurisdiction has raised any concerns about their agreements with Samoa.

Summary of the jurisdiction response – Samoa

	1.Treaty partners	2. Compliance with the standard	3. Signature of a complying instrument	4. Minimum standard provision used
1	New Zealand	Yes other		PPT

San Marino

A. Progress in the implementation of the minimum standard

San Marino has 23 tax agreements in force, as reported in its response to the Peer Review questionnaire. Ten of those agreements comply with the minimum standard.

San Marino signed the MLI in 2017 and deposited its instrument of ratification on 11 March 2020, listing its non-compliant agreements. The MLI entered into force for San Marino on 1 July 2020. The agreements modified by the MLI come into compliance with the minimum standard once the provisions of the MLI take effect.

San Marino is implementing the minimum standard through the inclusion of the preamble statement and the PPT.[150]

B. Conclusion

No jurisdiction has raised any concerns about their agreements with San Marino.

Summary of the jurisdiction response – San Marino

	1.Treaty partners	2. Compliance with the standard	3. Signature of a complying instrument	4. Minimum standard provision used
1	Austria	No	No	PPT
2	Azerbaijan*	No	No	PPT
3	Barbados	No	Yes MLI	PPT
4	Belgium	Yes MLI		PPT
5	Croatia	No	Yes MLI	PPT
6	Cyprus*	Yes MLI		PPT
7	Georgia	Yes MLI		PPT
8	Greece	No	Yes MLI	PPT
9	Hungary	No	Yes MLI	PPT
10	Italy	No	Yes MLI	PPT
11	Liechtenstein	Yes MLI		PPT
12	Luxembourg	Yes MLI		PPT
13	Malaysia	No	Yes MLI	PPT
14	Malta	Yes MLI		PPT
15	Portugal	Yes MLI		PPT
16	Qatar	Yes MLI		PPT
17	Romania	No	Yes MLI	PPT
18	Saint Kitts and Nevis	No	No	PPT
19	Serbia	Yes other		PPT
20	Seychelles	No	Yes MLI	PPT
21	Singapore	Yes MLI		PPT
22	United Arab Emirates	No	No	PPT
23	Viet Nam	No	No	PPT

[150] For its agreements listed under the MLI, San Marino is implementing the preamble statement (Article 6 of the MLI) and the PPT (Article 7 of the MLI). San Marino made a reservation pursuant to Article 7(15)(b) of the MLI not to apply Article 7(1) of the MLI with respect to agreements that already contain a PPT (covering three agreements).

Saudi Arabia

A. Progress in the implementation of the minimum standard

Saudi Arabia has 54 tax agreements in force, as reported in its response to the Peer Review questionnaire. Twenty-two of those agreements comply with the minimum standard.

Saudi Arabia signed the MLI in 2018 and deposited its instrument of ratification on 23 January 2020. The MLI entered into force for Saudi Arabia on 1 May 2020. The agreements modified by the MLI come into compliance with the minimum standard once the provisions of the MLI take effect.

Saudi Arabia has not listed its agreement with Latvia under the MLI but indicated in its response to the Peer Review questionnaire that steps have been taken (other than under the MLI) to implement the minimum standard in that agreement, as well as in the agreement with Iraq*.

Saudi Arabia is implementing the minimum standard through the inclusion of the preamble statement and the PPT.[151]

B. Conclusion

No jurisdiction has raised any concerns about their agreements with Saudi Arabia.

Summary of the jurisdiction response – Saudi Arabia

	1.Treaty partners	2. Compliance with the standard	3. Signature of a complying instrument	4. Minimum standard provision used
1	Albania	No	No	PPT
2	Algeria*	No	No	PPT
3	Austria	No	No	PPT
4	Azerbaijan*	No	No	PPT
5	Bangladesh*	No	No	PPT
6	Belarus	No	No	PPT
7	Bulgaria	Yes other		PPT
8	China (People's Republic of)	No	Yes MLI	PPT
9	Cyprus*	Yes MLI		PPT
10	Czech Republic	No	No	PPT
11	Egypt	Yes MLI		PPT
12	Ethiopia*	No	No	PPT
13	France	Yes MLI		PPT
14	Gabon	No	No	PPT
15	Georgia	No	No	PPT
16	Greece	No	Yes MLI	PPT
17	Hong Kong (China)	No	No	PPT
18	Hungary	No	Yes MLI	PPT
19	India	Yes MLI		PPT
20	Ireland	Yes MLI		PPT

[151] For its agreements listed under the MLI, Saudi Arabia is implementing the preamble statement (Article 6 of the MLI) and the PPT (Article 7 of the MLI).

21	Italy	No	Yes MLI	PPT
22	Japan	Yes MLI		PPT
23	Jordan	Yes MLI		PPT
24	Kazakhstan	Yes MLI		PPT
25	Korea	Yes MLI		PPT
26	Kyrgyzstan*	No	No	PPT
27	Luxembourg	Yes MLI		PPT
28	Malaysia	No	Yes MLI	PPT
29	Malta	Yes MLI		PPT
30	Mexico	No	Yes MLI	PPT
31	Netherlands	Yes MLI		PPT
32	North Macedonia	No	Yes MLI	PPT
33	Pakistan	Yes MLI		PPT
34	Poland	Yes MLI		PPT
35	Portugal	Yes MLI		PPT
36	Romania	No	Yes MLI	PPT
37	Russian Federation	Yes MLI		PPT
38	Singapore	Yes MLI		PPT
39	South Africa	No	Yes MLI	PPT
40	Spain	No	Yes MLI	PPT
41	Sweden	No	Yes MLI	PPT
42	Switzerland	Yes Other		PPT
43	Syria*	No	No	PPT
44	Tajikistan*	No	No	PPT
45	Tunisia	No	No	PPT
46	Turkey	No	Yes MLI	PPT
47	Turkmenistan*	No	No	PPT
48	Ukraine	Yes MLI		PPT
49	United Arab Emirates	Yes Other		PPT
50	United Kingdom	Yes MLI		PPT
51	Uzbekistan*	No	No	PPT
52	Venezuela*	No	No	PPT
53	Viet Nam	No	No	PPT

Other agreements

	1.Treaty partners	2. Inclusive Framework member
1	Kosovo*	No

Senegal

A. Progress in the implementation of the minimum standard

Senegal has 19 tax agreements in force, as reported in its response to the Peer Review questionnaire, including the multilateral Regulation 08/2008/COM adopting the rules for the avoidance of double taxation within the West African Economic and Monetary Union and the rule for assistance in tax matters (the UEMOA) concluded with seven partners. One of those agreements, the agreement with Luxembourg, complies with the minimum standard.

Senegal signed the MLI in 2017 and listed its non-compliant bilateral agreements. The agreements modified by the MLI come into compliance with the minimum standard once the provisions of the MLI take effect.

Senegal is implementing the minimum standard through the inclusion of the preamble statement and the PPT combined with the LOB.[152]

B. Conclusion

The UEMOA does not at this stage comply with the minimum standard and discussions to bring this agreement up to date should be contemplated.[153]

Recommendation

It is recommended that Senegal completes the steps to have the MLI take effect with respect to its agreements listed under the MLI as those agreements will only be modified by the MLI (and come into compliance with the minimum standard) once the provisions of the MLI take effect.

[152] For its agreements listed under the MLI, Senegal is implementing the preamble statement (Article 6 of the MLI) and the PPT (Article 7 of the MLI). Senegal has also adopted for the simplified LOB under Article 7(6) of the MLI and expressed a statement, in accordance with Article 7(17)(a) of the MLI, that while it accepts the application of the PPT under the MLI, it intends where possible to adopt an LOB provision through bilateral negotiation. Senegal has made a reservation pursuant to Article 6(4) of the MLI not to apply Article 6(1) of the MLI with respect to agreements, which already contain the relevant preamble language (covering one agreement). Senegal has also made a reservation pursuant to Article 7(15)(b) of the MLI not to apply Article 7(1) of the MLI with respect to agreements which already contain a PPT (covering one agreement).

[153] Revisions to the UEMOA require an agreement from its eight treaty partners.

Summary of the jurisdiction response – Senegal

	1.Treaty partners	2. Compliance with the standard	3. Signature of a complying instrument	4. Minimum standard provision used
1	Belgium	No	Yes MLI	PPT
2	Cabo Verde	Yes other		PPT
3	Canada	No	Yes MLI	PPT
4	France	No	Yes MLI	PPT
5	Italy	No	Yes MLI	PPT
6	Lebanon*	No	No	PPT
7	Luxembourg	Yes other		PPT
8	Malaysia	No	Yes MLI	PPT
9	Mauritania*	No	No	PPT
10	Morocco	No	Yes MLI	PPT
11	Norway	No	No	PPT
12	Portugal	No	Yes MLI	PPT
13	Qatar	No	Yes MLI	PPT
14	Spain	No	Yes MLI	PPT
15	Tunisia	No	Yes MLI	PPT
16	United Arab Emirates	No	Yes MLI	PPT
17	United Kingdom	No	Yes MLI	PPT

Other agreements

	1.Treaty partners	2. Inclusive Framework member
1	Benin	Yes
2	Burkina Faso	Yes
3	Chines Taipei	No
4	Côte d'Ivoire	Yes
5	Guinea-Bissau*	No
6	Mali*	No
7	Niger*	No
8	Togo*	No

Serbia

A. Progress in the implementation of the minimum standard

Serbia has 61 tax agreements in force, as reported in its response to the Peer Review questionnaire. Thirty-five of those agreements comply with the minimum standard.

Serbia signed the MLI in 2017 and deposited its instrument of ratification on 5 June 2018, listing its non-compliant agreements. The MLI entered into force for Serbia on 1 October 2018. The agreements modified by the MLI come into compliance with the minimum standard once the provisions of the MLI take effect.

Serbia is implementing the minimum standard through the inclusion of the preamble statement and the PPT.[154]

B. Conclusion

No jurisdiction has raised any concerns about their agreements with Serbia.

Summary of the jurisdiction response - Serbia

	1.Treaty partners	2. Compliance with the standard	3. Signature of a complying instrument	4. Minimum standard provision used
1	Albania	Yes MLI		PPT
2	Armenia	No	Yes MLI	PPT
3	Austria	Yes MLI		PPT
4	Azerbaijan*	No	No	PPT
5	Belarus	No	No	PPT
6	Belgium	Yes MLI		PPT
7	Bosnia-Herzegovina	Yes MLI		PPT
8	Bulgaria	No	Yes MLI	PPT
9	Canada	Yes MLI		PPT
10	China (People's Republic of)	No	Yes MLI	PPT
11	Croatia	No	Yes MLI	PPT
12	Cyprus*	Yes MLI		PPT
13	Czech Republic	Yes MLI		PPT
14	Democratic People's Republic of Korea*	No	No	PPT
15	Denmark	Yes MLI		PPT
16	Egypt	Yes MLI		PPT
17	Estonia	No	Yes MLI	PPT
18	Finland	Yes MLI		PPT
19	France	Yes MLI		PPT
20	Georgia	Yes MLI		PPT
21	Germany	No	No	PPT
22	Greece	No	Yes MLI	PPT
23	Hong Kong (China)	Yes other		PPT

154 For its agreements listed under the MLI, Serbia is implementing the preamble statement (Article 6 of the MLI) and the PPT (Article 7 of the MLI).

24	Hungary	No	Yes MLI	PPT
25	India	Yes MLI		PPT
26	Indonesia	Yes MLI		PPT
27	Iran*	No	No	PPT
28	Ireland	Yes MLI		PPT
29	Israel	Yes other		PPT
30	Italy	No	Yes MLI	PPT
31	Kazakhstan	Yes MLI		PPT
32	Korea	Yes MLI		PPT
33	Kuwait*	No	Yes MLI	PPT
34	Latvia	Yes MLI		PPT
35	Libya*	No	No	PPT
36	Lithuania	Yes MLI		PPT
37	Luxembourg	Yes MLI		PPT
38	Malta	Yes MLI		PPT
39	Moldova*	No	No	PPT
40	Montenegro	No	No	PPT
41	Netherlands	Yes MLI		PPT
42	North Macedonia	No	Yes MLI	PPT
43	Norway	Yes MLI		PPT
44	Pakistan	Yes MLI		PPT
45	Poland	Yes MLI		PPT
46	Qatar	Yes MLI		PPT
47	Romania	No	Yes MLI	PPT
48	Russian Federation	Yes MLI		PPT
49	San Marino	Yes other		PPT
50	Slovak Republic	Yes MLI		PPT
51	Slovenia	Yes MLI		PPT
52	Spain	No	Yes MLI	PPT
53	Sri Lanka	No	No	PPT
54	Sweden	No	No	PPT
55	Switzerland	No	No	PPT
56	Tunisia	No	Yes MLI	PPT
57	Turkey	No	Yes MLI	PPT
58	Ukraine	Yes MLI		PPT
59	United Arab Emirates	Yes MLI		PPT
60	United Kingdom	Yes MLI		PPT
61	Viet Nam	No	No	PPT

Seychelles

A. Progress in the implementation of the minimum standard

The Seychelles has 28 tax agreements in force, as reported in its response to the Peer Review questionnaire. None of those agreements comply with the minimum standard.

The Seychelles signed the MLI in 2017 and deposited its instrument of ratification on 14 December 2021, listing its non-compliant agreements. The MLI enters into force for the Seychelles on 1 April 2022. The agreements modified by the MLI come into compliance with the minimum standard once the provisions of the MLI take effect.

The Seychelles is implementing the minimum standard through the inclusion of the preamble statement and the PPT.[155]

B. Conclusion

No jurisdiction has raised any concerns about their agreements with the Seychelles.

Summary of the jurisdiction response - Seychelles

	1.Treaty partners	2. Compliance with the standard	3. Signature of a complying instrument	4. Minimum standard provision used
1	Bahrain	No	Yes MLI	PPT
2	Barbados	No	Yes MLI	PPT
3	Belgium	No	Yes MLI	PPT
4	Bermuda	No	No	
5	Botswana	No	No	
6	China (People's Republic of)	No	Yes MLI	PPT
7	Cyprus*	No	Yes MLI	PPT
8	Eswatini	No	No	
9	Ethiopia*	No	No	
10	Guernsey	No	Yes MLI	PPT
11	Indonesia	No	Yes MLI	PPT
12	Isle of Man	No	Yes MLI	PPT
13	Jersey	No	Yes MLI	PPT
14	Kenya	No	Yes MLI	PPT
15	Luxembourg	No	Yes MLI	PPT
16	Malaysia	No	Yes MLI	PPT
17	Mauritius	No	Yes MLI	PPT
18	Monaco	No	Yes MLI	PPT
19	Oman	No	Yes MLI	PPT
20	Qatar	No	Yes MLI	PPT
21	San Marino	No	Yes MLI	PPT
22	Singapore	No	Yes MLI	PPT

155 For its agreements listed under the MLI, the Seychelles is implementing the preamble statement (Article 6 of the MLI) and the PPT (Article 7 of the MLI). The Seychelles expressed a statement that while it accepts the application of the PPT under the MLI, it intends where possible to adopt an LOB provision through bilateral negotiation.

23	South Africa	No	Yes MLI	PPT
24	Sri Lanka	No	No	
25	Thailand	No	No	
26	United Arab Emirates	No	Yes MLI	PTP
27	Viet Nam	No	No	
28	Zambia	No	No	

Sierra Leone

A. Progress in the implementation of the minimum standard

Sierra Leone has three tax agreements in force, as reported in its response to the Peer Review questionnaire.

None of those agreements comply with the minimum standard.

Sierra Leone has not signed the MLI.

B. Conclusion

Recommendation

It is recommended that Sierra Leone formulates a plan for the implementation of the minimum standard in the agreements for which no steps have yet been taken and that were concluded with members of the BEPS Inclusive Framework (Norway, South Africa, and the United Kingdom)

Other agreements

This Table shows the agreements that are not compliant, not subject to a complying instrument, not covered by a general statement on the implementation of the detailed LOB and for which no steps have been taken to implement the minimum standard.

	1.Treaty partners	2. Inclusive Framework member
1	Norway	Yes
2	South Africa	Yes
3	United Kingdom	Yes

Singapore

A. Progress in the implementation of the minimum standard

Singapore has 88 tax agreements in force, as reported in its response to the Peer Review questionnaire. Forty-five of those agreements comply with the minimum standard.

Singapore signed the MLI in 2017 and deposited its instrument of ratification on 21 December 2018, listing its non-compliant agreements concluded with other members of the Inclusive Framework. The MLI entered into force for Singapore on 1 April 2019. The agreements modified by the MLI come into compliance with the minimum standard once the provisions of the MLI take effect.

Singapore is implementing the minimum standard in its tax agreements through the inclusion of the preamble statement and the PPT.[156]

B. Conclusion

No jurisdiction has raised any concerns about their agreements with Singapore.

Summary of the jurisdiction response - Singapore

	1.Treaty partners	2. Compliance with the standard	3. Signature of a complying instrument	4. Minimum standard provision used
1	Albania	Yes MLI		PPT
2	Australia	Yes MLI		PPT
3	Austria	Yes MLI		PPT
4	Bahrain	No	Yes MLI	PPT
5	Bangladesh*	No	No	PPT
6	Barbados	No	Yes MLI	PPT
7	Belarus	No	No	PPT
8	Belgium	Yes MLI		PPT
9	Brunei Darussalam	No	No	PPT
10	Bulgaria	No	Yes MLI	PPT
11	Cambodia*	No	No	PPT
12	Canada	Yes MLI		PPT
13	China (People's Republic of)	No	Yes MLI	PPT
14	Chinese Taipei*	No	No	PPT
15	Cyprus*	Yes MLI		PPT
16	Czech Republic	Yes MLI		PPT
17	Denmark	Yes MLI		PPT
18	Ecuador*	No	No	PPT
19	Egypt	Yes MLI		PPT
20	Estonia	No	Yes MLI	PPT
21	Ethiopia*	No	No	PPT
22	Fiji*	No	Yes MLI	PPT
23	Finland	Yes MLI		PPT

[156] For its agreements listed under the MLI, Singapore is implementing the preamble statement (Article 6 of the MLI) and the PPT (Article 7 of the MLI).

24	France	Yes MLI		PPT
25	Georgia	Yes MLI		PPT
26	Germany	Yes other		PPT
27	Ghana*	No	No	PPT
28	Guernsey	Yes MLI		PPT
29	Hungary	No	Yes MLI	PPT
30	India	Yes MLI		PPT
31	Indonesia	Yes MLI		PPT
32	Ireland	Yes MLI		PPT
33	Isle of Man	Yes MLI		PPT
34	Israel	Yes MLI		PPT
35	Italy	No	Yes MLI	PPT
36	Japan	Yes MLI		PPT
37	Jersey	Yes MLI		PPT
38	Kazakhstan	Yes MLI		PPT
39	Korea	Yes other		PPT
40	Kuwait*	No	Yes MLI	PPT
41	Lao People's Democratic Republic*	No	No	PPT
42	Latvia	Yes MLI		PPT
43	Libya*	No	No	PPT
44	Liechtenstein	Yes MLI		PPT
45	Lithuania	Yes MLI		PPT
46	Luxembourg	Yes MLI		PPT
47	Malaysia	No	Yes MLI	PPT
48	Malta	Yes MLI		PPT
49	Mauritius	Yes MLI		PPT
50	Mexico	No	Yes MLI	PPT
51	Mongolia	No	No	PPT
52	Morocco	No	Yes MLI	PPT
53	Myanmar*	No	No	PPT
54	Netherlands	Yes MLI		PPT
55	New Zealand	Yes MLI		PPT
56	Nigeria	No	Yes MLI	PPT
57	Norway	No	No	PPT
58	Oman	Yes MLI		PPT
59	Pakistan	No	Yes MLI	PPT
60	Panama	No	Yes MLI	PPT
61	Papua New Guinea	No	Yes MLI	PPT
62	Philippines*	No	No	PPT
63	Poland	Yes MLI		PPT
64	Portugal	Yes MLI		PPT
65	Qatar	Yes MLI		PPT
66	Romania	No	Yes MLI	PPT
67	Russian Federation	Yes MLI		PPT
68	Rwanda*	No	No	PPT
69	San Marino	Yes MLI		PPT
70	Saudi Arabia	Yes MLI		PPT
71	Seychelles	No	Yes MLI	PPT
72	Slovak Republic	Yes MLI		PPT
73	Slovenia	Yes MLI		PPT
74	South Africa	No	Yes MLI	PPT
75	Spain	No	Yes MLI	PPT
76	Sri Lanka	No	No	PPT

77	Sweden	No	No	PPT
78	Switzerland	No	No	PPT
79	Thailand	No	No	PPT
80	Tunisia	No	Yes MLI	PPT
81	Turkey	No	Yes MLI	PPT
82	Turkmenistan*	Yes other		PPT
83	Ukraine	Yes MLI		PPT
84	United Arab Emirates	Yes MLI		PPT
85	United Kingdom	Yes MLI		PPT
86	Uruguay	Yes MLI		PPT
87	Uzbekistan*	No	No	PPT
88	Viet Nam	No	No	PPT

Slovak Republic

A. Progress in the implementation of the minimum standard

The Slovak Republic has 69 tax agreements in force as reported in its response to the Peer Review questionnaire. Thirty-two of those agreements comply with the minimum standard.

The Slovak Republic signed the MLI in 2017 and deposited its instrument of ratification on 20 September 2018. The MLI entered into force for the Slovak Republic on 1 January 2019. The agreements modified by the MLI come into compliance with the minimum standard once the provisions of the MLI take effect.

The Slovak Republic has not listed its agreements with Armenia and the United Arab Emirates but indicated in its response to the Peer Review questionnaire that steps have been taken (other than under the MLI) to implement the minimum standard in the agreements with Armenia, Brazil, Ethiopia*, Iran*, and the United Arab Emirates. Armenia has listed its agreement with the Slovak Republic under the MLI.

The Slovak Republic is implementing the minimum standard through the inclusion of the preamble statement and the PPT combined with the LOB.[157]

B. Conclusion

No jurisdiction has raised any concerns about their agreements with the Slovak Republic.

Armenia has listed its agreement with the Slovak Republic under the MLI, which amounts to a request to implement the minimum standard.

Summary of the jurisdiction response – Slovak Republic

	1.Treaty partners	2. Compliance with the standard	3. Signature of a complying instrument	4. Minimum standard provision used
1	Armenia	No	No	PPT+LOB
2	Australia	Yes MLI		PPT
3	Austria	Yes MLI		PPT
4	Belarus	No	No	
5	Belgium	Yes MLI		PPT
6	Bosnia-Herzegovina	Yes MLI		PPT
7	Brazil	No	No	PPT+LOB
8	Bulgaria	No	Yes MLI	PPT
9	Canada	Yes MLI		PPT
10	China (People's Republic of)	No	Yes MLI	PPT
	Croatia	No	Yes MLI	PPT
12	Cyprus*	Yes MLI		PPT
13	Czech Republic	Yes MLI		PPT
14	Denmark	Yes MLI		PPT+LOB
15	Estonia	No	Yes MLI	PPT
16	Ethiopia*	No	No	PPT+LOB

157 For its agreements listed under the MLI, the Slovak Republic is implementing the preamble statement (Article 6 of the MLI) and the PPT (Article 7 of the MLI). The Slovak Republic has also adopted for the simplified LOB under Article 7(6) of the MLI.

17	Finland	Yes MLI		PPT
18	France	Yes MLI		PPT
19	Georgia	Yes MLI		PPT
20	Germany	No	Yes MLI	PPT
21	Greece	No	Yes MLI	PPT+LOB
22	Hungary	No	Yes MLI	PPT
23	Iceland	Yes MLI		PPT+LOB
24	India	Yes MLI		PPT+LOB
25	Indonesia	Yes MLI		PPT
26	Iran*	No	No	PPT+LOB
27	Ireland	Yes MLI		PPT
28	Israel	Yes MLI		PPT
29	Italy	No	Yes MLI	PPT
30	Japan	Yes MLI		PPT
31	Kazakhstan	Yes MLI		PPT+LOB
32	Korea	Yes MLI		PPT
33	Kuwait*	No	Yes MLI	PPT
34	Latvia	Yes MLI		PPT
35	Libya*	No	No	
36	Lithuania	Yes MLI		PPT
37	Luxembourg	Yes MLI		PPT
38	Malaysia	No	Yes MLI	PPT
39	Malta	Yes MLI		PPT
40	Mexico	No	Yes MLI	PPT+LOB
41	Moldova*	No	No	
42	Montenegro	No	No	
43	Netherlands	Yes MLI		PPT
44	Nigeria	No	Yes MLI	PPT
45	North Macedonia	No	Yes MLI	PPT
46	Norway	No	No	
47	Poland	Yes MLI		PPT
48	Portugal	Yes MLI		PPT
49	Romania	No	Yes MLI	PPT
50	Russian Federation	Yes MLI		PPT+LOB
51	Serbia	Yes MLI		PPT
52	Singapore	Yes MLI		PPT
53	Slovenia	Yes MLI		PPT
54	South Africa	No	Yes MLI	PPT
55	Spain	No	Yes MLI	PPT
56	Sri Lanka	No	No	
57	Sweden	No	Yes MLI	PPT
58	Switzerland	No	No	
59	Syrian Arab Republic*	No	No	
60	Tunisia	No	Yes MLI	PPT
61	Turkey	No	Yes MLI	PPT
62	Turkmenistan*	No	No	
63	Ukraine	Yes MLI		PPT
64	United Arab Emirates	No	No	
65	United Kingdom	Yes MLI		PPT
66	United States	No	No	
67	Uzbekistan*	No	No	
68	Viet Nam	No	No	PPT

Other agreements

	1.Treaty partners	2. Inclusive Framework member
1	Chinese Taipei*	No

Slovenia

A. Progress in the implementation of the minimum standard

Slovenia has 59 tax agreements in force as reported in its response to the Peer Review questionnaire. Thirty-four of those agreements comply with the minimum standard.

Slovenia signed the MLI in 2017 and deposited its instrument of ratification of the MLI on 22 March 2018. The MLI entered into force for Slovenia on 1 July 2018.The agreements modified by the MLI come into compliance with the minimum standard once the provisions of the MLI take effect.

Slovenia has signed a bilateral complying instrument with respect to its agreements with Sweden.

Slovenia has not listed its agreements with Germany and Montenegro under the MLI but indicated in its response to the Peer Review questionnaire that steps have been taken (other than under the MLI) to implement the minimum standard in these two agreements.

Slovenia is implementing the minimum standard through the inclusion of the preamble statement and the PPT.[158]

B. Conclusion

No jurisdiction has raised any concerns about their agreements with Slovenia.

Summary of the jurisdiction response - Slovenia

	1.Treaty partners	2. Compliance with the standard	3. Signature of a complying instrument	4. Minimum standard provision used
1	Albania	Yes MLI		PPT
2	Armenia	No	Yes MLI	PPT
3	Austria	Yes MLI		PPT
4	Azerbaijan*	No	No	PPT
5	Belarus	No	No	PPT
6	Belgium	Yes MLI		PPT
7	Bosnia-Herzegovina	Yes MLI		PPT
8	Bulgaria	No	Yes MLI	PPT
9	Canada	Yes MLI		PPT
10	China (People's Republic of)	No	Yes MLI	PPT
11	Croatia	No	Yes MLI	PPT
12	Cyprus*	Yes MLI		PPT
13	Czech Republic	Yes MLI		PPT
14	Denmark	Yes MLI		PPT
15	Estonia	No	Yes MLI	PPT
16	Finland	Yes MLI		PPT
17	France	Yes MLI		PPT
18	Georgia	Yes MLI		PPT

158 For its agreements listed under the MLI, Slovenia is implementing the preamble statement (Article 6 of the MLI) and the PPT (Article 7 of the MLI).

19	Germany	No	No	PPT
20	Greece	No	Yes MLI	PPT
21	Hungary	No	Yes MLI	PPT
22	Iceland	Yes MLI		PPT
23	India	Yes MLI		PPT
24	Iran*	No	No	PPT
25	Ireland	Yes MLI		PPT
26	Israel	Yes MLI		PPT
27	Italy	No	Yes MLI	PPT
28	Japan	Yes other		PPT
29	Kazakhstan	Yes MLI		PPT
30	Korea	Yes MLI		PPT
31	Kosovo*	No	No	PPT
32	Kuwait*	No	Yes MLI	PPT
33	Latvia	Yes MLI		PPT
34	Lithuania	Yes MLI		PPT
35	Luxembourg	Yes MLI		PPT
36	Malta	Yes MLI		PPT
37	Moldova*	No	No	PPT
38	Montenegro	No	No	PPT
39	Netherlands	Yes MLI		PPT
40	North Macedonia	No	Yes MLI	PPT
41	Norway	Yes MLI		PPT
42	Poland	Yes MLI		PPT
43	Portugal	Yes MLI		PPT
44	Qatar	Yes MLI		PPT
45	Romania	No	Yes MLI	PPT
46	Russian Federation	Yes MLI		PPT
47	Serbia	Yes MLI		PPT
48	Singapore	Yes MLI		PPT
49	Slovak Republic	Yes MLI		PPT
50	Spain	No	Yes MLI	PPT
51	Sweden	No	Yes other	PPT
52	Switzerland	No	No	PPT
53	Thailand	No	No	PPT
54	Turkey	No	Yes MLI	PPT
55	Ukraine	Yes MLI		PPT
56	United Arab Emirates	Yes MLI		PPT
57	United Kingdom	Yes MLI		PPT
58	United States	No	No	PPT
59	Uzbekistan*	No	No	PPT

South Africa

A. Progress in the implementation of the minimum standard

South Africa has 79 tax agreements in force as reported in its response to the Peer Review questionnaire. None of those agreements comply with the minimum standard.

South Africa signed the MLI in 2017. The agreements modified by the MLI come into compliance with the minimum standard once the provisions of the MLI take effect. South Africa has not listed its agreements with Germany, Grenada, Sierra Leone and Zambia. These agreements will therefore not, at this stage, be modified by the MLI.

South Africa indicated in its response to the Peer Review questionnaire that steps have been taken (other than under the MLI) to implement the minimum standard in its agreements with Germany, Malawi* and Zambia.

South Africa is implementing the minimum standard through the inclusion of the preamble statement and the PPT.[159]

B. Conclusion

South Africa is currently developing a plan, in consultation with the Secretariat, for the implementation of the minimum standard in its agreements with Grenada and Sierra Leone.

Recommendation

It is recommended that South Africa completes the steps to have the MLI take effect with respect to its agreements listed under the MLI as those agreements will only be modified by the MLI (and come into compliance with the minimum standard) once the provisions of the MLI take effect.

Summary of the jurisdiction response – South Africa

	1.Treaty partners	2. Compliance with the standard	3. Signature of a complying instrument	4. Minimum standard provision used
1	Algeria*	No	No	PPT
2	Australia	No	Yes MLI	PPT
3	Austria	No	Yes MLI	PPT
4	Belarus	No	No	PPT
5	Belgium	No	Yes MLI	PPT
6	Botswana	No	No	PPT
7	Brazil	No	No	PPT
8	Bulgaria	No	Yes MLI	PPT
9	Cameroon	No	Yes MLI	PPT

[159] For its agreements listed under the MLI, South Africa is implementing the preamble statement (Article 6 of the MLI) and the PPT (Article 7 of the MLI).

10	Canada	No	Yes MLI	PPT
11	Chile	No	Yes MLI	PPT
12	China (People's Republic of)	No	Yes MLI	PPT
13	Chinese Taipei*	No	No	PPT
14	Croatia	No	Yes MLI	PPT
15	Cyprus*	No	Yes MLI	PPT
16	Czech Republic	No	Yes MLI	PPT
17	Democratic Republic of the Congo	No	No	PPT
18	Denmark	No	Yes MLI	PPT
19	Egypt	No	Yes MLI	PPT
20	Eswatini	No	No	PPT
21	Ethiopia*	No	No	PPT
22	Finland	No	Yes MLI	PPT
23	France	No	Yes MLI	PPT
24	Germany	No	No	PPT
25	Ghana*	No	No	PPT
26	Greece	No	Yes MLI	PPT
27	Hong Kong (China)	No	Yes MLI	PPT
28	Hungary	No	Yes MLI	PPT
29	India	No	Yes MLI	PPT
30	Indonesia	No	Yes MLI	PPT
31	Iran*	No	No	PPT
32	Ireland	No	Yes MLI	PPT
33	Israel	No	Yes MLI	PPT
34	Italy	No	Yes MLI	PPT
35	Japan	No	Yes MLI	PPT
36	Kenya	No	Yes MLI	PPT
37	Korea	No	Yes MLI	PPT
38	Kuwait*	No	Yes MLI	PPT
39	Lesotho*	No	No	PPT
40	Luxembourg	No	Yes MLI	PPT
41	Malawi*	No	No	PPT
42	Malaysia	No	Yes MLI	PPT
43	Malta	No	Yes MLI	PPT
44	Mauritius	No	Yes MLI	PPT
45	Mexico	No	Yes MLI	PPT
46	Mozambique*	No	No	PPT
47	Namibia	No	No	PPT
48	Netherlands	No	Yes MLI	PPT
49	New Zealand	No	Yes MLI	PPT
50	Nigeria	No	Yes MLI	PPT
51	Norway	No	Yes MLI	PPT
52	Oman	No	Yes MLI	PPT
53	Pakistan	No	Yes MLI	PPT
54	Poland	No	Yes MLI	PPT
55	Portugal	No	Yes MLI	PPT
56	Qatar	No	Yes MLI	PPT
57	Romania	No	Yes MLI	PPT
58	Russian Federation	No	Yes MLI	PPT
59	Rwanda*	No	No	PPT
60	Saudi Arabia	No	Yes MLI	PPT
61	Seychelles	No	Yes MLI	PPT
62	Singapore	No	Yes MLI	PPT

63	Slovak Republic	No	Yes MLI	PPT
64	Spain	No	Yes MLI	PPT
65	Sweden	No	Yes MLI	PPT
66	Switzerland	No	Yes MLI	PPT
67	Tanzania*	No	No	PPT
68	Thailand	No	No	PPT
69	Tunisia	No	Yes MLI	PPT
70	Turkey	No	Yes MLI	PPT
71	Uganda*	No	No	PPT
72	Ukraine	No	Yes MLI	PPT
73	United Arab Emirates	No	Yes MLI	PPT
74	United Kingdom	No	Yes MLI	PPT
75	United States	No	No	LOB included in DTA
76	Zambia	No	No	PPT
77	Zimbabwe*	No	No	PPT

Other agreements

	1.Treaty partners	2. Inclusive Framework member
1	Grenada	Yes
2	Sierra Leone	Yes

Spain

A. Progress in the implementation of the minimum standard

Spain has 94 tax agreements in force as reported in its response to the Peer Review questionnaire. Four of those agreements comply with the minimum standard.

Spain signed the MLI in 2017 and deposited its instrument of ratification on 28 September 2021. The MLI enters into force for Spain on 1 January 2022. The agreements modified by the MLI come into compliance with the minimum standard once the provisions of the MLI take effect.

Spain reserved the right to delay the entry into effect of the provisions of the MLI until Spain has completed its internal procedures for this purpose with respect to each of its listed agreements.[160] Spain has not yet notified that it completed its internal procedures for the entry into effect of the MLI with respect to any of its agreements.

Spain has signed a bilateral complying instrument with respect to its agreement with Ukraine.

Spain has not listed its agreements with Netherlands, Norway, and Sweden under the MLI, but indicated in its response to the Peer Review questionnaire that steps have been taken (other than under the MLI) to implement the minimum standard in these three agreements.

Spain is implementing the minimum standard through the inclusion of the preamble statement and the PPT, combined with the LOB for its agreements with Japan and Mexico.[161]

B. Conclusion

Acknowledging that the MLI enters into force for Spain on 1 January 2022, no recommendation is made that Spain completes the steps to have the MLI take effect with respect to its agreements listed under the MLI in 2021.[162] Spain is expected to swiftly start the process to complete such steps in 2022, as those agreements will only be modified by the MLI (and come into compliance with the minimum standard) once the provisions of the MLI take effect.

Summary of the jurisdiction response - Spain

	1.Treaty partners	2. Compliance with the standard	3. Signature of a complying instrument	4. Minimum standard provision used
1	Albania	No	Yes MLI	PPT
2	Algeria*	No	No	
3	Andorra	No	Yes MLI	PPT

160 The reservation was made under Article 35(7)(a) of the MLI.

161 For its agreements listed under the MLI, Spain is implementing the preamble statement (Article 6 of the MLI) and the PPT (Article 7 of the MLI). Spain has made a reservation pursuant to Article 6(4) not to apply Article 6(1) of the MLI with respect to agreements that already contain the relevant preamble language (covering three agreements). Spain has also made a reservation pursuant to Article 7(15)(b) of the MLI not to apply Article 7(1) of the MLI with respect to agreements that already contain a PPT (covering three agreements).

162 By notifying the Depositary that it has completed its internal procedures for the entry into effect of the MLI with respect to its agreements (under Article 35(7)(b) MLI).

4	Argentina	No	Yes MLI	PPT
5	Armenia	No	Yes MLI	PPT
6	Australia	No	Yes MLI	PPT
7	Austria	No	Yes MLI	PPT
8	Azerbaijan*	No	No	
9	Barbados	No	Yes MLI	PPT
10	Belgium	No	Yes MLI	PPT
11	Bolivia*	No	No	
12	Belarus	No	No	
13	Bosnia-Herzegovina	No	Yes MLI	PPT
14	Brazil	No	No	
15	Bulgaria	No	Yes MLI	PPT
16	Cabo Verde	No	No	
17	Canada	No	Yes MLI	PPT
18	Chile	No	Yes MLI	PPT
19	China (People's Republic of)	Yes other		PPT
20	Colombia	No	Yes MLI	PPT
21	Costa Rica	No	Yes MLI	PPT
22	Croatia	No	Yes MLI	PPT
23	Cuba*	No	No	
24	Cyprus*	No	Yes MLI	PPT
25	Czech Republic	No	Yes MLI	PPT
26	Dominican Republic	No	No	
27	Ecuador*	No	No	
28	Egypt	No	Yes MLI	PPT
29	El Salvador*	No	No	
30	Estonia	No	Yes MLI	PPT
31	Finland	No	Yes MLI	PPT
32	France	No	Yes MLI	PPT
33	Georgia	No	Yes MLI	PPT
34	Germany	No	Yes MLI	PPT
35	Greece	No	Yes MLI	PPT
36	Hong Kong (China)	No	Yes MLI	PPT
37	Hungary	No	Yes MLI	PPT
38	Iceland	No	Yes MLI	PPT
39	India	No	Yes MLI	PPT
40	Indonesia	No	Yes MLI	PPT
41	Iran*	No	No	
42	Ireland	No	Yes MLI	PPT
43	Israel	No	Yes MLI	PPT
44	Italy	No	Yes MLI	PPT
45	Jamaica	No	Yes MLI	PPT
46	Japan	Yes other		PPT+LOB
47	Kazakhstan	No	Yes MLI	PPT
48	Korea	No	Yes MLI	PPT
49	Kuwait*	No	Yes MLI	PPT
50	Kyrgyzstan*	No	No	
51	Latvia	No	Yes MLI	PPT
52	Lithuania	No	Yes MLI	PPT
53	Luxembourg	No	Yes MLI	PPT
54	Malaysia	No	Yes MLI	PPT
55	Malta	No	Yes MLI	PPT
56	Mexico	Yes other		PPT+LOB

57	Moldova*	No	No	
58	Morocco	No	Yes MLI	PPT
59	Netherlands	No	No	
60	New Zealand	No	Yes MLI	PPT
61	Nigeria	No	Yes MLI	PPT
62	North Macedonia	No	Yes MLI	PPT
63	Norway	No	No	
64	Oman	No	Yes MLI	PPT
65	Pakistan	No	Yes MLI	PPT
66	Panama	No	Yes MLI	PPT
67	Philippines*	No	No	
68	Poland	No	Yes MLI	PPT
69	Portugal	No	Yes MLI	PPT
70	Qatar	No	Yes MLI	PPT
71	Romania	Yes other		PPT
72	Russian Federation	No	Yes MLI	PPT
73	Saudi Arabia	No	Yes MLI	PPT
74	Senegal	No	Yes MLI	PPT
75	Serbia	No	Yes MLI	PPT
76	Singapore	No	Yes MLI	PPT
77	Slovak Republic	No	Yes MLI	PPT
78	Slovenia	No	Yes MLI	PPT
79	South Africa	No	Yes MLI	PPT
80	Sweden	No	No	
81	Switzerland	No	No	
82	Tajikistan*	No	No	
83	Thailand	No	No	
84	Trinidad and Tobago	No	No	
85	Tunisia	No	Yes MLI	PPT
86	Turkey	No	Yes MLI	PPT
87	Ukraine	No	Yes other	PPT
88	United Arab Emirates	No	Yes MLI	PPT
89	United Kingdom	No	Yes MLI	PPT
90	United States	No	No	
91	Uruguay	No	Yes MLI	PPT
92	Uzbekistan*	No	No	
93	Venezuela*	No	No	
94	Viet Nam	No	No	

Sri Lanka

A. Progress in the implementation of the minimum standard

Sri Lanka has 43 tax agreements in force as reported in its response to the Peer Review questionnaire. None of those agreements, comply with the minimum standard.

Sri Lanka has not signed the MLI.

Sri Lanka indicated in its response to the Peer Review questionnaire that steps have been taken (other than under the MLI) to implement the minimum standard in its agreements with Belgium, the Czech Republic, Denmark, India, Luxembourg, Netherlands, Pakistan, Romania and Switzerland.

Sri Lanka is implementing the minimum standard through the inclusion of the preamble statement and the PPT, combined with the LOB for its agreement with India.

In their responses to the Peer Review questionnaire, Indonesia and Japan indicated that their agreements with Sri Lanka did not give rise to material treaty shopping concerns, for their respective jurisdictions.

B. Conclusion

Sri Lanka has developed a plan for the implementation of the minimum standard in its agreements with Australia, Bahrain, Belarus, Canada, China (People's Republic of), Finland, France, Germany, Indonesia, Italy, Japan, Korea, Malaysia, Mauritius, Norway, Oman, Poland, Qatar, Russian Federation, Seychelles, Singapore, the Slovak Republic, Sweden, Thailand, the United Arab Emirates, the United Kingdom and Viet Nam. Sri Lanka indicated in its response to the Peer Review questionnaire that bilateral negotiations would be pursued with respect to those agreements.

Summary of the jurisdiction response – Sri Lanka

	1.Treaty partners	2. Compliance with the standard	3. Signature of a complying instrument	4. Minimum standard provision used
1	Belgium	No	No	PPT
2	Czech Republic	No	No	PPT
3	Denmark	No	No	PPT
4	India	No	No	LOB
5	Luxembourg	No	No	PPT
6	Netherlands	No	No	PPT
7	Pakistan	No	No	PPT
8	Romania	No	No	PPT
9	Switzerland	No	No	PPT
10	United States	No	No	D-LOB

Other agreements

	1.Treaty partners	2. Inclusive Framework member
1	Australia	Yes
2	Bahrain	Yes
3	Bangladesh*	No

4	Belarus	Yes
5	Canada	Yes
6	China (People's Republic of)	Yes
7	Finland	Yes
8	France	Yes
9	Germany	Yes
10	Indonesia	Yes
11	Iran*	No
12	Italy	Yes
13	Japan	Yes
14	Korea	Yes
15	Kuwait*	No
16	Malaysia	Yes
17	Mauritius	Yes
18	Nepal*	No
19	Norway	Yes
20	Oman	Yes
21	Palestine*	No
22	Philippines*	No
23	Poland	Yes
24	Qatar	Yes
25	Russian Federation	Yes
26	Seychelles	Yes
27	Singapore	Yes
28	Slovak Republic	Yes
29	Sweden	Yes
30	Thailand	Yes
31	United Arab Emirates.	Yes
32	United Kingdom	Yes
33	Viet Nam	Yes

Sweden

A. Progress in the implementation of the minimum standard

Sweden has 81 tax agreements in force as reported in its response to the Peer Review questionnaire, including the multilateral Nordic Convention concluded with Denmark, the Faroe Islands, Finland, Iceland and Norway (the "Nordic Convention").[163] Three of those agreements, including the Nordic Convention, comply with the minimum standard.

Sweden signed the MLI in 2017 and deposited its instrument of ratification on 22 June 2018. The MLI entered into force for Sweden on 1 October 2018. The agreements modified by the MLI come into compliance with the minimum standard once the provisions of the MLI take effect.

Sweden reserved the right to delay the entry into effect of the provisions of the MLI until Sweden has completed its internal procedures for this purpose with respect to each of its listed agreements.[164] Sweden has not yet notified that it completed its internal procedures for the entry into effect of the MLI with respect to any of its agreements.

Sweden has not listed its agreements with Australia, Austria, Bosnia-Herzegovina, Brazil, Croatia, France, Germany, Montenegro, Namibia, Portugal, Serbia, Singapore, Slovenia, and Spain under the MLI. These agreements will therefore not, at this stage, be modified by the MLI. Australia, Bosnia-Herzegovina, Croatia, France, Portugal, Serbia and Singapore have listed their agreements with Sweden under the MLI.

Sweden has signed a bilateral complying instrument with respect to its agreements with Brazil, Portugal, Slovenia and the United Kingdom.

Sweden indicated in its response to the Peer Review questionnaire that steps have been taken (other than under the MLI) to implement the minimum standard in its agreements with Austria, France, Germany, Namibia, Singapore and Spain.

Sweden indicated in its response to the Peer Review questionnaire that the agreements with Australia, Bosnia-Herzegovina, Croatia, Kosovo*, Montenegro and Serbia do not give rise to material treaty-shopping concerns for Sweden.

Sweden is implementing the minimum standard through the inclusion of the preamble statement and the PPT.[165]

B. Conclusion

Australia, Bosnia-Herzegovina, Croatia, France, Serbia and Singapore have listed their agreements with Sweden under the MLI, which amount to requests to implement the minimum standard.

---

[163] See the Multilateral convention concluded by Denmark, Finland, the Faroe Islands, Iceland, Norway and Sweden: for the avoidance of double taxation with respect to taxes on income and on capital (1996, 1997, 2008 and 2018). In total, Sweden identified 85 "agreements" in its List of Tax agreements: 80 bilateral agreements and the Nordic Convention concluded with five treaty partners.

[164] The reservation was made under Article 35(7)(a) of the MLI.

[165] For its agreements listed under the MLI, Sweden is implementing the preamble statement (Article 6 of the MLI) and the PPT (Article 7 of the MLI).

Recommendation

It is recommended that Sweden completes the steps to have the MLI take effect with respect to its agreements listed under the MLI as those agreements will only be modified by the MLI (and come into compliance with the minimum standard) once the provisions of the MLI take effect.

It is also recommended that Sweden formulates a plan for the implementation of the minimum standard in its agreements for which no steps have yet been taken and that were concluded with members of the BEPS Inclusive Framework (Australia, Bosnia-Herzegovina, Croatia, and Serbia).

Summary of the jurisdiction response - Sweden

	1.Treaty partners	2. Compliance with the standard	3. Signature of a complying instrument	4. Minimum standard provision used
1	Albania	No	Yes MLI	PPT
2	Argentina	No	Yes MLI	PPT
3	Armenia	No	Yes MLI	PPT
4	Austria	No	No	
5	Azerbaijan*	No	No	
6	Bangladesh*	No	No	
7	Barbados	No	Yes MLI	
8	Belarus	No	No	
9	Belgium	No	Yes MLI	PPT
10	Bolivia*	No	No	
11	Botswana	No	No	
12	Brazil	No	Yes other	PPT+LOB
13	Bulgaria	No	Yes MLI	PPT
14	Canada	No	Yes MLI	PPT
15	Chile	No	Yes MLI	PPT
16	China (People's Republic of)	No	Yes MLI	PPT
17	Cyprus*	No	Yes MLI	PPT
18	Czech Republic	No	Yes MLI	PPT
19	Denmark	Yes other		PPT
20	Egypt	No	Yes MLI	PPT
21	Estonia	No	Yes MLI	PPT
22	Faroe Islands	Yes other		PPT
23	Finland	Yes other		PPT
24	France	No	No	
25	Gambia*	No	No	
26	Georgia	No	Yes MLI	PPT
27	Germany	No	No	
28	Greece	No	Yes MLI	PPT
29	Hungary	No	Yes MLI	PPT
30	Iceland	Yes other		PPT
31	India	No	Yes MLI	PPT
32	Indonesia	No	Yes MLI	PPT
33	Ireland	No	Yes MLI	PPT
34	Israel	No	Yes MLI	PPT
35	Italy	No	Yes MLI	PPT
36	Jamaica	No	Yes MLI	PPT

37	Japan	No	Yes MLI	PPT+LOB
38	Kazakhstan	No	Yes MLI	PPT
39	Kenya	No	Yes MLI	PPT
40	Korea	No	Yes MLI	PPT
41	Latvia	No	Yes MLI	PPT
42	Lithuania	No	Yes MLI	PPT
43	Luxembourg	No	Yes MLI	PPT
44	Malaysia	No	Yes MLI	PPT
45	Malta	No	Yes MLI	PPT
46	Mauritius	No	Yes MLI	PPT
47	Mexico	No	Yes MLI	PPT
48	Namibia	No	No	
49	Netherlands	No	Yes MLI	PPT
50	New Zealand	No	Yes MLI	PPT
51	Nigeria	No	Yes MLI	PPT
52	North Macedonia	No	Yes MLI	PPT
53	Norway	Yes other		PPT
54	Pakistan	No	Yes MLI	PPT
55	Philippines*	No	No	
56	Poland	No	Yes, MLI	PPT
57	Portugal	No	Yes other	
58	Romania	No	Yes MLI	PPT
59	Russian Federation	Yes other		PPT
60	Saudi Arabia	No	Yes MLI	PPT
61	Singapore	No	No	
62	Slovak Republic	No	Yes MLI	PPT
63	Slovenia	No	Yes other	PPT
64	South Africa	No	Yes MLI	PPT
65	Spain	No	No	
66	Sri Lanka	No	No	
67	Switzerland	Yes other		PPT
68	Tanzania*	No	No	
69	Thailand	No	No	
70	Trinidad and Tobago	No	No	
71	Tunisia	No	Yes MLI	PPT
72	Turkey	No	Yes MLI	PPT
73	Ukraine	No	Yes MLI	PPT
74	United Kingdom	No	Yes MLI/other	PPT
75	United States	No	No	
76	Venezuela*	No	No	
77	Viet Nam	No	No	
78	Zambia	No	No	
79	Zimbabwe*	No	No	

Other agreements

	1.Treaty partners	2. Inclusive Framework member
1	Australia	Yes
2	Bosnia-Herzegovina	Yes
3	Croatia	Yes
4	Kosovo*	No
5	Montenegro	Yes
6	Serbia	Yes

Switzerland

A. Progress in the implementation of the minimum standard

Switzerland has 107 tax agreements in force as reported in its response to the Peer Review questionnaire. Fourteen of those agreements comply with the minimum standard.

Switzerland signed the MLI in 2017 and deposited its instrument of ratification on 29 August 2019. The MLI entered into force for Switzerland on 1 December 2019. The agreements modified by the MLI come into compliance with the minimum standard once the provisions of the MLI take effect. Switzerland has listed twelve of its agreements under the MLI and indicated in its response to the Peer Review questionnaire that it would only list an agreement under the MLI if it agrees with its treaty partner on how the MLI modifies their agreement. Switzerland considers that the MLI amends a covered tax agreement like an amending protocol. An agreement with the other contracting jurisdiction on the precise wording of the amendments to the corresponding tax agreement through the MLI is therefore a requirement for Switzerland to include a tax agreement under the MLI.

Switzerland reserved the right to delay the entry into effect of the provisions of the MLI until Switzerland has completed its internal procedures for this purpose with respect to each of its listed agreements.[166] Switzerland notified that it completed its internal procedures for the entry into effect of the MLI with respect to its agreements with Luxembourg on 27 May 2020 and with respect to its agreements with the Czech Republic and Lithuania on 18 December 2020.

Switzerland has not listed its agreements with Albania, Antigua and Barbuda, Armenia, Australia, Barbados, Belarus, Belgium, Belize, British Virgin Islands, Bulgaria, Canada, China (People's Republic of), Colombia, Côte d'Ivoire, Croatia, Denmark, Dominica, Egypt, Estonia, Finland, France, Georgia, Germany, Greece, Grenada, Hong Kong (China), Hungary, India, Indonesia, Israel, Jamaica, Japan, Kazakhstan, Korea, Liechtenstein, Malaysia, Malta, Mongolia, Montenegro, Montserrat, Morocco, North Macedonia, Oman, Pakistan, Peru, Poland, Qatar, Romania, Russia, Saint Kitts and Nevis, Saint Lucia, Saint Vincent and the Grenadines, Serbia, Singapore, Slovak Republic, Slovenia, Spain, Sri Lanka, Thailand, Tunisia, United Arab Emirates, Uruguay and Viet Nam. These agreements will therefore not, at this stage, be modified under the MLI. Albania, Armenia, Australia, Barbados, Belize, China (People's Republic of), Colombia, Croatia, Egypt, Finland, France, Greece, Hong Kong (China), Hungary, India, Indonesia, Jamaica, Kazakhstan, Malaysia, Morocco, Oman, Pakistan, Peru, Poland, Romania, Serbia, Singapore, Slovak Republic, Slovenia, Spain, Tunisia, United Arab Emirates and Uruguay have listed their agreement with Switzerland under the MLI.

Switzerland has signed a bilateral complying instrument with respect to its agreements with Cyprus*, Iran*, Kuwait*, Liechtenstein, Malta and North Macedonia.

Switzerland indicated in its response to the Peer Review questionnaire that steps have been taken (other than under the MLI) to implement the minimum standard in its agreements with Albania, Algeria*, Armenia, Australia, Bangladesh*, Belarus, Belgium, Bulgaria, Canada, China (People's Republic of), Colombia, Côte d'Ivoire, Croatia, Denmark, Egypt, Estonia, Finland, France, Georgia, Germany, Greece, Hong Kong (China), Hungary, India, Indonesia, Israel, Jamaica, Japan, Kazakhstan, Kyrgyzstan*, Malaysia, Mongolia, Montenegro, Morocco, Oman, Pakistan, Peru, Philippines*, Poland, Qatar, Romania, Russia, Serbia, Singapore, the Slovak Republic, Slovenia, Spain, Sri Lanka, Tajikistan*, Thailand, Trinidad and Tobago, Tunisia, the United Arab Emirates, the United States, Uruguay and Viet Nam.

[166] The reservation was made under Article 35(7)(a) of the MLI.

Switzerland further indicated in its response to the Peer Review questionnaire that the agreements with Antigua and Barbuda, Azerbaijan*, Barbados, Belize, British Virgin Islands, Chinese Taipei*, Dominica, Ecuador*, Gambia*, Ghana*, Grenada, Malawi*, Moldova*, Montserrat, Saint Kitts and Nevis, Saint Lucia, Saint Vincent and the Grenadines, Turkmenistan*, Uzbekistan* and Venezuela* do not give rise to material treaty-shopping concerns for Switzerland.

Switzerland is implementing the minimum standard through the inclusion of the preamble statement and the PPT.[167]

In their responses to the Peer Review Questionnaire, Saint Kitts and Nevis, Saint Lucia and Saint Vincent and the Grenadines indicated that their agreements with Switzerland did not give rise to material treaty shopping concerns for their respective jurisdictions.

B. Conclusion

Albania, Armenia, Australia, Barbados, Belize, China (People's Republic of), Colombia, Croatia, Egypt, Finland, France, Greece, Hong Kong (China), Hungary, India, Indonesia, Kazakhstan, Malaysia, Morocco, Oman, Pakistan, Peru, Poland, Romania, Serbia, Singapore, Slovak Republic, Slovenia, Spain, Tunisia, United Arab Emirates and Uruguay have listed their agreements with Switzerland under the MLI, which amount to requests to implement the minimum standard.

Switzerland is encouraged to complete and notify its internal procedures for the entry into effect of the MLI with respect to its agreements that are covered tax agreements under the MLI and for which no such notification has yet been made.

Summary of the jurisdiction response - Switzerland

	1.Treaty partners	2. Compliance with the standard	3. Signature of a complying instrument	4. Minimum standard provision used
1	Albania	No	No	PPT
2	Algeria*	No	No	PPT
3	Argentina	No	Yes MLI	PPT
4	Armenia	No	No	PPT
5	Australia	No	No	PPT
6	Austria	No	Yes MLI	PPT
7	Bangladesh*	No	No	PPT
8	Belarus	No	No	PPT
9	Belgium	No	No	PPT
10	Brazil	Yes other		PPT
11	Bulgaria	No	No	PPT
12	Canada	No	No	PPT
13	Chile	No	Yes MLI	PPT
14	China (People's Republic of)	No	No	PPT
15	Colombia	No	No	PPT
16	Côte d'Ivoire	No	No	PPT
17	Croatia	No	No	PPT
18	Cyprus*	No	Yes other	PPT

[167] For its agreements listed under the MLI, Switzerland is implementing the preamble statement (Article 6 of the MLI) and the PPT (Article 7 of the MLI).

19	Czech Republic	No	Yes MLI	PPT
20	Denmark	No	No	PPT
21	Egypt	No	No	PPT
22	Estonia	No	No	PPT
23	Finland	No	No	PPT
24	France	No	No	PPT
25	Georgia	No	No	PPT
26	Germany	No	No	PPT
27	Greece	No	No	PPT
28	Hong Kong (China)	No	No	PPT
29	Hungary	No	No	PPT
30	Iceland	No	Yes MLI	PPT
31	India	No	No	PPT
32	Indonesia	No	No	PPT
33	Iran*	No	Yes other	PPT
34	Ireland	Yes other		PPT
35	Israel	No	No	PPT
36	Italy	No	Yes MLI	PPT
37	Jamaica	No	No	PPT
38	Japan	No	No	PPT+LOB
39	Kazakhstan	No	No	PPT
40	Korea	Yes other		PPT
41	Kosovo*	Yes other		PPT
42	Kuwait*	No	Yes other	PPT
43	Kyrgyzstan*	No	No	PPT
44	Latvia	Yes other		PPT
45	Liechtenstein	No	Yes other	PPT
46	Lithuania	No	Yes MLI	PPT
47	Luxembourg	Yes MLI		PPT
48	Malaysia	No	No	PPT
49	Malta	No	Yes other	PPT
50	Mexico	No	Yes MLI	PPT
51	Mongolia	No	No	PPT
52	Montenegro	No	No	PPT
53	Morocco	No	No	PPT
54	Netherlands	Yes other		PPT
55	New Zealand	Yes other		PPT
56	North Macedonia	No	Yes other	PPT
57	Norway	Yes other		PPT
58	Oman	No	No	PPT
59	Pakistan	No	No	PPT
60	Peru	No	No	PPT
61	Philippines*	No	No	PPT
62	Poland	No	No	PPT
63	Portugal	No	Yes MLI	PPT
64	Qatar	No	No	PPT
65	Romania	No	No	PPT
66	Russia	No	No	PPT
67	Saudi Arabia	Yes other		PPT
68	Serbia	No	No	PPT
69	Singapore	No	No	PPT
70	Slovak Republic	No	No	PPT
71	Slovenia	No	No	PPT

72	South Africa	No	Yes MLI	PPT
73	Spain	No	No	PPT
74	Sri Lanka	No	No	PPT
75	Sweden	Yes other		PPT
76	Tajikistan*	No	No	PPT
77	Thailand	No	No	PPT
78	Trinidad and Tobago	No	No	PPT
79	Tunisia	No	No	PPT
80	Turkey	No	Yes MLI	PPT
81	Ukraine	Yes other		PPT
82	United Arab Emirates	No	No	PPT
83	United Kingdom	Yes other		PPT
84	United States	No	No	D-LOB
85	Uruguay	No	No	PPT
86	Viet Nam	No	No	PPT
87	Zambia	Yes other		PPT

Other agreements

	1.Treaty partners	2. Inclusive Framework member
1	Antigua and Barbuda	Yes
2	Barbados	Yes
3	Belize	Yes
4	British Virgin Islands	Yes
5	Dominica	Yes
6	Gambia*	No
7	Grenada	Yes
8	Malawi*	No
9	Montserrat	Yes
10	Saint Kitts and Nevis	Yes
11	Saint Lucia	Yes
12	Saint Vincent and the Grenadines	Yes
13	Azerbaijan*	No
14	Chinese Taipei*	No
15	Ecuador*	No
16	Ghana*	No
17	Moldova*	No
18	Turkmenistan*	No
19	Uzbekistan*	No
20	Venezuela*	No

Thailand

A. Progress in the implementation of the minimum standard

Thailand has 61 tax agreements in force as reported in its response to the Peer Review questionnaire. None of those agreements, comply with the minimum standard.

Thailand has not signed the MLI.

Thailand indicated in its response to the Peer Review questionnaire that steps have been taken (other than under the MLI) to implement the minimum standard in its agreements with Netherlands and Norway.

Thailand indicated in its response to the Peer Review questionnaire that it intends to join the MLI. Thailand indicated and that its internal process of approving the MLI is ongoing and that it expects to be able to sign the MLI in early 2022.

In its response to the Peer Review questionnaire, Japan indicated that its agreement with Thailand did not give rise to material treaty shopping concerns for Japan.

B. Conclusion

Thailand has developed a plan for the implementation of the minimum standard in its agreements with Armenia, Australia, Austria, Bahrain, Belarus, Belgium, Bulgaria, Canada, Chile, China (People's Republic of), Czech Republic, Denmark, Estonia, Finland, France, Germany, Hong Kong (China), Hungary, India, Indonesia, Ireland, Israel, Italy, Japan, Korea, Luxembourg, Malaysia, Mauritius, New Zealand, Oman, Pakistan, Poland, Romania, Russian Federation, Seychelles, Singapore, Slovenia, South Africa, Spain, Sri Lanka, Sweden, Switzerland, Turkey, Ukraine, United Arab Emirates, United Kingdom, and Viet Nam. Thailand indicated in its response to the Peer Review questionnaire that it intends to sign the MLI in early 2022 and to list most of its agreements to be covered under the MLI.

Summary of the jurisdiction response - Thailand

	1.Treaty partners	2. Compliance with the standard	3. Signature of a complying instrument	4. Minimum standard provision used
1	Netherlands	No	No	
2	Norway	No	No	
3	United States	No	No	D-LOB

Other agreements

	1.Treaty partners	2. Inclusive Framework member
1	Armenia	Yes
2	Australia	Yes
3	Austria	Yes
4	Bahrain	Yes
5	Bangladesh*	No
6	Belarus	Yes
7	Belgium	Yes

8	Bulgaria	Yes
9	Cambodia*	No
10	Canada	Yes
11	Chile	Yes
12	China (People's Republic of)	Yes
13	Chinese Taipei*	No
14	Cyprus*	No
15	Czech Republic	Yes
16	Denmark	Yes
17	Estonia	Yes
18	Finland	Yes
19	France	Yes
20	Germany	Yes
21	Hong Kong (China)	Yes
22	Hungary	Yes
23	India	Yes
24	Indonesia	Yes
25	Ireland	Yes
26	Israel	Yes
27	Italy	Yes
28	Japan	Yes
29	Korea	Yes
30	Kuwait*	No
31	Lao People's Democratic Republic*	No
32	Luxembourg	Yes
33	Malaysia	Yes
34	Mauritius	Yes
35	Myanmar*	No
36	Nepal*	No
37	New Zealand	Yes
38	Oman	Yes
39	Pakistan	Yes
40	Philippines*	No
41	Poland	Yes
42	Romania	Yes
43	Russian Federation	Yes
44	Seychelles	Yes
45	Singapore	Yes
46	Slovenia	Yes
47	South Africa	Yes
48	Spain	Yes
49	Sri Lanka	Yes
50	Sweden	Yes
51	Switzerland	Yes
52	Tajikistan*	No
53	Turkey	Yes
54	Ukraine	Yes
55	United Arab Emirates	Yes
56	United Kingdom	Yes
57	Uzbekistan*	No
58	Viet Nam	Yes

Trinidad and Tobago

A. Progress in the implementation of the minimum standard

Trinidad and Tobago has 17 tax agreements in force, as reported in its response to the Peer Review questionnaire, including the multilateral agreement among the members of the CARICOM concluded with ten treaty partners (the CARICOM Agreement).[168]

None of those agreements comply with the minimum standard.

Trinidad and Tobago has not signed the MLI.

Trinidad and Tobago has made a general statement in its response to the Peer Review questionnaire that it intends to implement a detailed LOB as part of its commitment to implement the minimum standard.

B. Conclusion

The CARICOM Agreement does not at this stage comply with the minimum standard and discussions to bring this agreement up to date should be contemplated.[169]

Summary of the jurisdiction response – Trinidad and Tobago

	1.Treaty partners	2. Compliance with the standard	3. Signature of a complying instrument	4. Minimum standard provision used
1	Antigua and Barbuda	No	No	
2	Barbados	No	No	
3	Belize	No	No	
4	Brazil	No	No	
5	Canada	No	No	
6	China (People's Republic of)	No	No	
7	Denmark	No	No	
8	Dominica	No	No	
9	France	No	No	
10	Germany	No	No	
11	Grenada	No	No	
12	India	No	No	
13	Italy	No	No	
14	Guyana*	No	No	

[168] Agreement Among the Governments of the Member States of the Caribbean Community for the Avoidance of Double Taxation and the Prevention of Fiscal Evasion with Respect to Taxes on Income, Profits or Gains and Capital Gains and for the Encouragement of Regional Trade and Investment, St. Michael Barbados, 6 July 1994; between: Antigua and Barbuda (18 February 1998), Barbados (7 July 1995), Belize (30 November 1994), Dominica (19 June 1996), Grenada (1 March 1996), Guyana* (26 November 1997), Jamaica (16 February 1995), St. Kitts/Nevis (8 May 1997), St. Lucia (22 May 1995) St. Vincent (12 February 1998) and Trinidad & Tobago (29 November 1994). In total, Trinidad and Tobago identified 26 "agreements" in its List of Tax agreements: 16 bilateral agreements and the CARICOM Agreement concluded with ten of its treaty partners.

[169] Revisions to the CARICOM Agreement require an agreement from its eleven treaty partners.

15	Jamaica	No	No	
16	Luxembourg	No	No	
17	Norway	No	No	
18	Saint Kitts and Nevis	No	No	
19	Saint Lucia	No	No	
20	Saint Vincent and the Grenadines	No	No	
21	Spain	No	No	
22	Sweden	No	No	
23	Switzerland	No	No	
24	United Kingdom	No	No	
25	United States	No	No	
26	Venezuela*	No	No	

Tunisia

A. Progress in the implementation of the minimum standard

Tunisia has 56 tax agreements in force as reported in its response to the Peer Review questionnaire, including the Arab Maghreb Union Income Agreement concluded with four treaty partners (the UMA Agreement).[170] None of those agreements comply with the minimum standard.

Tunisia signed the MLI in 2018 and listed its non-compliant agreements.[171] The agreements modified by the MLI come into compliance with the minimum standard once the provisions of the MLI take effect.

Tunisia indicated in its response to the Peer Review questionnaire that steps have been taken (other than under the MLI) to implement the minimum standard in its agreements with Austria, Norway, Sudan* and Switzerland.

Tunisia is implementing the minimum standard through the inclusion of the preamble statement and the PPT.[172]

B. Conclusion

Recommendation

It is recommended that Tunisia completes the steps to have the MLI take effect with respect to its agreements listed under the MLI as those agreements will only be modified by the MLI (and come into compliance with the minimum standard) once the provisions of the MLI take effect.

Summary of the jurisdiction response - Tunisia

	1.Treaty partners	2. Compliance with the standard	3. Signature of a complying instrument	4. Minimum standard provision used
1	Algeria*	No	No	
2	Algeria* (UMA)	No	No	
3	Austria	No	No	PPT
4	Belgium	No	Yes MLI	PPT
5	Burkina Faso	No	Yes MLI	PPT
6	Cameroon	No	Yes MLI	PPT
7	Canada	No	Yes MLI	PPT

170 In total, Tunisia identified 59 "agreements" in its List of Tax agreements: 55 bilateral agreements and the UMA Agreement concluded with four of its treaty partners.

171 While Tunisia has not listed all its non-compliant agreements in its provisional list of reservations and notifications under the MLI (MLI Position), Tunisia has included these agreements to be covered under the MLI in its draft definitive MLI Position, for deposit upon Tunisia's deposit of its instrument of ratification of the MLI.

172 For its agreements listed under the MLI, Tunisia is implementing the preamble statement (Article 6 of the MLI) and the PPT (Article 7 of the MLI).

8	China (People's Republic of)	No	Yes MLI	PPT
9	Côte d'Ivoire	No	Yes MLI	PPT
10	Czech Republic	No	No	
11	Denmark	No	Yes MLI	PPT
12	Egypt	No	Yes MLI	PPT
13	Ethiopia*	No	No	
14	France	No	Yes MLI	PPT
15	Germany	No	No	
16	Greece	No	Yes MLI	PPT
17	Hungary	No	Yes MLI	PPT
18	Indonesia	No	No	
19	Iran*	No	No	
20	Italy	No	Yes MLI	PPT
21	Jordan	No	Yes MLI	PPT
22	Korea	No	Yes MLI	PPT
23	Kuwait*	No	Yes MLI	PPT
24	Lebanon*	No	No	
25	Libya*	No	No	
26	Libya* (UMA)	No	No	
27	Luxembourg	No	Yes MLI	PPT
28	Mali*	No	Non	
29	Malta	No	Yes MLI	PPT
30	Mauritania*	No	No	
31	Mauritania* (UMA)	No	No	
32	Mauritius	No	Yes MLI	PPT
33	Morocco	No	No	PPT
34	Morocco(UMA)	No	No	
35	Netherlands	No	Yes MLI	PPT
36	Norway	No	No	PPT
37	Oman	No	Yes MLI	PPT
38	Pakistan	No	Yes MLI	PPT
39	Poland	No	Yes MLI	PPT
40	Portugal	No	Yes MLI	PPT
41	Qatar	No	No	
42	Romania	No	Yes MLI	PPT
43	Saudi Arabia	No	Yes MLI	PPT
44	Senegal	No	Yes MLI	PPT
45	Serbia	No	Yes MLI	PPT
46	Singapore	No	Yes MLI	PPT
47	Slovak Republic	No	Yes MLI	PPT
48	South Africa	No	Yes MLI	PPT
49	Spain	No	Yes MLI	PPT
50	Sudan*	No	No	PPT
51	Sweden	No	Yes MLI	PPT
52	Switzerland	No	No	PPT
53	Syria*	No	No	
54	Turkey	No	Yes MLI	PPT
55	United Arab Emirates	No	Yes MLI	PPT
56	United Kingdom	No	Yes MLI	PPT
57	United States	No	Non	
58	Viet Nam	No	No	
59	Yemen*	No	No	

Turkey

A. Progress in the implementation of the minimum standard

Turkey has 87 tax agreements in force as reported in its response to the Peer Review questionnaire. One of those agreements, the agreement with Rwanda*, complies with the minimum standard.

Turkey signed the MLI in 2017 and listed its non-compliant agreements. The agreements modified by the MLI come into compliance with the minimum standard once the provisions of the MLI take effect.

Turkey indicated in its response to the Peer Review questionnaire that steps have been taken (other than under the MLI) to implement the minimum standard in its agreement with Korea.

Turkey is implementing the minimum standard through the inclusion of the preamble statement and the PPT.[173]

B. Conclusion

Recommendation

It is recommended that Turkey completes the steps to have the MLI take effect with respect to its agreements listed under the MLI as those agreements will only be modified by the MLI (and come into compliance with the minimum standard) once the provisions of the MLI take effect.

Summary of the jurisdiction response – Turkey

	1.Treaty partners	2. Compliance with the standard	3. Signature of a complying instrument	4. Minimum standard provision used
1	Albania	No	Yes MLI	PPT
2	Algeria*	No	No	PPT
3	Australia	No	Yes MLI	PPT
4	Austria	No	Yes MLI	PPT
5	Azerbaijan*	No	No	PPT
6	Bahrain	No	Yes MLI	PPT
7	Bangladesh*	No	No	PPT
8	Belarus	No	No	PPT
9	Belgium	No	Yes MLI	PPT
10	Bosnia-Herzegovina	No	Yes MLI	PPT
11	Brazil	No	No	PPT
12	Bulgaria	No	Yes MLI	PPT
13	Canada	No	Yes MLI	PPT
14	China (People's Republic of)	No	Yes MLI	PPT
15	Croatia	No	Yes MLI	PPT

173 For its agreements listed under the MLI, Turkey is implementing the preamble statement (Article 6 of the MLI) and the PPT (Article 7 of the MLI).

16	Czech Republic	No	Yes MLI	PPT
17	Denmark	No	Yes MLI	PPT
18	Egypt	No	Yes MLI	PPT
19	Estonia	No	Yes MLI	PPT
20	Ethiopia*	No	No	PPT
21	Finland	No	Yes MLI	PPT
22	France	No	Yes MLI	PPT
23	Gambia*	No	No	PPT
24	Georgia	No	Yes MLI	PPT
25	Germany	No	Yes MLI	PPT
26	Greece	No	Yes MLI	PPT
27	Hungary	No	Yes MLI	PPT
28	India	No	Yes MLI	PPT
29	Indonesia	No	Yes MLI	PPT
30	Iran*	No	No	PPT
31	Ireland	No	Yes MLI	PPT
32	Israel	No	Yes MLI	PPT
33	Italy	No	Yes MLI	PPT
34	Japan	No	Yes MLI	PPT
35	Jordan	No	Yes MLI	PPT
36	Kazakhstan	No	Yes MLI	PPT
37	Korea	No	No	PPT
38	Kosovo*	No	No	PPT
39	Kuwait*	No	Yes MLI	PPT
40	Kyrgyzstan*	No	No	PPT
41	Latvia	No	Yes MLI	PPT
42	Lebanon*	No	No	PPT
43	Lithuania	No	Yes MLI	PPT
44	Luxembourg	No	Yes MLI	PPT
45	Malaysia	No	Yes MLI	PPT
46	Malta	No	Yes MLI	PPT
47	Mexico	No	Yes MLI	PPT
48	Moldova*	No	No	PPT
49	Mongolia	No	No	PPT
50	Montenegro	No	No	PPT
51	Morocco	No	Yes MLI	PPT
52	Netherlands	No	Yes MLI	PPT
53	New Zealand	No	Yes MLI	PPT
54	North Macedonia	No	Yes MLI	PPT
55	Norway	No	Yes MLI	PPT
56	Oman	No	Yes MLI	PPT
57	Pakistan	No	Yes MLI	PPT
58	Philippines*	No	No	PPT
59	Poland	No	Yes MLI	PPT
60	Portugal	No	Yes MLI	PPT
61	Qatar	No	Yes MLI	PPT
62	Romania	No	Yes MLI	PPT
63	Russian Federation	No	Yes MLI	PPT
64	Rwanda*	Yes other		PPT
65	Saudi Arabia	No	Yes MLI	PPT
66	Serbia	No	Yes MLI	PPT
67	Singapore	No	Yes MLI	PPT
68	Slovak Republic	No	Yes MLI	PPT

69	Slovenia	No	Yes MLI	PPT
70	South Africa	No	Yes MLI	PPT
71	Spain	No	Yes MLI	PPT
72	Sudan*	No	No	PPT
73	Sweden	No	Yes MLI	PPT
74	Switzerland	No	Yes MLI	PPT
75	Syrian Arab Republic*	No	No	PPT
76	Tajikistan*	No	No	PPT
77	Thailand	No	No	PPT
78	Tunisia	No	Yes MLI	PPT
79	Turkish Republic of Northern Cyprus*	No	No	PPT
80	Turkmenistan*	No	No	PPT
81	Ukraine	No	Yes MLI	PPT
82	United Arab Emirates	No	Yes MLI	PPT
83	United Kingdom	No	Yes MLI	PPT
84	United States	No	No	PPT
85	Uzbekistan*	No	No	PPT
86	Viet Nam	No	No	PPT
87	Yemen*	No	No	PPT

Turks and Caicos Islands

A. Progress in the implementation of the minimum standard

The Turks and Caicos Islands has no tax agreements in force as reported in its response to the Peer Review questionnaire.

B. Conclusion

No jurisdiction has raised any concerns about the Turks and Caicos Islands.

Ukraine

A. Progress in the implementation of the minimum standard

Ukraine has 75 tax agreements in force as reported in its response to the Peer Review questionnaire. Thirty-one of those agreements comply with the minimum standard.

Ukraine signed the MLI in 2018 and deposited its instrument of ratification on 8 August 2019. The MLI entered into force for Ukraine on 1 December 2019. The agreements modified by the MLI come into compliance with the minimum standard once the provisions of the MLI take effect.

Ukraine has signed a bilateral complying instrument with respect to its agreements with Netherlands and Spain.

Ukraine has not listed its agreement with Qatar to be modified under the MLI, but indicated in its response to the Peer Review questionnaire that steps have been taken (other than under the MLI) to implement the minimum standard in its agreements with Germany and Qatar.

Ukraine is implementing the minimum standard through the inclusion of the preamble statement and the PPT.[174]

B. Conclusion

No jurisdiction has raised any concerns about their agreements with Ukraine.

Summary of the jurisdiction response - Ukraine

	1.Treaty partners	2. Compliance with the standard	3. Signature of a complying instrument	4. Minimum standard provision used
1	Algeria*	No	No	PPT
2	Armenia	No	Yes MLI	PPT
3	Austria	No	No	PPT
4	Azerbaijan*	No	No	PPT
5	Belarus	No	No	PPT
6	Belgium	Yes MLI		PPT
7	Brazil	No	No	PPT
8	Bulgaria	No	Yes MLI	PPT
9	Canada	Yes MLI		PPT
10	China (People's Republic of)	No	Yes MLI	PPT
11	Croatia	No	Yes MLI	PPT
12	Cyprus*	Yes MLI		PPT
13	Czech Republic	No	No	PPT
14	Denmark	Yes MLI		PPT
15	Egypt	Yes MLI		PPT
16	Estonia	No	Yes MLI	PPT
17	Finland	Yes MLI		PPT
18	France	Yes MLI		PPT

174 For its agreements listed under the MLI, Ukraine is implementing the preamble statement (Article 6 of the MLI) and the PPT (Article 7 of the MLI).

19	Georgia	No	No	PPT
20	Germany	No	No	PPT
21	Greece	No	Yes MLI	PPT
22	Hungary	No	Yes MLI	PPT
23	Iceland	Yes MLI		PPT
24	India	Yes MLI		PPT
25	Indonesia	No	No	PPT
26	Iran*	No	No	PPT
27	Ireland	Yes MLI		PPT
28	Israel	Yes MLI		PPT
29	Italy	No	Yes MLI	PPT
30	Japan	Yes MLI		PPT
31	Jordan	Yes MLI		PPT
32	Kazakhstan	Yes MLI		PPT
33	Korea	Yes MLI		PPT
34	Kuwait*	No	No	PPT
35	Kyrgyzstan*	No	No	PPT
36	Latvia	Yes MLI		PPT
37	Lebanon*	No	No	PPT
38	Libya*	No	No	PPT
39	Lithuania	Yes MLI		PPT
40	Luxembourg	Yes MLI		PPT
41	Malaysia	No	No	PPT
42	Malta	Yes MLI		PPT
43	Mexico	No	Yes MLI	PPT
44	Moldova*	No	No	PPT
45	Mongolia	No	No	PPT
46	Montenegro	No	No	PPT
47	Morocco	No	Yes MLI	PPT
48	Netherlands	No	Yes other	PPT
49	North Macedonia	No	Yes MLI	PPT
50	Norway	No	No	PPT
51	Pakistan	Yes MLI		PPT
52	Poland	Yes MLI		PPT
53	Portugal	Yes MLI		PPT
54	Qatar	No	No	PPT
55	Romania	No	Yes MLI	PPT
56	Russian Federation	Yes MLI		PPT
57	Saudi Arabia	Yes MLI		PPT
58	Serbia	Yes MLI		PPT
59	Singapore	Yes MLI		PPT
60	Slovak Republic	Yes MLI		PPT
61	Slovenia	Yes MLI		PPT
62	South Africa	No	Yes MLI	PPT
63	Spain	No	Yes other	PPT
64	Sweden	No	Yes MLI	PPT
65	Switzerland	Yes other		PPT
66	Syrian Arab Republic*	No	No	PPT
67	Tajikistan*	No	No	PPT
68	Thailand	No	No	PPT
69	Turkey	No	Yes MLI	PPT
70	Turkmenistan*	No	No	PPT
71	United Arab Emirates	Yes MLI		PPT

72	United Kingdom	Yes other		PPT
73	United States	No	No	PPT
74	Uzbekistan*	No	No	PPT
75	Viet Nam	No	No	PPT

United Arab Emirates

A. Progress in the implementation of the minimum standard

The United Arab Emirates has 105 tax agreements in force as reported in its response to the Peer Review questionnaire. Thirty-eight of those agreements comply with the minimum standard.

The United Arab Emirates signed the MLI in 2018 and deposited its instrument of ratification on 29 May 2019. The MLI entered in force for the United Arab Emirates on 1 September 2019. The agreements modified by the MLI come into compliance with the minimum standard once the provisions of the MLI take effect.

The United Arab Emirates has not listed its agreement with San Marino. This agreement will therefore not, at this stage, be modified by the MLI. San Marino has listed its agreement with the United Arab Emirates under the MLI.

The United Arab Emirates indicated in its response to the Peer Review questionnaire that steps have been taken (other than under the MLI) to implement the minimum standard in its agreement with Austria.

The United Arab Emirates is implementing the minimum standard through the inclusion of the preamble statement and the PPT.[175]

B. Conclusion

Recommendation

It is recommended that the United Arab Emirates formulates a plan for the implementation of the minimum standard in its agreement for which no steps have yet been taken and that were concluded with members of the BEPS Inclusive Framework (San Marino).

Summary of the jurisdiction response – United Arab Emirates

	1.Treaty partners	2. Compliance with the standard	3. Signature of a complying instrument	4. Minimum standard provision used
1	Albania	Yes MLI		PPT
2	Algeria*	No	No	PPT
3	Andorra	No	Yes MLI	PPT
4	Angola	Yes other		PPT
5	Argentina	No	Yes MLI	PPT
6	Armenia	No	Yes MLI	PPT
7	Austria	No	No	PPT
8	Azerbaijan*	No	No	PPT
9	Bangladesh*	No	No	PPT

175 For its agreements listed under the MLI, the United Arab Emirates is implementing the preamble statement (Article 6 of the MLI) and the PPT (Article 7 of the MLI).

10	Barbados	No	Yes MLI	PPT
11	Belarus	No	No	PPT
12	Belgium	Yes MLI		PPT
13	Belize	No	No	PPT
14	Bermuda	No	No	PPT
15	Bosnia-Herzegovina	Yes MLI		PPT
16	Botswana	Yes other		PPT
17	Brazil	Yes other		PPT
18	Brunei Darussalam	No	No	PPT
19	Bulgaria	No	Yes MLI	PPT
20	Burundi	No	No	PPT
21	Canada	Yes MLI		PPT
22	China (People's Republic of)	No	Yes MLI	PPT
23	Colombia	No	No	PPT
24	Comoros*	No	No	PPT
25	Croatia	No	Yes MLI	PPT
26	Cyprus*	Yes MLI		PPT
27	Czech Republic	No	No	PPT
28	Egypt	No	No	PPT
29	Estonia	No	Yes MLI	PPT
30	Ethiopia*	No	No	PPT
31	Fiji*	No	No	PPT
32	Finland	Yes MLI		PPT
33	France	Yes MLI		PPT
34	Georgia	No	No	PPT
35	Germany	No	No	PPT
36	Greece	No	Yes MLI	PPT
37	Guinea*	No	No	PPT
38	Hong Kong (China)	No	Yes MLI	PPT
39	Hungary	No	Yes MLI	PPT
40	India	Yes MLI		PPT
41	Indonesia	Yes MLI		PPT
42	Ireland	Yes MLI		PPT
43	Italy	No	Yes MLI	PPT
44	Japan	Yes MLI		PPT
45	Jersey	Yes MLI		PPT
46	Jordan	Yes MLI		PPT
47	Kazakhstan	Yes MLI		PPT
48	Kenya	No	Yes MLI	PPT
49	Korea	Yes MLI		PPT
50	Kosovo*	No	No	PPT
51	Kyrgyzstan*	No	No	PPT
52	Latvia	Yes MLI		PPT
53	Lebanon*	No	No	PPT
54	Liechtenstein	Yes MLI		PPT
55	Lithuania	Yes MLI		PPT
56	Luxembourg	Yes MLI		PPT
57	Malaysia	No	Yes MLI	PPT
58	Maldives	No	No	PPT
59	Malta	Yes MLI		PPT
60	Mauritania*	No	No	PPT
61	Mauritius	Yes MLI		PPT
62	Mexico	No	Yes MLI	PPT

63	Moldova*	No	No	PPT
64	Montenegro	No	No	PPT
65	Morocco	No	Yes MLI	PPT
66	Mozambique*	No	No	PPT
67	Netherlands	Yes MLI		PPT
68	New Zealand	Yes MLI		PPT
69	North Macedonia	No	Yes MLI	PPT
70	Pakistan	Yes MLI		PPT
71	Panama	No	Yes MLI	PPT
72	Paraguay	No	No	PPT
73	Philippines*	No	No	PPT
74	Poland	Yes MLI		PPT
75	Portugal	Yes MLI		PPT
76	Romania	No	Yes MLI	PPT
77	Russian Federation	Yes MLI		PPT
78	Saint Vincent and the Grenadines	Yes other		PPT
79	Saudi Arabia	Yes other		PPT
80	Senegal	No	Yes MLI	PPT
81	Serbia	Yes MLI		PPT
82	Seychelles	No	Yes MLI	PPT
83	Singapore	Yes MLI		PPT
84	Slovak Republic	No	No	PPT
85	Slovenia	Yes MLI		PPT
86	South Africa	No	Yes MLI	PPT
87	Spain	No	Yes MLI	PPT
88	Sri Lanka	No	No	PPT
89	Sudan*	No	No	PPT
90	Switzerland	No	No	PPT
91	Syrian Arab Republic*	No	No	PPT
92	Tajikistan*	No	No	PPT
93	Thailand	No	No	PPT
94	Tunisia	No	Yes MLI	PPT
95	Turkey	No	Yes MLI	PPT
96	Turkmenistan*	No	No	PPT
97	Ukraine	Yes MLI		PPT
98	United Kingdom	Yes MLI		PPT
99	Uruguay	Yes MLI		PPT
100	Uzbekistan*	No	No	PPT
101	Venezuela*	No	No	PPT
102	Viet Nam	No	No	PPT
103	Yemen*	No	No	PPT

Other agreements

	1.Treaty partners	2. Inclusive Framework member
1	San Marino	Yes
2	Zimbabwe*	No

United Kingdom

A. Progress in the implementation of the minimum standard

The United Kingdom has 131 tax agreements in force as reported in its response to the Peer Review questionnaire. Fifty-three of those agreement comply with the minimum standard.

The United Kingdom signed the MLI in 2017 and deposited its instrument of ratification on 29 June 2018. The MLI entered into force for the United Kingdom on 1 October 2018. The agreements modified by the MLI come into compliance with the minimum standard once the provisions of the MLI take effect.

The United Kingdom has signed a bilateral complying instrument with respect to its agreements with Germany and Sweden.

The United Kingdom indicated in its response to the Peer Review questionnaire that steps have been taken (other than under the MLI) to implement the minimum standard in its agreements with Chinese Tapei* and Montserrat.

The United Kingdom is implementing the minimum standard through the inclusion of the preamble statement and the PPT.[176]

B. Conclusion

No jurisdiction has raised any concerns about their agreements with the United Kingdom.

Summary of the jurisdiction response – United Kingdom

	1.Treaty partners	2. Compliance with the standard	3. Signature of a complying instrument	4. Minimum standard provision used
1	Albania	Yes MLI		PPT
2	Algeria*	No	No	PPT
3	Antigua and Barbuda	No	No	PPT
4	Argentina	No	Yes MLI	PPT
5	Armenia	No	Yes MLI	PPT
6	Australia	Yes MLI		PPT
7	Austria	Yes other		PPT
8	Azerbaijan*	No	No	PPT
9	Bahrain	No	Yes MLI	PPT
10	Bangladesh*	No	No	PPT
11	Barbados	No	Yes MLI	PPT
12	Belarus	Yes other		PPT
13	Belgium	Yes MLI		PPT
14	Belize	No	Yes MLI	PPT
15	Bolivia*	No	No	PPT
16	Bosnia-Herzegovina	Yes MLI		PPT

176 For its agreements listed under the MLI, the United Kingdom is implementing the preamble statement (Article 6 of the MLI) and the PPT (Article 7 of the MLI). The United Kingdom has made a reservation pursuant to Article 6(4) of the MLI not to apply Article 6(1) of the MLI with respect to agreements that already contain the relevant preamble language (covering three agreements).

17	Botswana	No	No	PPT
18	Brunei Darussalam	No	No	PPT
19	Bulgaria	No	Yes MLI	PPT
20	Canada	Yes MLI		PPT
21	Chile	No	Yes MLI	PPT
22	China (People's Republic of)	No	Yes MLI	PPT
23	Chinese Taipei*	No	No	PPT
24	Colombia	Yes other		PPT
25	Côte d'Ivoire	No	Yes MLI	PPT
26	Croatia	No	Yes MLI	PPT
27	Cyprus*	Yes other		PPT
28	Czech Republic	Yes MLI		PPT
29	Denmark	Yes MLI		PPT
30	Egypt	Yes MLI		PPT
31	Estonia	No	Yes MLI	PPT
32	Eswatini	No	No	PPT
33	Ethiopia*	No	No	PPT
34	Faroe Islands	No	No	PPT
35	Fiji*	No	Yes MLI	PPT
36	Finland	Yes MLI		PPT
37	France	Yes MLI		PPT
38	Gambia*	No	No	PPT
39	Georgia	Yes MLI		PPT
40	Germany	No	Yes other	PPT
41	Ghana*	No	No	PPT
42	Gibraltar	Yes other		PPT
43	Greece	No	Yes MLI	PPT
44	Grenada	No	No	PPT
45	Guernsey	Yes other		PPT
46	Guyana*	No	No	PPT
47	Hong Kong (China)	No	Yes MLI	PPT
48	Hungary	No	Yes MLI	PPT
49	Iceland	Yes MLI		PPT
50	India	Yes MLI		PPT
51	Indonesia	Yes MLI		PPT
52	Ireland	Yes MLI		PPT
53	Isle of Man	Yes other		PPT
54	Israel	Yes other		PPT
55	Italy	No	Yes MLI	PPT
56	Jamaica	No	Yes MLI	PPT
57	Japan	Yes MLI		PPT+LOB
58	Jersey	Yes other		PPT
59	Jordan	Yes MLI		PPT
60	Kazakhstan	Yes MLI		PPT
61	Kenya	No	Yes MLI	PPT
62	Kiribati*	No	No	PPT
63	Korea	Yes MLI		PPT
64	Kosovo*	No	No	PPT
65	Kuwait*	No	Yes MLI	PPT
66	Latvia	Yes MLI		PPT
67	Lesotho*	No	No	PPT
68	Libya*	No	No	PPT
69	Liechtenstein	Yes MLI		PPT

70	Lithuania	Yes MLI		PPT
71	Luxembourg	Yes MLI		PPT
72	Malawi*	No	No	PPT
73	Malaysia	No	Yes MLI	PPT
74	Malta	Yes MLI		PPT
75	Mauritius	Yes MLI		PPT
76	Mexico	No	Yes MLI	PPT
77	Moldova*	No	No	PPT
78	Mongolia	No	No	PPT
79	Montenegro	No	No	PPT
80	Montserrat	No	No	PPT
81	Morocco	No	Yes MLI	PPT
82	Myanmar*	No	No	PPT
83	Namibia	No	No	PPT
84	Netherlands	Yes MLI		PPT
85	New Zealand	Yes MLI		PPT
86	Nigeria	No	Yes MLI	PPT
87	North Macedonia	No	Yes MLI	PPT
88	Norway	Yes MLI		PPT
89	Oman	Yes MLI		PPT
90	Pakistan	Yes MLI		PPT
91	Panama	No	Yes MLI	PPT
92	Papua New Guinea	No	Yes MLI	PPT
93	Philippines*	No	No	PPT
94	Poland	Yes MLI		PPT
95	Portugal	Yes MLI		PPT
96	Qatar	Yes MLI		PPT
97	Romania	No	Yes MLI	PPT
98	Russian Federation	Yes MLI		PPT
99	Saint Kitts and Nevis	No	No	PPT
100	Saudi Arabia	Yes MLI		PPT
101	Senegal	No	Yes MLI	PPT
102	Serbia	Yes MLI		PPT
103	Sierra Leone	No	No	PPT
104	Singapore	Yes MLI		PPT
105	Slovak Republic	Yes MLI		PPT
106	Slovenia	Yes MLI		PPT
107	Solomon Islands*	No	No	PPT
108	South Africa	No	Yes MLI	PPT
109	Spain	No	Yes MLI	PPT
110	Sri Lanka	No	No	PPT
111	Sudan*	No	No	PPT
112	Sweden	No	Yes other	PPT
113	Switzerland	Yes other		PPT
114	Tajikistan*	No	No	PPT
115	Thailand	No	No	PPT
116	Trinidad and Tobago	No	No	PPT
117	Tunisia	No	Yes MLI	PPT
118	Turkey	No	Yes MLI	PPT
119	Turkmenistan*	No	No	PPT
120	Tuvalu*	No	No	PPT
121	Uganda*	No	No	PPT
122	Ukraine	Yes MLI		PPT

123	United Arab Emirates	Yes MLI		PPT
124	United States	No	No	PPT
125	Uruguay	Yes MLI		PPT
126	Uzbekistan*	Yes other		PPT
127	Venezuela*	No	No	PPT
128	Viet Nam	No	No	PPT
129	Zambia	No	No	PPT
130	Zimbabwe*	No	No	PPT

Other agreements

	1.Treaty partners	2. Inclusive Framework member
1	Falkland Islands*	No

United States

A. Progress in the implementation of the minimum standard

The United States has 66 tax agreements in force as reported in its response to the Peer Review questionnaire. None of those agreements comply with the minimum standard.

The United States made a general statement in its response to the Peer Review questionnaire that it intends to implement a detailed LOB rule as part of its commitment to implement the minimum standard in all of its bilateral agreements. The detailed LOB is not available through the MLI and requires substantive bilateral discussions and modifications with respect to each treaty.

The United States has implemented LOB clauses in most of its agreements. It started to include anti-treaty-shopping measures in 1962,[177] and since the seventies, LOB clauses (which initially targeted investment or holding companies) have appeared in agreements concluded by the United States. All of the United States' agreements are supplemented by its domestic anti-conduit regulations.[178]

The 2016 US Model Convention contains an express statement that the tax treaty should not create opportunities for non-taxation or reduced taxation through tax evasion or avoidance (including through treaty-shopping arrangements aimed at obtaining reliefs provided in this Convention for the indirect benefit of residents of third states).

The United States' agreements with the following 45 jurisdictions contain an LOB rule and are supplemented by domestic anti-conduit rules: Australia, Austria, Bangladesh*, Barbados, Belgium, Bulgaria, Canada, China (People's Republic of), Cyprus*, Czech Republic, Denmark, Estonia, Finland, France, Germany, Iceland, India, Indonesia, Ireland, Israel, Italy, Jamaica, Japan, Kazakhstan, Latvia, Lithuania, Luxembourg, Malta, Mexico, Netherlands, New Zealand, Portugal, Russian Federation, the Slovak Republic, Slovenia, South Africa, Spain, Sri Lanka, Sweden, Switzerland, Thailand, Tunisia, Turkey, Ukraine, Venezuela*. Signed conventions with Hungary and Poland contain an LOB rule and are supplemented by domestic anti-conduit rules. The agreements with Egypt, Korea, Morocco, Norway, and Trinidad and Tobago have a limited anti-treaty shopping rule and are supplemented by domestic anti-conduit rules. The agreement with the United Kingdom contains an LOB and anti-conduit rules and is supplemented by domestic anti-conduit rules.

B. Conclusion

No jurisdiction has raised any concerns about their agreements with the United States.

---

[177] With respect to the United States' agreement with Luxembourg.

[178] See I.R.C. §7701(l), added to the Internal Revenue Code by section 13238 of the Omnibus Budget Reconciliation Act of 1993, P.L. 103-66 (allowing the Internal Revenue Service to re-characterise any multiple-party financing transaction as being a transaction directly among any two or more of its parties whenever appropriate to prevent the avoidance of the United States' tax); Treas. Reg. § 1.881-3 (as amended in 2020) (providing additional guidance relating to conduit financing arrangements). In addition, the United States has judicial doctrines such as substance-over-form and economic substance that may achieve a similar result in addressing conduit arrangements.

Summary of the jurisdiction response – United States

	1.Treaty partners	2. Compliance with the standard	3. Signature of a complying instrument	4. Minimum standard provision used
1	Armenia	No	No	
2	Australia	No	No	
3	Austria	No	No	
4	Azerbaijan*	No	No	
5	Bangladesh*	No	No	
6	Barbados	No	No	
7	Belarus	No	No	
8	Belgium	No	No	
9	Bulgaria	No	No	
10	Canada	No	No	
11	China (People's Republic of)	No	No	
12	Cyprus*	No	No	
13	Czech Republic	No	No	
14	Denmark	No	No	
15	Egypt	No	No	
16	Estonia	No	No	
17	Finland	No	No	
18	France	No	No	
19	Georgia	No	No	
20	Germany	No	No	
21	Greece	No	No	
22	Hungary	No	No	
23	Iceland	No	No	
24	India	No	No	
25	Indonesia	No	No	
26	Ireland	No	No	
27	Israel	No	No	
28	Italy	No	No	
29	Jamaica	No	No	
30	Japan	No	No	
31	Kazakhstan	No	No	
32	Korea	No	No	
33	Kyrgyzstan*	No	No	
34	Latvia	No	No	
35	Lithuania	No	No	
36	Luxembourg	No	No	
37	Malta	No	No	
38	Mexico	No	No	
39	Moldova*	No	No	
40	Morocco	No	No	
41	Netherlands	No	No	
42	New Zealand	No	No	
43	Norway	No	No	
44	Pakistan	No	No	
45	Philippines*	No	No	
46	Poland	No	No	
47	Portugal	No	No	
48	Romania	No	No	
49	Russian Federation	No	No	

50	Slovak Republic	No	No	
51	Slovenia	No	No	
52	South Africa	No	No	
53	Spain	No	No	
54	Sri Lanka	No	No	
55	Sweden	No	No	
56	Switzerland	No	No	
57	Tajikistan*	No	No	
58	Thailand	No	No	
59	Trinidad and Tobago	No	No	
60	Tunisia	No	No	
61	Turkey	No	No	
62	Turkmenistan*	No	No	
63	Ukraine	No	No	
64	United Kingdom	No	No	
65	Uzbekistan*	No	No	
66	Venezuela*	No	No	

Uruguay

A. Progress in the implementation of the minimum standard

Uruguay has 22 tax agreements in force as reported in its response to the Peer Review questionnaire. Fourteen of those agreements comply with the minimum standard.

Uruguay signed the MLI in 2017 and deposited its instrument of ratification on 6 February 2020, listing its non-compliant agreements. The MLI entered into force for Uruguay on 1 June 2020. The agreements modified by the MLI come into compliance with the minimum standard once the provisions of the MLI take effect.

Uruguay is implementing the minimum standard through the inclusion of the preamble statement and the PPT combined with the LOB.[179]

B. Conclusion

No jurisdiction has raised any concerns about their agreements with Uruguay.

Summary of the jurisdiction response – Uruguay

	1.Treaty partners	2. Compliance with the standard	3. Signature of a complying instrument	4. Minimum standard provision used
1	Belgium	Yes MLI		PPT
2	Chile	Yes Other		PPT and LOB
3	Ecuador*	No	No	PPT and LOB
4	Finland	Yes MLI		PPT
5	Germany	No	No	
6	Hungary	No	Yes MLI	PPT
7	India	Yes MLI		PPT and LOB
8	Italy	Yes Other		PPT
9	Korea	Yes MLI		PPT
10	Liechtenstein	Yes MLI		PPT
11	Luxembourg	Yes MLI		PPT
12	Malta	Yes MLI		PPT
13	Mexico	No	Yes MLI	PPT and LOB
14	Paraguay	Yes Other		PPT and LOB
15	Portugal	Yes MLI		PPT
16	Romania	No	Yes MLI	PPT
17	Singapore	Yes MLI		PPT
18	Spain	No	Yes MLI	PPT
19	Switzerland	No	No	
20	United Arab Emirates	Yes MLI		PPT
21	United Kingdom	Yes MLI		PPT
22	Viet Nam	No	No	PPT

[179] For its agreements listed under the MLI, Uruguay is implementing the preamble statement (Article 6 of the MLI) and the PPT (Article 7 of the MLI). Uruguay has also adopted for the simplified LOB under Article 7(6) of the MLI.

Viet Nam

A. Progress in the implementation of the minimum standard

Viet Nam has 76 tax agreements in force as reported in its response to the Peer Review questionnaire. None of those agreements comply with the minimum standard.

Viet Nam has not signed the MLI.

Viet Nam indicated in its response to the Peer Review questionnaire that it intends to join the MLI in early 2022.

In its response to the Peer Review questionnaire, Japan indicated that its agreement with Viet Nam did not give rise to material treaty shopping concerns for Japan.

B. Conclusion

Viet Nam has developed a plan for the implementation of the minimum standard in its agreements with Australia, Austria, Belarus, Belgium, Brunei Darussalam, Bulgaria, Canada, China (People's Republic of), Croatia, Czech Republic, Denmark, Estonia, Finland, France, Germany, Hong Kong (China), Hungary, Iceland, India, Indonesia, Ireland, Israel, Italy, Japan, Kazakhstan, Korea, Latvia, Luxembourg, Macau (China), Malaysia, Malta, Mongolia, Morocco, Netherlands, New Zealand, Norway, Oman, Pakistan, Panama, Poland, Portugal, Qatar, Romania, Russian Federation, San Marino, Saudi Arabia, Serbia, the Seychelles, Singapore, Slovak Republic, Spain, Sri Lanka, Sweden, Switzerland, Thailand, Tunisia, Turkey, Ukraine, United Arab Emirates, United Kingdom and Uruguay.

Viet Nam indicated in its response to the Peer Review questionnaire that it intends to sign the MLI in early 2022and list those agreements to be covered.

Other agreements

This Table shows the agreements that are not compliant, not subject to a complying instrument, not covered by a general statement on the implementation of the detailed LOB and for which no steps have been taken to implement the minimum standard.

	1.Treaty partners	2. Inclusive Framework member
1	Australia	Yes
2	Austria	Yes
3	Azerbaijan*	No
4	Bangladesh*	No
5	Belarus	Yes
6	Belgium	Yes
7	Brunei Darussalam	Yes
8	Bulgaria	Yes
9	Cambodia*	No
10	Canada	Yes
11	China (People's Republic of)	Yes
12	Chinese Taipei*	No
13	Croatia	Yes
14	Cuba*	No

15	Czech Republic	Yes
16	Democratic People's Republic of Korea*	No
17	Denmark	Yes
18	Estonia	Yes
19	Finland	Yes
20	France	Yes
21	Germany	Yes
22	Hong Kong (China)	Yes
23	Hungary	Yes
24	Iceland	Yes
25	India	Yes
26	Indonesia	Yes
27	Iran*	No
28	Ireland	Yes
29	Israel	Yes
30	Italy	Yes
31	Japan	Yes
32	Kazakhstan	Yes
33	Korea	Yes
34	Kuwait*	No
35	Lao People's Democratic Republic*	No
36	Latvia	Yes
37	Luxembourg	Yes
38	Macau (China)	Yes
39	Malaysia	Yes
40	Malta	Yes
41	Mongolia	Yes
42	Morocco	Yes
43	Mozambique*	No
44	Myanmar*	No
45	Netherlands	Yes
46	New Zealand	Yes
47	Norway	Yes
48	Oman	Yes
49	Pakistan	Yes
50	Palestinian Authority	No
51	Panama	Yes
52	Philippines*	No
53	Poland	Yes
54	Portugal	Yes
55	Qatar	Yes
56	Romania	Yes
57	Russian Federation	Yes
58	San Marino	Yes
59	Saudi Arabia	Yes
60	Serbia	Yes
61	Seychelles	Yes
62	Singapore	Yes
63	Slovak Republic	Yes
64	Spain	Yes
65	Sri Lanka	Yes
66	Sweden	Yes

67	Switzerland	Yes
68	Thailand	Yes
69	Tunisia	Yes
70	Turkey	Yes
71	Ukraine	Yes
72	United Arab Emirates	Yes
73	United Kingdom	Yes
74	Uruguay	Yes
75	Uzbekistan*	No
76	Venezuela*	No

Zambia

A. Progress in the implementation of the minimum standard

Zambia has 23 tax agreements in force as reported in its response to the Peer Review questionnaire. One of those agreements, the agreement with Switzerland, complies with the minimum standard.

Zambia has not signed the MLI.

Zambia indicated in its response to the Peer Review questionnaire that steps have been taken (other than under the MLI) to implement the minimum standard in its agreements with India and South Africa.

Zambia is implementing the minimum standard through the inclusion of the preamble statement and the PPT.

In their responses to the Peer Review questionnaire, Germany and Japan indicated that their agreements with Zambia did not give rise to material treaty shopping concerns, for their respective jurisdictions.

B. Conclusion

Zambia is currently developing a plan, in consultation with the Secretariat, for the implementation of the minimum standard in its agreements with Botswana, Canada, China (People's Republic of), Denmark, Finland, France, Germany, Ireland, Italy, Japan, Kenya, Morocco, Netherlands, Norway, Romania, the Seychelles, Sweden and the United Kingdom.

Summary of the jurisdiction response - Zambia

	1.Treaty partners	2. Compliance with the standard	3. Signature of a complying instrument	4. Minimum standard provision used
1	India	No	No	
2	South Africa	No	No	PPT
3	Switzerland	Yes other		PPT

Other agreements

	1.Treaty partners	2. Inclusive Framework member
1	Botswana	Yes
2	Canada	Yes
3	China (People's Republic of)	Yes
4	Denmark	Yes
5	Finland	Yes
6	France	Yes
7	Germany	Yes
8	Ireland	Yes
9	Italy	Yes
10	Japan	Yes
11	Kenya	Yes
12	Morocco	Yes
13	Netherlands	Yes

14	Norway	Yes
15	Romania	Yes
16	Seychelles	Yes
17	Sweden	Yes
18	Tanzania*	No
19	Uganda*	No
20	United Kingdom	Yes

www.ingramcontent.com/pod-product-compliance
Ingram Content Group UK Ltd.
Pitfield, Milton Keynes, MK11 3LW, UK
UKHW051457290926
15471UKWH00008B/1262

9 789264 826588